ROCK OF CHICKAMAUGA

The Life of General George H. Thomas

MAJOR GENERAL GEORGE H. THOMAS

Mathew Brady took this photograph, probably on a warm day
in his Washington studio after the close of the Civil War in 1865.

From an original print in the author's collection

ROCK OF CHICKAMAUGA

The Life of
GENERAL GEORGE H. THOMAS

By Freeman Cleaves

UNIVERSITY OF OKLAHOMA PRESS

NORMAN

LC: 85-40939
ISBN: 0-8061-1978-0

Copyright © 1948 by the University of Oklahoma Press, Norman, Publishing
Division of the University. All rights reserved. Manufactured in the U.S.A.

8   9   10   11   12   13   14

For Gwendoline

Acknowledgments

M
ANY PERSONS have helped smooth the way for the biographer. In particular I owe much to the lively interest of Dr. Frederick M. Dearborn of New York City who loaned copies of original letters and manuscripts and also supplied Thomas portraits and other pictures from his extensive Civil War collection. I had some enlightening correspondence with Dr. W. H. T. Squires and Percy S. Stephenson of Norfolk, W. C. Thomas of Wytheville, and H. B. Staley of Marion, Virginia, concerning the Thomas family history.

Miss Mabel R. Gillis of the California State Library kindly sent photostats and typewritten copies of newspaper clippings, while other photostat and microfilm material was obtained from the Henry E. Huntington Library, San Marino, California; the Chicago Historical Society; the Pennsylvania Historical Society; and the Library of Congress.

Miss Elizabeth B. Drewry located material and placed it at my disposal at the National Archives in Washington. Division of Manuscripts Chief St. George L. Sioussat and Thomas P. Martin and C. Percy Powell assisted in many ways at the Library of Congress. Research at the United States Military Academy was expedited through the courtesy and co-operation of Lieutenant Colonel W. J. Morton, librarian, and Corporal Sidney Foreman.

For helpful assistance at the New York Public Library, where the bulk of the research was done, I am indebted to Robert W. Hill, Miss Henrietta Quigley, Miss Shirley Barker, Ivor Avellino, and the indefatigable Sylvester Vigilante. My wife, Gwendoline Chase Cleaves, patiently read the manuscript. For special help in locating out-of-the-way material I am indebted to Thomas Robson Hay of Locust Valley, Long Island, New York.

FREEMAN CLEAVES

New York City

The Contents

The Illustrations

The Maps

ROCK OF CHICKAMAUGA

The Life of General George H. Thomas

1

Virginia and West Point

M ISS Judith Thomas of Southampton County, Virginia, sat down at a table with an unanswered letter before her. She was not quite sure what to say to her correspondent. She fingered the letter and looked it over again. Inscribed "Division of the Atlantic," it bore the spread-eagle seal of the United States Army and read:

"Governor's Island, April 12, 1890
"Dear Miss Thomas:
"Your good brother was my instructor in artillery at the Military Academy and in later years I was on duty with him a great deal. Recently I have been asked to write an article upon his life and character. Now if you or your sister would write me any incidents you can remember about him, I should be very grateful. . . . "

The letter was signed by Oliver O. Howard, major general, United States Army, and was addressed to "Miss Judith E. Thomas, near Newsom's Depot, Southampton County, Virginia."[1]

This unwelcome inquiry from the North could hardly be dealt with according to family policy. Since the beginning of the War Between the States, George Henry Thomas had been regarded by his family as one who had never been born. Judith Thomas remembered how it all began. When George was a boy, he would hang around the Negro quarters and swap the loaf sugar he had pilfered for raccoons and possums. George was

[1] Military Order of the Loyal Legion of the U. S., New York Commandery, *Personal Recollections*, Series I (1891), 286.

3

disobedient. He would even teach the Negro children, against his parents' wishes, the lessons he had learned at church and at school. Indeed, he seemed to love the Negro quarters more than his own house. After his father died, George, then only sixteen, had begun to manage the farm, but he had never liked farm work. True, he was always self-reliant, but he was also independent of mind. He would visit the saddle maker's to learn how to make his own saddles, or go to the cabinetmaker's to find out how to make furniture. And he still insisted on teaching the Negroes unnecessary things. Perhaps this in itself had done little harm, but he had gone much further during the war. The aged woman stirred uneasily in her chair as she recalled how her brother had armed and drilled Negro troops for service against his native South. Neither she nor her sister Fanny had ever forgiven him, although their brother Benjamin, now living at Vicksburg, had made his peace with the traitor.

The date of the letter, Judith Thomas noticed, was just twenty-five years to the day since General Lee's surrender. General Lee! That noble man had stood by his state while her own nearest kin had joined the despoilers. Judith turned the letter over and seized a pencil in a trembling hand: "General Howard," she wrote on the back, "In answer to your inquiry concerning the character of the late George H. Thomas, I can only inform you that he was as all other boys are who are well born and well reared."[2] Surely that was not giving aid or comfort to the enemy. Behind Judith Thomas, a large framed picture hung with its face to the wall.

What the eighty-year-old Judith had written symbolized the South's long silence concerning the career of George H. Thomas. If the silence was broken, it was only to abuse him. Because he became a great military leader of whose services the Confederacy was deprived, Southern newspapers questioned his motives even after the war. The story was often repeated that he had fought for the Union only because he had been refused a commission in the Confederate Army. It is true that such a commission was discussed in the Virginia Assembly in April, 1861; but if the offer was ever made, it came too late. On April 13, Thomas made

[2] *Ibid.*

4

GEORGE H. THOMAS

in 1866, aged fifty, wearing the badge of the Army of the Cumberland with its five-pointed star, in the center of which is a triangle enclosing an acorn, standard army fare

From an engraving by H. B. Hall & Sons

his decision from a sense of duty to the flag he served, a flag which had been fired upon the day before at Fort Sumter. Of Welsh and Huguenot ancestry, George Thomas was unalterably firm in his attitudes; he was a Regular Army man who clung to his old coats and old ways. His maiden sisters, whom he promptly notified once his decision was made, were also unswerving in their loyalty. They promptly turned his picture to the wall, then destroyed all his letters, and never wrote to him again except to suggest that he change his name. Their neighbors even heard them remark that if he ever came home, they would show him how to use the fine gift sword which stood behind the front door. The sword had been given him by Southampton County friends in commemoration of his long service in Florida and in the Mexican War, but obviously he had forfeited all rights to it. The General's attempts at reconciliation brought no word of forgiveness, and he never went home again.

Some years after Thomas's death in San Francisco in 1870, General William Tecumseh Sherman expressed the hope that he might be forgiven. Speaking before a great crowd of veteran soldiers at the unveiling of the equestrian statue in Thomas Circle, Washington City, Sherman predicted that the day would come when Southerners would be making pilgrimages to the monument. "Brave George Thomas," said Sherman, "will become the idol of the South."[3] But no delegation of Southerners has ever appeared with wreaths to lay at the statue. Local historians have taken no notice of the General. Although the several score volumes of the *Virginia Magazine of History* and the *William and Mary Quarterly* are filled with Southern family lore and ancestral details, reference to George Henry Thomas of Southampton County is confined to one footnote. The historian of Nat Turner's Insurrection, the most famous event in Southampton County, talked with Thomas's maiden sisters, who survived that bloody incursion, but found nothing to relate concerning their brother. General Sherman, who had roomed with Thomas at West Point, once said that President Andrew Jackson had signed his appointment to the Military Academy as a

[3] Richard W. Johnson, *Memoir of Major General George H. Thomas,* 288.

reward for riding from one house to another with a message during Nat Turner's approach.[4] Although the historian relates that Jackson rewarded another Virginia youth, who helped defend his father's house against the marauders, by giving him a midshipman's commission, he took no notice of any heroic action on Thomas's part, and it is not exactly clear what Thomas may have done.

Nat Turner's Insurrection began on the night of August 21, 1831, and continued throughout most of the following day. Not since the era of sporadic Indian raids had such scenes taken place in Southampton County, and then on a much smaller scale. It was difficult, for a time, for the isolated farmers and housewives to comprehend their peril, and many lost their lives because of this incredulousness. The farms were widely scattered and unsuited for joint defense. Apple orchards abounded in that fertile country; corn, cotton, and tobacco grew plentifully in fields and orchards. Each farm had its apple-brandy still, a reliable source of income, and with an abundance of cheap labor there was little reason for a man to be poor. Because of its large Negro population, the whites being outnumbered by nearly three to two, Southampton County was considered a part of the "black belt" which ran over the border into North Carolina.

On one of the county's fine farms an enormous oak tree of almost perfect symmetry towered above a spacious white house. Here lived the widow of John Thomas and her family of two girls, Judith and Fanny, and two boys. On the afternoon of August 22, 1831, a neighbor, James Gurley, rode into the yard to give warning that sixty drunk and blood-stained Negro farm hands were approaching by a back road. Gurley did not know just how many people they had killed; but after the bodies were finally counted, there were fifty-five dead adults, children, and infants. Leading the raid was Nat Turner, a religious fanatic who had taught himself to read the Bible and was reputed to interpret signs in the heavens. One day Nat plainly heard celestial voices bidding him free all the Negroes from bondage; then another sign appeared in the heavens. He collected a few Negroes and served in the woods a midnight repast accompanied by ap-

[4] Society of the Army of the Cumberland, 1875 Reunion, *Report*, 56.

ple brandy mixed with gunpowder. First his master, Joseph Travis, Mrs. Travis, and their children were murdered; then the drunken insurgents kept up their bloody work until they had depopulated a good-sized area during the course of a foray covering twenty-seven miles. As the Negroes whom Nat Turner swept up approached the Thomas house, they were carrying a variety of weapons—knives, axes, hatchets, scythes, swords, clubs, and guns. Some of the marauders rode horseback. Mrs. Thomas drove away in a buggy with her two daughters, but fearing that she might be overtaken, she left her carriage on the road and fled through the woods to Jerusalem. Nat Turner's men entered the Thomas stables and forced the Negroes there to accompany them on horseback. Sam, the overseer, kept a cool head. He told his son Leonard to hang back and escape at the first opportunity. He was to tell his mother to get the keys, which Sam had hidden in the cider press, and look after the farm. The insurgents were turned back by only a dozen armed white men on their way to Jerusalem. Sam dashed into the woods with the other Thomas Negroes and reported to his mistress in the village. Since danger existed of their being shot on sight by enraged whites, they were lodged in jail for safekeeping until the next morning.

It was some hours before a concerted blow could be struck at Nat Turner. Help came from several neighboring counties. Late on that second day of the raid, the insurgents were rounded up, several killed, and nearly all the rest captured and tied up or manacled. Nat Turner, who hid in a hole in the woods, was not discovered for six weeks. The Thomas family visited one of the insurgent Negroes in jail and learned of their narrow escape. They were told that if they had remained at home a few minutes longer, they "would not be here now."[5]

George Henry Thomas had been born on July 31, 1816, on the family homestead near Newsom's Depot, five miles from the North Carolina line. His father, John, was of Welsh descent; his

[5] William Sidney Drewry, *The Southampton Insurrection*, 27f; Henry Howe, *Historical Collections of Virginia*, 472; Dr. John Allen Wyeth, *With Sabre and Scalpel*, 261 n.

7

mother, Mary Rochelle, could trace her line to the Huguenot, George de Rochelle, who found America a healthier place than France for Protestants during the reign of Louis XIV. The Thomas forebears lived in England a generation or two before coming to Virginia. Exactly when they sailed is not known, but the Southampton County line is said to go back to a Captain Robert Thomas of Isle of Wight County who signed a power of attorney in 1678 and was listed as a justice of the peace. Too many papers have been lost, however, and too many members of the family died intestate to permit any tracing of the line from Robert to John and George Henry Thomas.[6]

The father died in 1830 from a "farm accident," which is unexplained.[7] George managed to keep himself busy with little or no parental direction after graduation from the local academy. An observant boy, skillful with his hands, it was thought that he might do something better than farming. When he was eighteen years old, he entered the law office of his uncle, James Rochelle, county clerk at Jerusalem. He helped prepare the usual documents but indicated no special liking for reading law. One day in early spring, 1836, Congressman John Young Mason of the district called at Rochelle's office and let it be known that he had a Military Academy appointment to fill. Since no cadet from his district had ever succeeded in graduating from West Point, Mason wanted to find someone whose prospects were at least fair. He had heard some good things of young Thomas and was willing to gamble on him. George agreed to undertake the examination. Mason expressed himself satisfied with his appearance, and upon returning to Washington he sent this note to Secretary of War Lewis Cass: "Sir: I have the honor to recommend George Thomas of Southampton County, Virginia, for admission into the Academy at West Point as a Cadet. He is Seventeen or Eighteen years of age, of fine size, and

6 *William & Mary Quarterly*, VII, 268; Charles W. Baird, *History of the Huguenot Emigration to America*, I, 296; Goodridge Wilson, *Smythe County History and Tradition*, 125, 177, 180–81; John Bennett Boddie, *Seventeenth Century Isle of Wight County*, 255–57; W. H. T. Squires, *The Days of Yester-Year*, 184–85.

7 Henry Coppée, *General Thomas*, 3; T. B. Van Horne, *Major General George H. Thomas*, 2.

of excellent talents with a good preparatory education."[8] Actually, Thomas was approaching his twentieth birthday and was two years older than the average plebe cadet.

The recommendation was accepted and the appointment signed by President Jackson. Visiting Washington in April, Thomas called upon Congressman Mason to offer his thanks. Whether or not Mason had any misgivings, he took the opportunity to remind his visitor of the miserable record of other students from his district at West Point. "If you should fail to graduate," he warned the young man in parting, "I never want to see your face again."[9]

This was warning enough. To brush up on his studies, Thomas arrived at West Point several weeks in advance of the start of the school year. Throughout his whole life he would leave nothing undone in preparation for any set task. He discovered, however, that a command of the three "R's" was the only academic requirement at West Point, and he easily passed the physical tests. Grown to man's size, he stood five feet, ten inches tall, was muscular and vigorous, and rode a horse well. Two plebes from other parts of the country, William Tecumseh Sherman of Ohio and Stewart Van Vliet of Vermont, were assigned a room with him in the Old South Barracks. Red-haired "Cump" Sherman, nervous, talkative, and careless in dress, was then a wiry youth of sixteen; Van Vliet, oldest of the trio at twenty-one, would prove himself a meticulous and hard-working student. They observed in Thomas a handsome youth of fair complexion, light brown hair, deep blue eyes, and square jaw, who "bore a remarkable resemblance," according to Cadet William Starke Rosecrans, "to Stuart's portrait of Washington."[10] Dignified, self-possessed, and steady in manner, Thomas became known to the cadets as "Old Tom" and "George Washington."

The newcomers examined the rules for storing away clothing and equipment. Trunks were to be placed under the iron

[8] Mason to Lewis Cass, March 1, 1836, War Department Files, National Archives.

[9] Coppée, *Thomas,* 5.

[10] Army of the Cumberland, 1879 Reunion, *Report,* 173.

bedsteads, dress caps neatly arranged on a shelf behind the door, books on the shelf farthest from the door, clothes on pegs over bedsteads, muskets in gun racks with locks sprung, and so on. Order and neatness perfectly suited Van Vliet, who acquired only ten demerits in his first year and an absolutely clean slate thereafter, a marvelous record of shoe-shining, button-polishing, and punctuality. Sherman could stand the pace for only a year, moving to other quarters. While he was actually brilliant in his studies, an empty stomach made him restless at night. Few nocturnal excursions for food were organized without him. Some supplementary effort was needed to eke out the scanty provisions furnished by a profit-wise contractor, and it was in such cause that Sherman, known as the best hash-maker at West Point, acquired 109 demerits as a plebe. Thomas averaged less than 22 demerits a year, or 87 all told. This number, however, had little effect on his scholastic rank.

Cadets from one part of the country ordinarily were suspicious, at first sight, of those from other sections but upon further acquaintance found them not so bad after all. North, South, and West soon became very good friends in the barracks. "A warm friendship commenced in that room which continued, without a single break, during our lives," observed Stewart Van Vliet in later years. "We were all three sturdy fellows, which prevented our being annoyed by older cadets. They commenced to haze us . . . but Thomas put a stop to it. One evening a cadet came into our room and commenced to give us orders. He had said but a few words when Old Tom . . . stepped up to him and said, 'Leave this room immediately or I will throw you through the window.' . . . There were no more attempts to haze us."[11]

Following the entrance examinations came several days of displaying the chest, drawing in the stomach and chin, keeping elbows straight, shoulders drawn back, and the feet at an angle of forty-five degrees. "It was heads up, eyes to the front, and one seldom saw his boots,"[12] according to Cadet Samuel G. French of New Jersey. Cadet William Dutton left a complete record of his trials:

[11] Coppée, *Thomas*, 323 n.
[12] Samuel G. French, *Two Wars*, 11.

"At 5 A.M. which is ½ an hour after the morning gun, the drums are beat by the barracks, & the cry grows—'fall in there,' when we all have to be in the ranks or be reported. The roll is then called, we go to our rooms & have 15 minutes to roll up our blankets, put them up, wash, clean the room etc., when *every thing must* be in order. We have no matresses & only 2 blankets to lay on the floor.... We then march to the mess hall, & if one speaks, raises his hand, looks to the right or left ... we are reported, indeed we are reported for everything.... When we arrive at the tables, the command is given 'take seats' & then such a scrambling you never saw. For breakfast we have the remains of the meat of the former days dinner, cut up with potato with considerable gravy—& not more than two-thirds of them can get a bit.—bread cut in chunks, butter and coffee. We have to eat as fast as we can, & before we get enough the command is given 'Squad rise,' at dinner we have 'Roast Beef,' and boiled potato & bread—no butter, at Tea, bread & butter & tea. We have to drill twice a day & a good many faint away.... After we have marched from tea, we stay in our room till ½ hour past 9 when we can go to bed if we choose, & at taps at 10 every light must be out & after that the inspector happens in all times of night."[13]

Sometimes in winter, when ice choked the river and a deep fall of snow blocked traffic on the roads, short rations grew even shorter. Although beset by countless small difficulties, plebes from comfortable homes managed to accustom themselves to the sudden change in regimen. During the last week in June they marched from the barracks into tents pitched upon the plain. Soon they were weary with drill and other military duties on hot summer days and nights. The open-air exercise stimulated large appetites. "I would like above all things to get into Aunt Dorcas's cupboard a *moment*," Cadet Dutton notified his uncle.[14] Sherman, according to an observer, usually had a grease spot on his pants from feasts after hours. The students ate their fill once a year at a Fourth of July dinner and until 1838 were allowed to

[13] U. S. Military Academy Library *Bulletin* No. 1, *Cadet Life Before the Mexican War*, 12–13.
[14] *Ibid.*, 8.

drink wine on this holiday occasion. "We had glorious times on the fourth," wrote a Class of 1837 cadet. "Nearly the whole Corps, and invited Citizens too, were quite patriotick, or to speak unequivocally, most celestially befuddled."[15]

The summer uniform, which Thomas filled out well, was a gray coat with a short tail, white vest and belt, tight pantaloons, stiff, standing collar, and dress cap of black felt. He stood his regular turn at guard duty, which meant walking a post one hour in every three during the day and night. The students sweated on formal parades and flocked about six small brass field-pieces for artillery drill. There were few idle moments. "All I want of those Editors who say that 'the lily-fingered cadets lounge on their velvet lawns, attend their brilliant balls & take pay for it' as I saw in the paper yesterday—is that they may go through *but one plebe encampment,*" ran a cadet's reply to current newspaper criticisms of an institution considered altogether too aristocratic for a plain homespun democracy to support.[16] The halls of Congress occasionally resounded with declamations against West Point, which was Episcopal rather than Methodist or Baptist in religion, with the military rather than the laity in charge.

The cadets were satisfied to return to the shelter of their barracks during the last week in August. Thomas opened the grim-looking textbooks of two new subjects, mathematics and French. For a future artilleryman and student of textbooks which stemmed from the Napoleonic era and were read in the original tongue, these studies were highly important, but the Virginian made progress rather slowly. At the end of the school year he was rated twenty-sixth in his class, not quite halfway down, but he made better progress thereafter. He preferred the scientific subjects which came during his last two years—astronomy, mineralogy, and geology, whatever was akin to nature. For outside reading on his own time, he selected Thomson's *Botany.* The required church service and the Sunday noonday meal were no sooner over than he would join a band of student prospectors who roamed about the Hudson River country col-

15 *Ibid.,* 22.
16 *Ibid.,* 9.

lecting various specimens. The boys would climb to the pinnacled Crow's Nest, the highest point roundabout, or ferry over to asbestos-filled "Cotton Rock" on the other side of the river. Indian arrows dug from the ruins of old Fort Montgomery, six miles down the Hudson, were a find. Occasionally an old she-bear and her cubs were encountered in the mountains, but the family would have vanished by the time the cadets returned with their guns.

Third-year courses differed little from those in any other scientific school. "Natural and experimental philosophy" as assigned included mechanics, optics, magnetism, and electricity, and to these were added astronomy, chemistry, drawing, and topography. The curriculum broadened in the final year with a review of artillery, the science of war and fortification, infantry tactics, civil engineering, mineralogy, geology, rhetoric, moral philosophy, and political science, including constitutional and international law.[17] West Pointers who put their training to the test in actual campaigning would discover that for all this wealth of subjects, their formal education fell far short of education for war. An officer who fought under Thomas in the Civil War criticized the tactical education of the cadet as going no further than the evolution of the battalion. "For nearly all," remarked General Jacob D. Cox, "it was the education of the soldier in the ranks and not the officer."[18]

There was little training in leadership or in the independent solving of practical problems encountered in the field. A graduate cadet had yet to learn such routine tasks as how to make official returns and how to do business with the Adjutant General's Office or the Ordnance, Quartermaster's, and Subsistence departments. Those who advanced to the rank of brigadier or major general would have to discover also how to guide great masses of men whether on parade or under fire. Only the more gifted improvisers such as Grant, Sherman, and the untrained Nathan Bedford Forrest of the Confederate cavalry would rise to the top. Of the Union's four leading generals in the Civil War,

[17] Roswell Park, *Sketch of the History and Topography of West Point*, 102–107.
[18] *Military Reminiscences*, I, 178.

none were honor men at West Point, and none except Thomas held the rank of cadet-sergeant at graduation. Although Sherman once wore a sergeant's stripes, somewhere along the 380 demerits he accumulated, he was demoted to private. West Point was too strait-laced for Grant and Philip Henry Sheridan, who advanced no further than private during their four-year course. Among the forty-two graduates of the Class of 1840, Sherman attained sixth place and Thomas stood twelfth, just ahead of Richard S. Ewell, a Virginian who would wear the gray. Leading the class was Paul O. Hebert, a future governor of Louisiana, while Van Vliet, for all his tidiness, stood ninth.[19] Since he knew the place for everything and how to put it away, he became a highly efficient supply officer during the Civil War.

Thomas saw four classes come and as many go, not realizing, of course, that every class roll was studded with the names of future heroes. Sherman, Grant, Rosecrans, Buell, and Hooker would be numbered among his Civil War associates, Braxton Bragg, Bushrod Johnson, William J. Hardee, and Daniel H. Hill would be on the other side of the battle line at Chickamauga. But the graduating West Pointers were chafing because there was no real war in sight and only actual fighting presented a quick and sure means of promotion.

Of course there was always Florida Territory, a perennial battleground ever since Andrew Jackson's unceremonious invasion of the peninsula in 1818. Thomas thumbed through a book he had found in the Academy library, *The Territory of Florida,* by John Lee Williams. The author had ascended many of Florida's rivers, explored its lagoons and bays, traced ancient Indian works and scattered ruins. A rare and ancient Spanish manuscript which had come into his hands had detailed much of the country's early history. Thomas pored over the descriptions of lakes and waterways and augmented his knowledge of snakes, birds, fish, and animals up to black bear and panther size. New and strange vegetable growths and fruits were depicted, and the author's tales of the aborigines stimulated curiosity concerning Indian life and customs.

19 G. W. Cullum, *Biographical Register of Officers and Cadets of the U. S. Military Academy,* 232–34; L. Lewis, *Sherman: Fighting Prophet,* 57, 62.

Current newspapers carried accounts of another sort—how the savages had been frightening planters from their fields and raiding the settlements during the spring months. In one such raid a band of Seminoles had ambushed a troupe of actors traveling to St. Augustine with a small military escort. Survivors of the first volley scattered, and then the Indians raided the actors' baggage and returned to their villages in grotesquely satisfying costumes.[20] Existing military forces in Florida were obviously too small for their job, but it was rumored that reinforcements were to be sent. Thomas received his diploma and second lieutenant's commission, said good-bye to his classmates, and went home on leave.

[20] John T. Sprague, *The Florida War*, 249 f.

II

Indians and Mexicans

ORDERS to Thomas, after his furlough, assigned him to Company D, Third Artillery, which the Lieutenant joined at Fort Columbus in New York Harbor. Here on Governor's Island, four companies of regulars were being recruited for service in the Florida war, and some recent West Point graduates were conducting drill on the parade ground. Thomas met Lieutenant Braxton Bragg, a dour and punctilious young officer of the Class of 1837 who had some tales of Florida to relate. The scattered army forces found themselves outnumbered, as a rule, at luckless moments. The jungle was a devilish place, the Indians dashing in and out of it like lightning on their murderous raids.

Bragg, whose home was in North Carolina not far from the Virginia line, was eager to visit there before resuming military duties in Florida. But the few miles which separated his birthplace from Virginia made all the difference in the world, Bragg thought, in respect to military privilege. Ever since the days of Washington, the army had been ruled by a Virginia hierarchy; now in command were native sons Thomas S. Jesup, Winfield Scott, Zachary Taylor, Walker Armistead, and Edmund P. Gaines. About the middle of November, when embarkation orders were posted, Bragg formally requested that he be allowed to make the first stage of the journey by rail in order to visit his aged and ailing father. In a note to Major Justin Dimock, commanding, he intimated that leave to go home was almost, though not quite, a part of his birthright. "I was not lucky enough to be born in Virginia, but I was born in a county of North Carolina bordering on Virginia," he said, "and therefore I ask leave to proceed by land."[1] The letter was accorded the silent treatment; and on November 23, 1840, the coastwise vessel *Zenobia* sailed for Savannah, Georgia, with Lieutenants Bragg and Thomas on board.

At Savannah more recruits were collected, several new companies were added to the Third Artillery, and two hundred soldiers were crowded into two small ships which shuttled between Savannah and the Florida ports. Thomas sailed with his company in the *Forester,* which dropped anchor at Fort Lauderdale; and the other companies were scattered along the coast from St. Augustine, where Bragg was stationed, to Key Biscayne. William Tecumseh Sherman, attached to Company A, was learning the ropes at Fort Pierce with his former roommate Stewart Van Vliet a member of the same company. Van Vliet was destined to accomplish a rare thing in Florida—shoot and kill an Indian.

Disembarking at Lauderdale, Thomas discovered a cluster of weather-beaten cane-built huts and a few Indian wigwams, all very dirty and overrun with cockroaches. The shabby little settlement stood about two hundred feet from the ocean, and behind it ran a deep and slow-moving river which now meanders through the center of the modern town. Farther back lay the jungle of tropical growth where thorn-clad vine tangled thickly about the swamp cypress, each limb hanging heavy with Spanish moss. Fires from Indian encampments lit up the far horizon. It was a picturesque scene at twilight, but Thomas enjoyed little sleep the first few nights. The buzzing of mosquitoes and other winged insects was almost continuous, and an army of fleas infested every cot. From the upland and swampy jungle came the scream of the panther, the hoarse bellow of the alligator, the shrill call of the whippoorwill, and the dismal cry of the loon. Foxes yelped and owls hooted, and the single solace of the evening was the nightingale's sweet song.

The soldiers soon learned to fish for pompano, redfish, snappers, and green turtles with net and line. The task of feeding the detachment fell on Thomas, who discovered he could stretch green-turtle steaks just so far. So much fine sea food was provided that the soldiers began to clamor for beef, which was

[1] *North American Review*, October, 1888, 364–65.

scarce and poor in quality, and they even welcomed an occasional serving of barreled mess pork. Thomas devoted much of his time to the quest for supplies, entering the woods for deer and wild turkey. Since he proved unusually attentive to duty and could be counted on to keep sober, he received the additional tasks of quartermaster, adjutant, and ordnance officer. All these responsibilities kept him closely confined to camp while officers on line duty had the more exciting job of rounding up small bands of savages, perhaps a family or two, to be transported to new hunting grounds in Indian Territory.

In July, 1841, Thomas encountered Lieutenant Van Vliet, wearing a satisfied smile, on his way south from Fort Pierce with Major Thomas Childs and sixty men; after taking sixty additional troops from Lauderdale, they penetrated the Everglades in an attempt to oust the renowned Seminole Chief Sam Jones from his cornfields. "I have been left behind to take care of this infernal place in consequence of being commissary, etc.," Thomas informed a former West Point comrade now on duty at Watervliet Arsenal on the Hudson. "What do you ordnance officers do for quartermasters and commissaries? Do you do the duty yourselves, or have you staff officers at your arsenals to perform those duties?" It was a natural question. "Old Van," Thomas continued, "has become so much pleased with line duty that I hardly think he could be bribed to accept an appointment on a staff corps. This will be the only opportunity I shall have of distinguishing myself, and not to be able to avail myself of it is too bad."[2]

The expedition was only partially successful, however, and after nearly a year of wrestling with problems of supply and demand, Thomas received an assignment which raised his spirits. Early in November, Captain Richard D. A. Wade, commanding at Lauderdale, was ordered to descend the river and ransack some of the native villages. Appointed second in command, Thomas went along with a detachment of sixty men and the post surgeon. A dozen canoes were paddled silently along the river; operating by stealth, Captain Wade landed on the shore of an inlet and captured a lone Seminole fishing in the bay.

2 Coppée, *Thomas*, 7–8.

The Indian was persuaded to lead the party fifteen miles overland to his village. Concealing themselves behind trees and brush, the soldiers surrounded it just after sundown and at a given signal burst in. A volley or two felled six grown Indians and two boys, who tried to escape; then the remnants of the several families were rounded up and placed under guard. All the stores in the village—pumpkins, beans, and other supplies— were piled up and burned, as well as all canoes not needed to transport the bag of twenty prisoners. One of the Indians slyly informed Captain Wade that although he had once been a great friend of Chief Sam Jones, they had recently quarreled. He offered to lead the party to one of the Chief's villages about thirty miles distant. The troops slept on their arms and rose early to march through bog and saw grass and over pine barrens, dodging rattlesnakes. Again they made their stealthy approach, but this time the savages were so completely surprised that they had no choice but to surrender. Again pushing forward a few miles, the detachment reached another settlement to make war upon a field of pumpkins, a single canoe, and a few huts. An additional prisoner was taken, but the game had petered out.[3]

As Indian expeditions went, this was accounted one of the most successful. Besides the eight men and boys killed, Captain Wade reported the capture of fourteen warriors, sixteen women, ten boys, fifteen girls, thirteen rifles, twelve powder horns, and quantities of buckshot and ball. Destroyed were thirty canoes and large stores of provisions. The Captain's report carried his thanks to Thomas for his "valuable and efficient aid," and Colonel W. J. Worth, commanding, recommended him for brevet to first lieutenant.[4] The brevet, "for gallantry and good conduct," was received as of November 6, and Wade himself was brevetted major. Still it was a rather shabby war, although, as Lieutenant Sherman explained it, "These excursions possessed to us a peculiar charm, for the fragrance of the air, the abundance of game and fish, and just enough of adventure, gave to life a rel-

[3] *Army and Navy Chronicle*, November 25, 1941; Sprague, *The Florida War*, 392–93; Johnson, *Thomas*, 18–20.
[4] Johnson, *Thomas*, 21.

ish."[5] The news of Captain Wade's success quickly spread; and another scout was organized, with Sherman, Van Vliet, Thomas, and several other West Pointers joining an expedition which again combined the forces at Forts Pierce and Lauderdale, but not a single Indian was seen.

Returning from this second November expedition, Thomas stepped from his boat to greet a new commanding officer at Lauderdale, Captain Erasmus Darwin Keyes, West Point, 1832. Recently promoted from first lieutenant, Keyes had been transferred from a comfortable staff job in Washington, and so far his two days of existence in Florida had taught him the meaning of the soldiers' phrase, "infested prison-house of the Army." For his first breakfast at Fort Lauderdale, he was served muddy coffee without milk, brown sugar, hard bread, tough buckwheat cakes, and semifluid rancid butter floating in a cracked teacup. For dinner, bean soup was substituted for the buckwheat cakes and harsh commissary whiskey for the coffee.[6] Keyes recalled the rich soups, juicy meats, and dry wines which comprised his customary fare in Washington, and shuddered.

Thomas heard his complaints sympathetically and promptly set about getting together a decent bill of fare. A man of strong likes and dislikes, Keyes could never say too much in praise of George Thomas. Although he saw little of him other than in the Florida service, he devoted several pages to him in his memoirs—almost as much as to General-in-Chief Scott. "The shape and carriage of his head and the expression of his handsome face corresponded with my idea of a patrician of Ancient Rome," wrote Keyes. "Thomas possessed an even temperament and was never violently demonstrative. He was seldom much in advance of the appointed time in his arrival at the post of duty, and I never knew him to be late or in a hurry. All his movements were deliberate, his self-possession was supreme, and he received and gave orders with equal serenity. From the first we were companions, and my confidence in him was complete. He did his duty and kept all his appointments precisely. . . . His deportment was dignified, and in the presence of strangers and casual

5 William T. Sherman, *Personal Memoirs*, I, 27.
6 Erasmus D. Keyes, *Fifty Years' Observation of Men and Events*, 163–64.

acquaintances he was reserved. . . . His nature was not only absolutely just but it was also highly sympathetic and genial. The happiest illusions of my youth and the most joyous encounters of my life have left no more benignant traces in my memory than my associations with George H. Thomas."[7]

Keyes relieved the lieutenant of his quartermaster duties, and the two officers devoted many quiet evening hours to an exchange of ideas and experiences. One of Keyes' favorite anecdotes concerned a scientific method, expounded by Thomas, of locating "Officer B." It was that officer's habit to sit reading in his hut while regaling himself with plug tobacco. Turning his head to the right, he could spit in the fireplace, or to the left, out of the window. "Now," said Thomas, "you may come in at the window and follow up the line of tobacco juice on the floor, or you may descend the chimney and trace from that, and at the intersection of the two lines you will discover 'B'."[8] Typical of Thomas's heavy humor, this made a hit with Keyes.

The final autumn campaign against the Indians, which accomplished nothing materially, did prove, nevertheless, that the Seminoles had fled to the safety of the Everglades in the interior. This result was cheering news in East Florida. Several new blockhouses had been erected during the year and additional tracts of land were cultivated in their shelter. The current phase of the war, it was apparent, was nearing its close. Sometime during December, Thomas and his company sailed around the peninsula to army headquarters at the head of Tampa Bay, and early in February, 1842, proceeded to New Orleans to refit. The army transport came up the Mississippi River to the city on the pile-built, broad levee, its wharves crowded with ships and laden with cotton bales, molasses casks, and hogsheads of sugar and tobacco. The old French forts within the city limits were deserted and crumbling, but farther out from the town were the modern bastions named for War of 1812 heroes. The vagueness of history concerning routine troop movements provides no clue to where Thomas was stationed, but there is little doubt that he attended the opera at the Theatre d'Orleans and dined at the domed Hotel St. Charles.

[7] *Ibid.,* 166–67, 179.
[8] *Ibid.,* 169.

The city was open-handed and gay, its dim filigreed streets luring the soldiers on nocturnal excursions. News from Florida that spring told of an actual victory following a pitched battle in a swamp. Other Third Artillery companies began to arrive at New Orleans, where Captain Keyes was pleased to rejoin his favorite subaltern in June. Since the thermometer soared well above ninety degrees in June, few were reluctant to leave the city for Charleston, South Carolina, when the regiment was ordered to sail on July 1. To escape the heat in the Gulf, officers and men kept to their berths or in the ship's cabin during the day and walked the deck at night. After lying uncomfortably becalmed for sixteen days, they reached port on July 26, eager to stretch their legs on land. Their new post was Fort Moultrie on Sullivan's Island with its bowers of roses and fine summer homes, a desirable haven for every young officer. Prominent Charleston families who sojourned on the island in summer were honored guests at dinner parties at the fort, bringing their lofty secessionist ideas with them. Wherever Old Blackburn Madeira and Scotch whiskey flowed, the officers kept on their guard; but their superiors had issued warning to refrain from political argument.

Captain Keyes recalled many pleasant hours at Fort Moultrie in the company of his two subalterns, George H. Thomas and Thomas W. Sherman of Rhode Island. Cump Sherman of Ohio, now a first lieutenant, and Stewart Van Vliet were there, as also were Lieutenants John F. Reynolds of Pennsylvania and Bragg of North Carolina, and Captain Robert Anderson of Kentucky, one of Thomas's instructors in the old days at West Point. Across the harbor these officers could watch the cotton ships from Northern ports dumping ballast for the foundation of a new fort which would bear the name of South Carolina's Revolutionary hero, Thomas Sumter. The command of this fort one day would fall to Major Anderson, and every available man in Charleston Harbor would be summoned for its defense on the eve of the great war.

Leave from duty after the customary two-year interval came to Thomas in November. Traveling with Lieutenant John Pope, who was going to Baltimore, he took the boat for Wilmington, North Carolina, then entrained for Goldsboro, where he encountered another artillery mate, Lieutenant Samuel G. French. With Pope already in tow, Thomas persuaded French to accompany him on the Weldon and Norfolk Railroad, which had a stop not far from his home in Southampton County. French recalled some of the discomforts of the trip which were still vivid in his declining years. The trio rode as far as Weldon in the northern part of the state and spent a chilly night at a ramshackle country inn. "On the way to Norfolk the rails were covered with frost and the driving wheels slipped so we all had to get out of the cars and help push the train over a slight ascent to a bridge."[9] French and Pope said good-bye to Thomas without thanking him for the experience and took a northbound boat at Portsmouth.

Early in December the lieutenant rejoined his company at Fort McHenry on Whetstone Point near Baltimore. The fort not only had won historic honors during the perilous fight of 1814 but was considered socially one of the most desirable posts in the country. There was much gaiety in the city, and many delicately inscribed invitations to parties and masquerade balls found their way to the fort. The West Pointers who had seen Indian service had little difficulty in winning social distinction and in turn wrote extravagant tributes to the beauty and grace of the young women they met. "The ladies of Baltimore from their ancestors inherited beauty, and from their environments naturally acquired retiring manners, low and sweet voices, gentleness and attractive grace," wrote Lieutenant French, a New Jerseyman who would defend the South in the great war.[10] Thomas moved in these social circles for a season, but service at Fort McHenry was not prolonged. After being promoted to first lieutenant, he was transferred in July to Company E, which was ordered back to Fort Moultrie in the fall. Captain Keyes was no longer at Charleston, but Cump Sherman recently had returned from special duty in Georgia and Alabama and could tell of riding from Rome to Bellefonte and from Kennesaw Mountain to Augusta. These trips, as it happened, took him over "the very

9 French, *Two Wars*, 24.
10 *Ibid.*, 26.

ground where in after years I had to conduct vast armies and fight great battles," as Sherman modestly wrote in his *Memoirs*.[11]

Life had been serene and happy during the quiet months since leaving Florida, and, except for three years to be spent as an instructor at West Point, Thomas would never know another period like it. A hint of imminent war with Mexico came with his transfer to recruiting service in Charleston during the winter, and again with the passage of a Congressional resolution which plainly invited the Republic of Texas to enter the Union. Certain Whigs in Congress protested that Texas was then at war with Mexico. "If we annex Texas, we will annex the war," exclaimed Senator Henry Clay of Kentucky. War or no war, Texas belonged to the Union, the Southern Democrats asserted. Since more Democratic heads than Whig could be counted in Congress, a future theater of conflict beckoned to the soldiers at Charleston. Uprooted from their comfortable quarters by a majority decision, members of Company E sailed for New Orleans on June 27, 1845.[12]

Commanding the artillery company was Braxton Bragg, now a captain, whom Keyes, hitting the bull's-eye, described as "ambitious and of a saturnine disposition and morbid temperament." Bragg had been sorely tried at a Fourth of July dinner party at Fort Moultrie when an ardent local aristocrat referred to North Carolina as a "strip of land lying between two states."[13] A duel had been avoided only when Sherman and Reynolds, acting as peacemakers, managed to postpone the affair. Of course, Bragg never forgot the indignity, which apparently served to stimulate his endless industry and his ambition to command. Thomas, plain and modest in manner, bearing no trace of false pride, managed to continue on very good terms with Bragg during their service together, although bitter personal enmity lay somewhere ahead.

After waiting several weeks in New Orleans for an artillery battery to arrive, Company E left for Corpus Christi on the Texas frontier, followed some weeks later by General Zachary

11 Sherman, *Personal Memoirs*, I, 32.
12 Richmond *Enquirer*, July 15, 1845.
13 *North American Review*, October, 1888, 365.

Taylor and his staff and several infantry companies. Other forces, both infantry and volunteers, had arrived meantime, as events elsewhere led up to the war. Annexation of Texas by the United States was agreed to by the Texas Congress and ratified by the people of that republic, who convened in boisterous holiday spirit on July 4. While Taylor's camp was pitched at the mouth of the Nueces River, the Democratic administration was on the march, claiming all the territory extending to the Río Grande, about 180 miles away. Taylor was instructed that even an attempt by a Mexican army to cross the Río Grande would be considered an invasion; and when the Mexicans declined to oblige, he was instructed to approach the river to repel "any attempted invasion." Since Mexico had committed many nuisances but no overt act, Taylor thought the proposal a little raw, and requested more definite instructions. Nothing was heard from the War Department for a time. Excitement in Congress concerning the Texas question was diverted by the "fifty-four forty or fight" clamor over Oregon, and since the Administration wanted only one fight at a time, a way would be found to accept the British offer of the forty-ninth parallel.

The soldiers at Corpus Christi went hunting for snipe, geese, deer, and turkeys, or gambled on the speed of their Mexican ponies. Bragg and Thomas, with Lieutenants John F. Reynolds and Daniel H. Hill, industriously practiced with their artillery teams. Friendly Mexicans who came to Corpus Christi during the winter described to Taylor the preparations their government was making for war. Some half-hearted diplomacy failing, the General was instructed to proceed to the Río Grande while the Pacific fleet held itself in readiness to blockade or occupy the Mexican province of California. Cump Sherman was still stuck with a recruiting job in the East, although he escaped it in time to sail around Cape Horn and take up quartermaster's duties in a California coastal town. Thomas found himself caught up in the march of events when orders came to Taylor to start for the Río Grande early in February, 1846. Taylor, who happened to be somewhat unprepared, hurriedly called for more wagons and mules, and the army continued to wait while the mules were trained. On February 22, a supply depot was established forty miles in advance; and two weeks later some four thousand regulars and volunteers packed up their souvenirs and equipment. A few Mexican skirmishers but no sizable force was encountered north of the Río Grande. Arriving on the left bank on March 28, Taylor threw up a massive six-sided work which was christened Fort Texas, but before it was finished, a few thousand Mexicans under General Mariano Arista got busy across the river and erected a series of earthworks and gun emplacements within easy shooting distance of the American work.[14]

Uneasily eyeing enemy activity, several dozen troops deserted the Americans to join the gaudily clad warriors and *senoritas* on the other side of the river. All the news discussed in the American camp was bad. Several small detachments sent on reconnoitering missions during April were surprised and scattered by a jubilant enemy. After learning of the capture of Captain Seth B. Thornton and some sixty dragoons on April 26, Taylor announced that the war was on. Several days later he discovered Arista to be strongly reinforced, while Fort Texas obviously required more adequate supplies of munitions and food. Officers of Company E, with their twelve-pound field guns, took their positions in the fort as the General started back to Point Isabel, a supply base twenty-eight miles in the rear. The Seventh Infantry, Major Jacob Brown commanding, four eighteen-pound guns, the camp women, and the sick were also left behind in the fort.

Although the work was strong enough to withstand a long siege, there was no telling how soon Taylor might return and how far supplies on hand could be stretched. Thomas witnessed a burst of energy among the artillerymen as the first shots were exchanged on the morning of May 3, but he worked his own gun sparingly.[15] Not only were the Mexican redoubts difficult to hit, but he wished to reserve his store of shells for a later day. An enemy cross fire did little damage except to keep everyone awake. The defenders of the fort grew heavy eyed and haggard from loss of sleep; food and water were doled out sparingly as

14 Justin H. Smith, *The War With Mexico*, I, 148–58.
15 Donn Piatt, *General George H. Thomas*, 67.

supplies dwindled. Insults shouted in several languages came to the ears of the pickets. The garrison suffered the loss of its commander on the third day when a shell fragment struck Major Brown in the leg. Worn out by fatigue, Brown survived the necessary amputation only a few hours, leaving his name to the fort and to the present city of Brownsville.

General Arista, who was blockading the road to Point Isabel, sent an emissary to the fort with a message advising surrender. The enemy openly boasted that the Americans would never hear from their General Taylor again. Remembering the Alamo, the defenders "promptly and most positively declined" the summons.[16] Three more wearisome days and nights went by with much dust and noise, thirst and hunger. Enemy shells continued to scream overhead or blast the thick walls of the fort. Estimates of shot and shell expended by the Mexicans reached 2,700 by the end of the siege, although only thirteen privates were wounded and one army noncom killed in addition to the commander. "The small loss could hardly be credited," wrote a Seventh Regiment officer.[17] On May 8, General Taylor approached within a few miles of the fort with loaded wagon trains. After battering his way through Arista's advance line at Palo Alto, he joined battle with the Mexicans next day at Resaca de la Palma, a covering growth from which a cavalry charge finally routed the foe. "Haggard faces put on smiles"[18] as Company E poured a galling fire into the mob of fugitives which streamed past the fort and sought safety across the river. Lieutenant Thomas, who still had a few shells stacked up, considered the target well worth waiting for as he sped the Mexicans homeward.[19]

[16] W. S. Henry, *Campaign Sketches of the War With Mexico*, 103.

[17] *Ibid.*

[18] Smith, *The War With Mexico*, I, 176.

[19] Cullum, *Biographical Register of Officers and Cadets of the United States Military Academy*, II, 36.

III

Monterrey and Buena Vista

"I would have rather fought 20 battles than passed through the bombardment of Fort Brown," declared one officer.[1] The lessons of the siege were not wasted on Lieutenant Thomas. He had seen Taylor extend his lines too far, a move dictated by political rather than military necessity, and so the General had been forced to hurry off for supplies before joining battle with the foe which had surprised him. Although Fort Brown had managed to hold out, a more skillful and determined enemy could have cut off the relieving force and destroyed the half-starved garrison at its leisure. The experience contributed to Thomas's innate store of caution and helped to make him less an improviser than a leader who operated on fixed principles, with absolute readiness his first rule. Whenever in command of an independent force during the Civil War, Thomas insisted on establishing fixed bases of supplies and making his lines of communication sure before advancing very far into the enemy country, and on other occasions he earnestly counseled his superior commander to observe this rule. On the other hand, General William Tecumseh Sherman moved faster and got farther than Thomas because he learned from Grant early in the war how to cut loose from fixed bases of supplies. The difference between these generals has been epitomized by the sayings: "Thomas never lost a battle," and "Sherman never won a battle or lost a campaign."

But on the day following Resaca de la Palma, Thomas thought only of food and fresh water and a bath in the muddy Río Grande. The dead on both sides were buried, the fort policed up, and the soldiers replenished their haversacks and

[1] Henry, *Campaign Sketches of the War With Mexico*, 104.

28

canteens. After a good night's sleep, Thomas crossed with his company into Matamoros. Priests and other natives brought complaints to Taylor that the retreating Mexican mob was raiding the countryside; sixty miles up the river the town of Reynosa appealed for the "protection" of the American troops, whose conduct, as it turned out, could not have been worse. Principal offenders were a mounted force of Texas Rangers who were carrying on a racial war against their hated neighbors, and following the campaign against Monterrey, Taylor sent them home.

Placed in command of two twelve-inch fieldpieces, Thomas marched ahead with some Seventh Infantry regulars and a company of Texans. The winding road coursed nearly due west through a fertile country with cornfields in sprout. Sleepy natives and their demure donkeys were aroused by bawdy shouts; wherever liquor was to be found, small parties of troops would get out of hand, looting and slaying. Arriving at Reynosa late in June, the soldiers feasted on ripe watermelon. The town was perched on a high outcropping of limestone and was obviously a healthy spot, quite well suited for an army base. However, when Taylor came along, he ordered the detachment to Camargo on the San Juan River, three miles from its junction with the Río Grande. Since it had been raining, the advance force had a difficult march while Taylor and the rest of the army came along in steamboats.

The town offered no opposition to the American detachment which plodded in on July 16. The soldiers found it a pestilential spot. Cut off from refreshing breezes by limestone hills, Camargo was one of the hottest places in all that region.[2] Most of the houses had been wrecked by recent freshets and there was an outpouring of scorpions, tarantulas, centipedes, and little frogs. "Scarcely a respectable house is left standing," chronicled Major Philip N. Barbour of Kentucky, who arrived with the main force early in August. "The troops (7th Infantry and a section of Bragg's Battery under Lieut. Thomas) are encamped in the plaza. The men occupy the buildings on the four sides to lounge in during the heat of the day. Dined with Thomas and

2 Smith, *The War With Mexico*, I, 212.

fared well. They had a most excellent dish that I never saw before, though it is an exceedingly simple one, viz.: fried peaches. Thomas told me there were plenty of fine peaches in town just ripening."[3] The fruit helped slacken the thirst of abstemious officers who regarded commissary whiskey and drinking water from the infested San Juan River as equally unpalatable. Soon the troops became sickly. Desolated Camargo, with its fierce heat, was dubbed a "Yawning Grave Yard."

"The mortality in our camp was appalling," wrote a soldier. "The dead march was ever wailing in our ears. . . . The groans and lamentations of the poor sufferers during those sickly, sultry nights were heartrending."[4] Yet it was here that Taylor chose to remain until September 5. Thomas yearned for an opportunity to quit the place early, but selected to lead the next advance were two infantry divisions under General William Jenkins Worth and General David E. Twiggs.

The next goal was the ancient city of Monterrey, a stronghold of adobe and stone perched on heavily fortified heights about one hundred miles southwest of Camargo. Early in September, Thomas took up the march with the rest of his company under Captain Bragg, a second artillery company led by Captain Randolph Ridgeley, and a brace of twenty-four-pound siege howitzers under Captain Edward Webster, son of the famous Daniel. Four companies of dragoons accompanied General Taylor and the artillery. Several hundred volunteers were left behind with the sick.

Leaving the dusty alluvial lands along the river, the men began to breathe deeply again. The town of Cerralvo, which they passed, was an attractive and healthy place, far better suited for a base than Camargo, but the rudiments of military hygiene were not yet part and parcel of official knowledge. Fields of corn and sugar cane, groves of ebony, oak, pecan, and mesquite trees abounded. "One broad plain shone with Spanish dahlias . . . every few miles a stream of cool, sparkling water leaped across the road. . . . In one town after another, grapes, figs and pome-

[3] Rhoda Doubleday (ed.), *Journal of Major Philip Norbourne Barbour*, 95.

[4] N. W. Stephenson, *Texas and the Mexican War*, 198.

granates delighted the eye."[5] When the soldiers caught their
first glimpse of the pale blue summits of the jagged Sierra Madre,
wagers were laid as to whether the lofty spectacle was mountains
or clouds. The peaks revealed themselves by rising higher each
day and darkening at sunset against a brilliant sky.

The food supply was no problem in that lush season. Fat
cattle grazed in the meadows, cornfields were in silk, and melons
and tree fruits fast ripening in the sun. "We had oranges, lem-
ons, limes, pomegranates, bananas and grapes," sighed Lieutenant Samuel G. French who marched with Thomas and Company E.[6] The army kept on the alert against a thousand mounted
Mexicans who, by hovering in front, separated Taylor from his
two infantry divisions. The march, however, was undisturbed
save for occasional depredations by foraging dragoons. Two
weeks on the road brought the army in sight of the soaring
cathedral towers and the looming defenses of Monterrey, "holy
city of the frontier." An extensive plain bordered by a grove of
pecan and walnut trees stood out from the northern ramparts.
An immense fortification, known as the Citadel but christened
"Black Fort" by the troops, guarded the approaches; and as
Taylor ventured within firing range, several cannon shot
whizzed past, miraculously injuring no one. In the city a deep-
toned bell was tolling. The Americans had come. Taylor retreated to the grove and pitched camp at a place called "Walnut
Springs."

Besides Black Fort, four other stout works, including the
heavily fortified Bishop's Palace on a western height, guarded
the city. Mexican sharpshooters protected by sandbags swarmed
over the housetops and the roof of the Cathedral. Commanded
by General Pedro de Ampudia, a wealthy native, the defenders
were variously estimated to number 8,000 or 10,000 against
about 6,600 officers and men under Taylor.

Built largely of adobe and stone, which made stubborn
walls, the city posed a large problem in generalship, which Taylor attacked by sending General Worth on a wide detour to
cut off the main supply route to the south while the artillery was

5 Smith, *The War With Mexico*, 236.
6 French, *Two Wars*, 59.

unlimbered before Black Fort. On Sunday, September 20, the siege began, as the West Pointers banged away at the massive walls. Thomas kept hard at work with his guns; but with no real siege ordnance near at hand, Webster being posted elsewhere, the artillery action served merely as a diversion.

Actual fighting commenced in the streets of the city the next day. During the forenoon, Bragg's battery was summoned on the gallop; but advancing a little too far, Thomas and his men found themselves pent up in a narrow alley between two walls of stone. Bullets were showering down from near-by housetops while only a single piece of artillery could be brought into action. Some of the men were badly hit; four horses were killed and several wounded.[7] Ordered to retreat, Thomas paused to load his piece once more and give the enemy a parting shot.[8] The gun carriage had to be raised up by hand and wheeled around; then Thomas waited until fresh horses could be brought up to haul it away. He managed to find his way out safely, but the First Ohio Volunteers, swinging into action, encountered Bragg's battery "in very bad plight . . . a perfect wreck" on the outskirts of the town. "A few of his artillerymen and more than a dozen horses were down in the same spot, making the ground about the guns slippery with their gasped foam and blood." Nevertheless, the West Pointers continued with the work at hand. Still exposed to enemy fire, they were desperately stripping the harness from the dead and disabled animals "determined that not a buckle or strap should be lost."[9]

The guns from the Citadel now turned on the Ohio Volunteers. Led by a bold Mexican female dressed as a captain, a body of enemy lancers lifted their banners and raced from the fort.[10] The volunteers dropped to the ground, lifted their rifles, and grew shaky. They were seriously considering retreat when help came from an unexpected quarter. Friendly guns boomed, grape and canister from Bragg's revived battery poured into the Mexi-

[7] S. C. Reid, *Scouting Expedition of McCulloch's Texas Rangers*, 172.

[8] Coppée, *Thomas*, 15; Van Horne, *Thomas*, 5.

[9] L. Giddings, *Campaign in Northern Mexico*, 168–69.

[10] Henry, *Campaign Sketches of the War With Mexico*, 233.

can ranks, and men and horses went down in struggling heaps as the confused lancers scurried back to the protection of Black Fort. Standing firm and grim-faced, Bragg, Thomas, and French were having a final go at the enemy, do or die.

On Tuesday, September 22, the exhausted battery refitted. On the other side of town, General Worth had cut the main supply road and was preparing to storm the Bishop's Palace, a heavily sandbagged sharpshooters' hive. Captain Webster's big guns were hammering away at the Cathedral, a storehouse for munitions, its roof alive with troops. The Bishop's Palace was taken after prolonged and bloody fighting that day, but the Cathedral in the central plaza and most of the city itself still remained in enemy hands.

It took still another hard day to drive the Mexicans from the plaza and the housetops. On September 23, as Bragg's battery began playing on the Cathedral, Lieutenant French was ordered to clear away a barricaded street leading into the plaza. He gained his position in time to witness the arrival of several companies of volunteers and regulars, who began fighting their way to the housetops. General Taylor then arrived without fanfare. French described the novel parade: "General Taylor and staff came down the street on foot, and very imprudently he passed the cross street, escaping the many shots fired at him. There he was, almost alone. He tried to enter the store on the corner. The door being locked, he and the Mexican within had a con fab, but not understanding what was said he called to Colonel Kinney, the interpreter. . . . The Colonel said 'damn,' and went over at double-quick and made the owner open the door. The store was empty. Here General Quitman joined him with some troops and a gun in charge of Lieutenant G. H. Thomas. Quitman directed me to take my howitzer to the next cross street but to save my men and horses. I suggested that Thomas should put his gun in position first and let us pass over through the smoke. Comprehending the matter at once, he said: 'No, you remain here and let Thomas pass over when you fire.' [Under cover of the smoke] Thomas moved to the next street and turned his gun into it. That street was barricaded also and defended by a piece of artillery. The infantry and riflemen now

33

made good progress in gaining possession of the houses and driving the enemy toward the plaza."[11]

The sight of General Taylor and the Mexican shopkeeper jabbering away at each other as guns popped and bullets flew thickly must have been diverting. Thomas and French kept on the move, peppering the barricades and silencing enemy guns. The infantrymen worked their way from house to house, knocking in doors with axes and smashing connecting walls by detonating shells. General Worth's command meantime was fighting its way toward the Cathedral from another direction, and by sunset the enemy were herded into the plaza and surrounded. The two pieces of artillery under Thomas and French were ordered back to camp with appropriate compliments. Concerned over a slight wound which French had received, Thomas took charge of his gun and hurried him off to the surgeon's tent.

Honors of war made Bragg a major by brevet and Thomas a brevet captain for good conduct and gallantry under fire. Another nickname fell his way, "Old Reliable."[12] Taylor, who was more conciliatory than implacable toward a beaten foe, was content to arrange an armistice, permitting Ampudia to retain side arms and a field battery of six pieces and to march from the city with his army intact. The terms were defended on the ground that too many lives would have been expended in taking Black Fort and that facilities were lacking to handle the thousands of Mexicans who would have become prisoners. But although the capture of Monterrey was hailed as a great victory nearly everywhere in the States, it contributed very little to the progress of the war.

While Taylor's recent triumph was variously praised and deprecated along party lines at Washington, officers and men went hunting for blue-winged teal and snipe. They regaled themselves at an American circus which unexpectedly showed up, patronized the gambling places which began to fill the city, and attended services in the sparsely filled Cathedral where an accomplished organist interspersed sacred music with operatic

11 French, *Two Wars,* 66.
12 W. F. G. Shanks, *Personal Recollections of Distinguished Generals,* 79.

airs. Many visited the Bishop's Palace, which commanded a grand view, and the troops also inspected the luxurious gardens and baths of General Arista's palace, its corridors and marble-paved halls now crowded with the wounded and sick. Although the climate was called "delicious," many soldiers were stricken with chills and fever, a reaction, it was thought, "from the active and exciting life we have been leading and to the injudicious use of fruits, such as oranges and pomegranates," Lieutenant George Gordon Meade informed his family. "Nearly one-third of the army is down with it," he wrote from Monterrey on October 20.[13]

Taking cognizance of the cool attitude of President Polk toward the recent victory, the West Pointers arrayed themselves solidly behind their leader. Despite some injudicious campaigning methods, Taylor's stout-hearted, homespun manner, devoid of pettiness and pomp, his unfamiliarity with fear, and his rumpled old clothes made him a great favorite. But Polk seemed dissatisfied with the armistice terms arranged with Ampudia and also uneasy about a Whig-sponsored presidential boom for the General. Taylor, therefore, was directed to send the portion of his force which still remained at Camargo and beyond to Tampico on the Mexican coast.

Lieutenant Meade of the Engineers expressed the prevailing indignation at this "outrage upon all military propriety . . . cutting up a commanding general's force,"[14] but what had been begun as a politically inspired war was to end as one. Orders were sent over Taylor's head to General Robert E. Patterson, commanding in the Río Grande Valley, to explore the mountain passes leading to Tampico, but Taylor decided that he could do this as well himself and ordered Patterson to follow along. Early in November, disregarding orders to remain where he was, Taylor sent General Worth to Saltillo, sixty-five miles to the south, and led another advance by an easterly route as far as Montemorelos. General John A. Quitman, who was selected to lead the advance toward Tampico, requested artillery support, nominating Thomas, Reynolds, and French of Bragg's battery,

[13] George Meade (ed.), *Life and Letters of General Meade*, I, 145.
[14] *Ibid.*

35

with the Virginian in command. Quitman's immediate goal was Victoria, village capital of the state of Tamaulipas (High Mountains). He organized the volunteer infantry assigned him into two brigades and marched along a beautiful and fertile valley in frosty December weather. The soldiers feasted their eyes on the lofty Sierra Madres which towered on the right in one unbroken chain. Their "sharp serrated edge," according to Lieutenant French, "looked thin enough for a man to sit astride of."[15]

Ushered in by a damp and rainy holiday evening, Christmas Day found the expedition on a hilly road near Villa Gran, a village surrounded by groves of orange trees and vast sugar estates. French went into the mountains to try to bag a holiday turkey but returned empty-handed; Reynolds and Thomas, meantime, had obtained some eggs and other ingredients for eggnog, lacking only the necessary stimulant. The trio then summoned the army physician and made him a prisoner until he could provide suitable ransom in the shape of a bottle of brandy or rum. So a note was carried to the steward and the missing ingredient supplied, the doctor jovially partaking of his own prescription and the holiday spirit.[16] Word filtered back that a large force of enemy lancers was somewhere ahead, but since the Mexicans were prone to exaggerate both their numbers and their capacity, Quitman's detachment of 2,000 men continued on its way undisturbed and marched into the great square at Victoria on December 29. The enemy, it was learned, had abandoned the place only a few hours before their arrival.

Quitman was resolved on staging fitting ceremonies in taking over the town. The General and his staff entered the square on formal parade, followed by Thomas's battery and several columns of infantry with bayonets gleaming. The artillery filed out of column and massed in the center, the officers to the front, facing the Alcazar. Arms were presented, the alcade and other town officials came forward, and after making a complimentary address, the alcade presented Quitman with the keys to the city.

15 French, *Two Wars*, 69.
16 *Ibid.*, 69–70.

Down came the Mexican standard, and the Stars and Stripes were thrown to the breeze; but as the band began to play, "all at once 3 or 4 jackasses began to bray and bray, and drowned out all proceedings amidst roars of laughter that could not be restrained, especially among the volunteers."[17]

The soldiers made their camp in a near-by field. Northers blew, flattening every tent and filling the air with a fine black dust. Then, on January 4, 1847, Taylor arrived with a division of regulars under General Twiggs, and a day or two later 1,500 men under General Patterson showed up. A force of some 5,000 troops was now congregated about the little town, but Taylor lingered on for several days as if uncertain regarding his personal prospects. On January 12, with supplies running short, he ordered Twiggs and Patterson to proceed to Tampico in the hope that he himself would be allowed to follow, but dispatches from Washington dictated another course entirely. General Winfield Scott had been decided upon as the army's new commander-in-chief, and not only were Twiggs and Patterson to reinforce him at Tampico but Worth's division of regulars was to march north from Saltillo to the Río Grande to accompany him on the voyage south. Ordinarily calm, Taylor was so non-plused at the news that, according to the story noised about camp, he dished mustard instead of sugar into his coffee.[18] Thomas and his two field batteries, two squadrons of dragoons, and Quitman's volunteer infantry still remained; but counting the forces left to him at Saltillo and Monterrey, Taylor now had less than 800 regular troops and fewer than 5,000 volunteers, most of them newcomers and raw recruits. Nearly all his seasoned officers were leaving to join Scott. Beset by gloom and uncertainty, the General faced about for Monterrey.

The hearty dislike which Thomas would always entertain for political interference in military matters could have had its source in this unfortunate handling of a successful campaign. Nothing could have pleased the West Pointers more than to cut off all communication with Washington and get on with the war. The turn of events separated the routes now taken by three

17 *Ibid.*, 70; John R. Kenly, *Memoirs of a Maryland Volunteer*, 191–92.
18 French, *Two Wars*, 71.

officers who were to become better acquainted at other places and times—Lieutenant Thomas, who accompanied Taylor on the return north; Captain Robert E. Lee, who rode with Worth for the Río Grande; and Lieutenant Ulysses S. Grant of Twigg's division, who marched overland to Tampico to join the combined forces of Worth and Scott as they steamed south.

The natural law of compensation may now have induced Polk to show kindness to some general, but, rather unfortunately for Taylor's depleted force, it was Antonio López de Santa Anna who became the recipient of extraordinary courtesy. A former Mexican president and a general in the war against Texas in 1836, Santa Anna had been permitted to return from exile in Cuba to help make peace, as Polk fatuously hoped, but the enemy freebooter had a quite different idea. One of Scott's couriers bearing orders to Taylor revealing how his force was to be weakened had been swept from his horse and murdered at Villa Gran. Discovering how Taylor stood, Santa Anna planned first to cut the northern army to pieces and then descend upon Scott, an ingenious and worthy plan. Taylor halted his force at Villa Gran on his way north and set up court in the main plaza, demanding the killer of the captured courier. He threatened the trembling alcade with hanging if he did not reveal him and questioned several witnesses, but all seemed confused and ignorant of any murder. A village priest anxiously hovered about the exasperated General, who, upon adjourning court, threatened the villagers with a fine of $50,000 if the offender were not produced, but there the matter ended.[19] Reaching Monterrey, Taylor went into his old camp at Walnut Springs, where Thomas resumed practice with his battery and wrote a few letters home.

The road now led southward again as Taylor reinforced the garrison at Saltillo early in February. Thomas's laboring mount—the rider, aged thirty, easily topped two hundred pounds—climbed to an elevation of 4,400 feet during the leisurely four-day march and the detachment continued some twenty miles farther on to Agua Nueva where Taylor pitched camp with 4,650 men. To advance this far, however, was un-

19 *Ibid.,* 72.

necessary and useless. When reconnoitering parties sent out to uncover enemy plans, discovered Santa Anna approaching in force, Taylor retreated to a more favorable position, selecting ground at La Angostura (The Narrows), a short distance south of the hacienda of Buena Vista. The country was broken and heavily seamed on both sides of the road. On the left, deep gorges ran back to the mountains, and gullies on the other side left but a narrow passage at one place to defend. As Santa Anna's army came closer, the Americans, on February 21, made their camp on the plain just south of The Narrows. There was little confidence among the troops who shivered that night from cold and dread.

On February 22, a beautiful morning, the bands played "Hail Columbia," the watchword "Honor of Washington" was passed, and the men began to take heart. It was Taylor's plan to protect his base at Saltillo by blocking the road at The Narrows and carrying the fight well beyond. A battery of five field-pieces and two companies of Illinois Volunteers guarded The Narrows, six more infantry companies took positions in advance, while farther along two lines of infantry were arranged *en échelon* on a high plateau extending toward the mountains. Thomas commanded a field gun on the right of the Second Illinois Regiment near the front line, with French guarding the left flank. Just in front, the Second Indiana edged over toward a long ravine. Captain Thomas W. Sherman, with two guns in reserve, commanded this section of the battery, and Bragg was posted on the other side of the road.

Soldiers filing into their places caught sight of spiral clouds of dust rising lazily aloft to the southward. The banners of the Mexican cavalry soon came in sight, then the artillery and infantry with bands playing national airs. Enemy uniforms of every color of the sunset shone on the plain; even the horses were clad in gorgeous tassels and silks. Several hours were consumed in field evolutions. Presuming that Taylor might have been impressed by this demonstrated power, Santa Anna sent his surgeon general forward with a written suggestion that the American leader surrender. "I wish to save you from a catastrophe," Santa Anna proposed gallantly, adding that his force numbered 20,000 men.[20] Taylor declined the offer briefly and bluntly. At 3:00 P.M. an enemy gun boomed. Thomas watched a contest near the mountain on his left as General Ampudia's infantry outflanked two dismounted companies of Arkansas and Kentucky cavalry, but the principal force was not drawn into the fight that day.

Chilly winds again penetrated the blankets of the men as they slept that night beside their arms. It was frigid enough on the plateau but even colder on the mountain to the right where the Second Kentucky clung to the heights. The fighting opened at daybreak with the American advantage of position clearly apparent on this side of the road. The guns at The Narrows tore into the enemy left flank and the volunteer infantry slaughtered their hundreds. The line of battle began to center about the artillery position on the left where Mexicans in overwhelming numbers were arrayed in a huge semicircle about the hopeful defenders. Fortunately the broken country prevented the enemy from operating en masse. Peppered by a desultory infantry fire, Thomas replied with round and hollow shot as rapidly as his men could serve the gun. The advancing Mexicans took shelter in a gorge, caught their breath, and crept closer. Trouble arose on the left of the American ranks when a befuddled Indiana colonel countermanded an order to charge, and confusion swept the Hoosier ranks.

The artillery was opening wide and bloody paths in front, but although the enemy masses gave way momentarily before the shock, angry shouting tides of men quickly filled the gaps and came on. Lieutenant John Paul Jones O'Brien, commanding three guns just in front of Thomas, was forced to retreat with the Hoosiers.[21] The Second Illinois, with Thomas and French on each side, was holding firm. Infantry reinforcements came on the run from the right flank, Bragg rushed up with two of his pieces, and another was unlimbered from reserve when French was wounded and had to retire. A charge by Colonel Jefferson Davis's Mississippi Rifles swept the enemy horse

[20] James Henry Carleton, *The Battle of Buena Vista*, 36–37; Holman Hamilton, *Zachary Taylor*, 233.

[21] Smith, *The War With Mexico*, 394; Carleton, *Buena Vista*, 113.

and foot toward the mountain, and the begrimed gunners hemmed them in with their steady fire. O'Brien now returned to the line, advancing well to the front with Thomas about one hundred yards to his right and rear.

With so many cannon now available, Bragg and Sherman swung over to strengthen the left. All might have gone well if several disturbed Mexican officers had not galloped to Taylor with a tentative offer of terms. The American guns were silenced as the men watched a flag of truce come forward, but the enemy fire did not slacken. The Mexicans hemmed in against the mountain took advantage of the respite to escape the trap and re-form. Summoning a powerful reserve, Santa Anna resumed the offensive. The American volunteers in their advanced position ran head on into thousands of enemy soldiers slithering out of a broad ravine and joining forces with those who had escaped the big guns. The Second Kentucky and First Illinois were decimated by surprisingly accurate fire from the right flank. The volunteers wheeled about despairingly and sought shelter in the nearest gorge. The Americans were slaughtered like sheep as part of the Mexican column reached the rim of the gorge despite the heavy canister charges of O'Brien and Thomas, and Santa Anna flung the rest of his men toward the guns in their front. Each recoil of his pieces carried O'Brien slowly back, although hardly as fast as the enemy approached; and with most of his men lying dead or wounded about him, the Lieutenant fired one last charge in the teeth of the foe and hobbled away. Left almost alone on the bare plateau, Thomas kept busily at work; but still there was no faltering in the enemy ranks, which were now very close.

Speaking in defense of his deliberate movements, Thomas afterward related: "I saved my section of Bragg's battery at Buena Vista by being a little slow." Help came just in time. Bragg and Sherman returned to the line; Colonel Davis with his Mississippi Regiment and Colonel Joseph Lane of the Second Indiana worked their way back and sent volley after volley into the threatening masses in their front. "The cannonade on both sides was incessant, the roar of musketry loud and continuous; it was impossible, above the general clamor and din, to distinguish the report of any single gun. . . . The whole air vibrated with the rushing current of balls."[22] Taylor rode up on his white horse and casually ordered Bragg to double-shot his guns and "give 'em hell."[23] The head of the Mexican column was blasted skyward, the onward rush slackened, and the gaudy and blood-stained enemy ranks wavered and sought shelter again in the broad ravine.

The artillery continued to play on enemy guns in fixed positions. Clusters of men who held out in other parts of the field were soon surrounded and subdued, receiving little mercy from soldiers who had seen their own wounded stabbed to death on the ground. Estimates of Mexican losses ran to 1,800 killed and wounded to 673 casualties for the Americans, or nearly 15 per cent of the 4,690 officers and men whom Taylor sent into the fight. Congratulations went out to the artillery officers. "Lieutenant Thomas," reported Captain Sherman, "more than sustained the reputation he has long enjoyed in his regiment as an accurate and scientific artillerist."[24] According to General Taylor, the artillery "was always in action at the right place and the right time."[25] But for the support of the guns, declared another officer, "we would not have maintained our position a single hour."[26] Thomas left an account of the conflict in a brief and bare summary of his early military career: "The Battle of Buena Vista was fought on the 22 Feb. '47 and I was under fire from 6 o.c. A.M. until 4 P.M."[27] A biographer must look elsewhere for further details.

[22] *Ibid.*, 116.

[23] Hamilton, *Zachary Taylor*, 240.

[24] Van Horne, *Thomas*, 6.

[25] Brainerd Dyer, *Zachary Taylor*, 237.

[26] Van Horne, *Thomas*, 6.

[27] Unsigned letter written by Thomas at Camp Cooper, Texas, September 21, 1859, Henry E. Huntington Library.

IV

Service East and West

THE war in the north ended triumphantly at Buena Vista. Taylor gave his men three days' rest, except for burial duty, then advanced to Agua Nueva in pursuit of Santa Anna, picking up dead and wounded Mexicans along the way. Permanent camp was made at Buena Vista. For gallantry in action, all the artillery officers received new brevet commissions which at least entitled them to higher pay. Bragg could now sign himself brevet lieutenant colonel, while T. W. Sherman, Thomas, Reynolds, and French were named brevet majors. This was the third brevet rank in succession for Thomas, an honor of rare precedent. Some of the officers who accompanied General Scott on the march from Veru Cruz to Mexico City would go a little farther as the result of victories at Contreras, Churubusco, Molino del Rey, and Chapultepec. Robert E. Lee, Scott's chief engineer, was promoted to lieutenant colonel of regulars; George B. McClellan and George Gordon Meade became captains, but all three had been graduated from West Point some years before Thomas. Thomas Jonathan Jackson, West Point, 1834, was still a first lieutenant as the war came to a close, as was Ulysses S. Grant.

Taylor's supply line was now so extended that the mails were slow and irregular, not coming through for weeks. On March 18, 1847, Thomas notified a former artillery mate, now with General Scott: "All communication with Camargo has been cut off and we have had no news from the states since the 1st February. . . . We are all anxiously awaiting news from your collum for upon its success depends the duration of the war."[1]

1 Thomas to Lt. Col. James Duncan, March 18, 1847, Duncan Papers, U. S. Military Academy Library.

A few days after this letter was written, Scott bombarded and took Vera Cruz, and following a series of brilliant victories, he entered Mexico City on September 15. Most of the northern army meanwhile remained in its orphan-like situation at Buena Vista, guarding the northern provinces while Congress debated whether or not to annex Mexico and that unhappy country endeavored to fix upon some stable form of government. Early in November, Thomas rode to Monterrey where he joined in a farewell to General Taylor, who was leaving on a triumphal return to New Orleans and his plantation home at Baton Rouge. Not until February 2, 1848, was the peace signed, but the northern army still remained in the field. Thomas rejoined Company E at Buena Vista and was detained there until June.

However, the mails from home brought a welcome letter detailing proceedings at a public meeting of Southampton County citizens. When an Eighth Infantry officer had returned to that neighborhood to recuperate from a long illness, he described the valor of the artillery officers in fitting detail. Resolutions were passed at the meeting heralding the "military skill, bravery and noble deportment of our fellow Countryman . . . George H. Thomas as exhibited in the Campaigns of Florida, at Fort Brown, Monterrey and Buena Vista."[2] A collection for a handsomely decorated gift sword was taken up, and the souvenir ultimately reached Thomas late in March. "Next to the consciousness of having done his duty the sympathy of friends is the highest reward of the soldier," the Virginian responded.[3]

During June the army withdrew from Buena Vista, then retired from Monterrey, and crossed the Río Grande at last on August 9. Although the Third Artillery was allowed to go home, Thomas remained for another six months at Brazos Santiago near the mouth of the river. He was thus unable to witness a rollicking political campaign in the States, but he had the satisfaction of learning that General Taylor had triumphed again and would enter the White House as twelfth president of the

[2] Piatt, *Thomas*, 67–68; original documents in Henry E. Huntington Library.

[3] Thomas to Capt. James Maget, March 31, 1848, Henry E. Huntington Library.

United States on March 4. From California, also, had come exciting news. Lieutenant Cump Sherman, still in service there, had reported the discovery of valuable yellow pebbles on the American Fork of the Sacramento River, sending $3,000 worth of the nuggets, packed in a tea caddy, to Washington.[4] Thomas did not lack for interesting topics to remark upon when he returned home to the Virginia farmhouse late in February, 1849, bringing with him new suits and pairs of shoes for the Negro hands.

A vacancy in the artillery department at West Point was being discussed in army circles. Braxton Bragg, then on leave at the home of his brother in Mobile, declined it but still took an interest in seeing that it went to the right man. While Thomas was still in Texas, Bragg wrote a letter to former Congressman John Young Mason, who was serving as secretary of the navy under President Polk. "The vacancy, I think," wrote Bragg, "would suit your young friend Brevet Major George H. Thomas 3rd Artillery and it is one for which he eminently qualified. Without knowing his views, I presume on requesting your influence in his behalf. . . . No officer of the army has been so long in the field without relief, and to my personal knowledge no one has rendered more arduous, faithful and brilliant service. . . . He is certainly entitled to some consideration from his government."[5] Although Mason doubtless was pleased to hear that Thomas was highly regarded in army circles, the appointment went to another Third Artillery officer, Lieutenant William H. Shover of Ohio, who outranked Thomas by about two years.

After staying in Virginia until August, 1849, Thomas rejoined his regiment at Fort Adams, Rhode Island, as a member of Company B. Nearly as much time was consumed in going and coming as was spent on duty there, since the call soon went out for troops to serve again in Florida. With dwindling military strength in that sector, the Indians were becoming active again, and the dignity of that new state (since 1845) was in danger of

4 Lewis, *Sherman*, 79.

5 Bragg to J. Y. Mason, November 17, 1848, formerly among Thomas F. Madigan mss., New York City.

being compromised. Early in September, Company B embarked for Palatka on the St. Johns River.

Duty in Florida was not of Thomas's asking, and it became even more irksome than during his first tour when he found himself under the jurisdiction of one of the few personal enemies he made during his thirty years of army service. This officer was Brigadier General Twiggs of Georgia, an uncongenial and pompous martinet. The white-haired Twiggs was not at all popular in the service, and it did not benefit Thomas that he had refused the General's request for a team of mules for his personal use at headquarters shortly after the Battle of Monterrey. Thomas's ingrained sense of duty prevented him from being of service to the General, and after resorting to much red tape, he was able to keep his mules.[6] The fact that Twiggs was enjoying the favors of a comely Mexican lady may have "strengthened his refusal," as it was put.

One or two anecdotes concerning the General, a good drinker and a lady-killer despite his advanced years, went the rounds of the camp. During the campaign in Mexico the conduct of an officer named Tree, who possessed similar frailties, came to Twiggs's attention. Tree earned his freedom by responding to the General's inquiry: "You cannot blame me; just as the Twigg is bent so is the Tree inclined."[7] Repeated also was the toast offered at an officers' celebration dinner toward the close of Scott's campaign: "To General Twiggs, the man with a hoary top and a stony bottom." Although no open conflict arose between the General and his self-willed subordinate in Florida, Thomas realized that he was being closely watched. During most of his tour of duty, however, he kept on the move with a congenial fellow officer of the Victoria campaign—Captain George Gordon Meade, who was surveying the ground for a chain of forts extending from Tampa Bay to Indian River.[8] Thomas supplied and garrisoned each new outpost, and in a region flourishing with specimens he pursued his old hobby of collecting rare flowers and mineral fragments.

6 Johnson, *Thomas*, 32.
7 French, *Two Wars*, 102.
8 Meade (ed.), *Life and Letters of George Gordon Meade*, I, 200–202.

A show of military strength sufficed to put an end to tribal aggression. Late in November, 1850, Thomas embarked for New Orleans where the two Third Artillery companies under his command had a few weeks of garrison duty before leaving for their next assignment at Fort Independence, Boston. The ship *Thomas Leonard,* which later set out, ran into a violent storm off Cape Hatteras, and the safety of all hands was imperiled by the confused orders of a drunken captain. Unable to control the situation, the first officer of the vessel appealed to Thomas, who summarily ordered the captain to keep to himself in his cabin and gave the mate full charge. The vessel managed to outride the gale safely, but several men became cholera victims; and upon reaching port, Thomas reported the deaths of nine soldiers and two members of the crew.[9]

To abandon sunny Florida for cold and damp Fort Independence in Boston Harbor was moving from one extreme to the other, but the thirty-four-year-old officer was becoming used to army ways. Fort Independence, erected during the John Adams administration, was a massive ancient work which had collected its share of legends. The most famous yarn concerned a young Virginia lieutenant, Robert F. Massie, in service there some years after the War of 1812. During the long evenings at the fort, gambling at cards was almost incessant, and Massie was accused by a senior officer, a captain, of cheating. The usual challenge was passed, and in a duel on Christmas morning, 1817, Massie was mercilessly shot. He had been a very popular youth, and eyes were turned on the slayer. After taking up a collection for a marble monument to be placed at Massie's grave, his friends vowed to settle accounts with the captain. One evening they met for a protracted drinking bout to which the officer was welcomed, all apparently in very good humor, but when the selected victim had become suitably befuddled, he was hurried off to a windowless subterranean casemate and was there gagged, shackled, and chained to the floor. The casemate opening was then sealed with bricks and mortar as tightly as the lips of the plotters.

Some ten years after the incident, Edgar Allan Poe was

9 Van Horne, *Thomas,* 11; *United Service Journal,* January 18, 1851, 29.

serving as an army regular in self-imposed exile at Fort Independence, where he must have learned the story, since he used a similar situation in his epic of malignity, "The Cask of Amontillado." In Thomas's day no one could be sure that the story was true, but it was eagerly related again early in the present century when a group of workmen digging into the sealed casemate discovered there a dusty skeleton clad in the remnants of an officer's uniform of the War of 1812.[10]

The artillery instructor's position at West Point again became open upon the death of Captain Shover early in 1853. Recommended this time by Captain William Starke Rosecrans, supervising engineer at Fort Adams, Thomas received the appointment in March and returned on short notice to familiar scenes on the west bank of the Hudson. A number of landmarks had been altered during his eleven-year absence. Gone were the old North and South Barracks, which were now replaced by a huge stone dormitory 360 feet long. New ordnance and artillery laboratories, an astronomical observatory, and a grim-looking library building had been completed, while the West Point Hotel had a new wing.[11] Moving his few possessions into the officers' quarters, Thomas borrowed some French military textbooks from the Academy library and entered upon the training of future Union and Confederate officers.

"Clever fellows and worthy gentlemen they were," wrote a cadet of the period.[12] High on the roll of first classmen was William D. Whipple of New York, Thomas's future chief of staff. Another graduate of 1851, Kenner Garrard of Kentucky, would serve many months with Thomas in Kentucky, Tennessee, and Georgia. Graduating in 1852 were two famous cavalrymen who joined opposite sides—David S. Stanley of Ohio and George B. Cosby of Kentucky. Round-faced Alexander McD. McCook of Ohio, another 1852 man, would see a good deal of his instructor during Army of the Cumberland campaigns in the West and South. Another Ohioan, George Crook, "modest,

10 Edward R. Snow, *Castle Island* (pamphlet), 25–27, 40.
11 Douglas S. Freeman, *Robert E. Lee*, I, 319.
12 Wharton J. Green, *Recollections and Reflections*, 73.

retiring, shy almost as a girl"; James B. McPherson; "Little Phil" Sheridan; John M. Schofield; and Oliver O. Howard, a "Bible-class man" from Maine—all would know Thomas both as an Academy instructor and as a soldier of the West. John B. Hood, wearer of the gray, would learn more of him in Georgia and Tennessee. Head man of the Class of 1854 was George Washington Custis Lee of Virginia; number seven was James Deshler of Alabama, a dead Rebel general at Chickamauga; number thirteen, the pugnacious James E. B. Stuart, who would come to his end resisting Sheridan in Virginia.

These youngsters dubbed Thomas, who received the additional duty of cavalry instructor, "Old Slow Trot." A little too heavy for an ideal cavalry commander, although this was the branch of the service which Thomas loved best, he was at pains never to labor his mount. During exercises on the plain, after the command to trot had been given and the cadets began to anticipate a gallop, "the deep and sonorous voice of Thomas would check their ardor with the order 'slow trot'!"[13]

West Point was the favored retreat for Mexican War veterans. Thomas's assistant was Lieutenant Fitz John Porter of New Hampshire, an officer twice brevetted for gallantry in the campaign with Scott. Captain Seth Williams of Maine, cited for valor at Cerro Gordo, was a faculty member; also Lieutenant John J. Reynolds of Indiana, lifelong friend of Thomas's Academy classmate Grant. In September, 1852, an alert, graceful figure took the chair as ninth superintendent at West Point. Recovered from wounds received during the storming of Chapultepec, Lieutenant Colonel Robert E. Lee was to direct Academy affairs for the next three years. Professor of drawing was Robert W. Weir of New York, whose "Embarkation of the Pilgrims" has graced a panel in the National Capitol since 1845. The painting created a sensation in the artist's studio when it was completed. A reverential cadet who viewed it there confessed that he sat speechless before it for half an hour, "my eyes riveted on this Divine Painting while feelings almost too good for human nature depraved filled me with rapturous delight."[14]

13 Coppée, *Thomas*, 183.
14 U. S. Military Academy Library *Bulletin* No. 1, 23.

The record so far has been bare concerning any love affair of Thomas's, for there is nothing to reveal that he had ever had any. He had reached his thirty-sixth year still a bachelor, but during the spring of 1852 the list of his borrowings from the Academy library, which up to now had been rather few, took a singular turn. Although Thomas's choices of reading matter during his first year as instructor had been professionally sedate, he now began to check out romantic novels, volumes of poems, and biographies of military heroes and kings.[15] The chances are that he, himself, never read any of them. A regular visitor at West Point during the spring and summer season was the widow of a prosperous hardware merchant of Troy, Mrs. Abigail Paine Kellogg. One of her interests at the Military Academy was a nephew, Lyman M. Kellogg, a member of the Class of 1852, but West Point was also known to be strategic ground for a lady with unmarried daughters. Mrs. Kellogg was accompanied by her daughters, Frances and Julia; and when Thomas began to pay court to Frances, the older of the two, it was only natural that he be made aware of the family's tastes in reading. The Virginian did not dally with his courtship. On November 17, 1852, between borrowings of Knapp's *Chemistry* and Hawthorne's *Twice Told Tales*, the marriage vows were taken at the home of the bride's uncle, Daniel Southwick of Troy.[16]

Younger than her husband by five years, Frances Kellogg Thomas was an exact match, it was said, for his stature of nearly six feet. The groom's fellow officers described her as a "noble" woman, "good natured and congenial." Thomas's splendid sword, the gift of his Southampton County neighbors, which he wore for the only time at his wedding, was duly inspected by members of the bride's family, which included the Paines and the Warrens of Troy. Its blade was of the "truest and prettiest steel," its silver scabbard "beautifully enriched with engraved scroll work encircling military trophies with the words Florida, Ft. Brown, Monterrey, Buena Vista, and an engraved vignette

15 U. S. Military Academy Library has the list of books borrowed by Thomas.

16 Timothy Hopkins, *The Kelloggs in the Old World and the New,* I, 27; Coppée, *Thomas,* 23; Troy (N. Y.) *Times,* March 29, 1870.

of the Battle of Monterrey." The hilt was of basket form, "very elaborately chased," the grip of solid silver, engraved with scrolls and an elephant, and the gold pommel grasped an amethyst.[17] Following a wedding tour to New York City, the couple returned to West Point early in January, and Thomas resumed his library borrowings with the Hawthorne, a *Memoir of Josephine,* the *Court and Camp of Boneparte,* and two novels by James Fenimore Cooper.

Thomas received a captain's commission, which was long overdue, during his honeymoon. It had been nearly ten years since he had been made a first lieutenant. Although life at West Point left little to be desired by a home-loving officer, the three-year rule uprooted Thomas from his agreeable domestic life less than six months after his marriage. His hopes sank as he read his assignment. Although there were numerous posts where he might have been stationed in the East, he was now ordered to the most remote station in the country—Fort Yuma. It was situated near the junction of the Colorado and Gila Rivers along the California and Arizona border, where temperatures of 115 degrees in the shade were not uncommon. The story of the soldier who died and went to Hell, returning to Yuma for blankets to make himself warm, was told every newcomer. General Twiggs, who had stood in the way of Thomas's promotion, was responsible for the assignment. On May 1, the Captain said good-bye to Colonel Lee and his bride and took his leave of the Academy, where he was succeeded by his old friend Major Keyes. He had been named commander of Company A, Third Artillery, but was ordered to escort four artillery companies to Fort Yuma.

The boat trip to the Isthmus of Panama, an overland march of some fifty miles across the Isthmus to the Pacific, and the voyage north to San Francisco consumed all of thirty days. Many of the men were sick, and, finding no suitable hospital facilities at Benecia Barracks where he was stationed, Thomas prodded the War Department with a suggestion that unused army quarters at the Spanish-built Presidio be converted into an infirmary. Thomas remained some two weeks in the city awaiting the ar-

[17] Van Horne, *Thomas,* 9.

rival of army baggage which had been delayed in crossing the Isthmus.[18] William Tecumseh Sherman, now retired from military service, was enjoying temporary prosperity in San Francisco as manager of one of the local banks which had sprouted following the gold rush. Thomas participated in much interesting talk at Sherman's dinner parties and established an account with his firm of Lucas and Turner, which fortunately withstood a crisis and a run the following winter.[19] Fort Yuma, he learned, was almost completely isolated. River traffic from the Gulf of California was irregular, and army detachments reached it only by crossing fearfully hot and dry Imperial Valley, a dangerous march in midsummer. A coastwise steamer took Thomas and his command to San Diego. The overland trek of nearly two hundred miles taxed the soldiers to the utmost, more especially because the last stages of the journey came in July, one of the worst months of the year for desert travel.

Thomas did not mince words in his report to Pacific Division headquarters: "The excessive heat and scarcity of water on the Desert caused the most intensive suffering, and it was only by the exercise of the utmost precaution that I have succeeded in reaching the post with the command in an *exhausted condition.* For the six days we were on the Desert the Thermometer ranged from 115 to 130 in the sun, rendering it necessary to make our march at night and to lay by during the day. This naturally broke in upon the rest of men and animals, and if I had not finally determined to make a depot of all the heavier stores . . . and make forced marches with the men in the waggons, I doubt if I should have succeeded in getting half the command here." In the future, he warned his superiors, "troops should never be marched across the Desert during the summer."[20]

The Fort Yuma reservation occupied land on both sides of the Colorado River, which separated the California and Arizona Territory. On the Arizona side a new village called Colo-

18 Thomas to Major E. D. Townsend, June 1, 1854, War Department Files, National Archives.

19 Lewis, *Sherman,* 90–91.

20 Thomas to Major E. D. Townsend, July 14, 1854, War Department Files, National Archives.

rado City—the present Yuma—was sprouting. Supplies were brought up the river from the Gulf by chartered steamboats, but the troops occasionally had to be put on short rations when the vessels failed to arrive. The first side-wheeler placed in service lacked sufficient power to overcome the rapid current. A much larger craft which replaced it exploded in September, and the garrison had to clear away the wreck. Thomas entered a plea that the army engage and manage its own steamboats, but since conditions at Yuma were not fully appreciated at Washington, private management continued with various successive craft and costly mishaps. Adverse river conditions were not easily overcome. Rising thirty feet during the spring, the Colorado would dwindle to a sluggish brick-red stream during the summer, and as the water receded, puffing steamers would catch on sticky mudbanks while the unfortunate passengers sweltered in the fierce heat.[21]

The military reservation provided a sanctuary for peaceful Indians, a resting place for immigrant parties, and a base for exploring and punitive expeditions. Dead bodies of lost or slain prospectors occasionally were brought in from the desert and attempts made to rescue Indian captives. Thomas looked into the mystery of the celebrated captivity of the Oatman sisters, Mary Ann and Olive, seven and fifteen years old respectively, who had been seized by Apaches in the fall of 1852 after their Mormon parents had become separated from their wagon train and had·been murdered. Mary Ann then wasted away during a tribal famine, but Olive survived and was rescued after Thomas had set an inquiry on foot.[22]

The days were long at Fort Yuma. Thomas collected some plant and mineral specimens and a singular variety of the bat which he turned over to an exploring party to be taken to the Smithsonian Institution at Washington. He spent several weeks with Indian interpreters studying the language of the Yuma tribe and, after learning to speak it, made an attempt to reduce it to writing.[23]

21 Will H. Robinson, *Story of Arizona*, 110–12.
22 California Historical Society *Quarterly*, June, 1942, 97 f.
23 Andrew D. Rodgers, *John Torrey*, 242.

53

Political and military matters were reviewed in an exchange of letters with Sherman and Bragg, the latter now stationed at Fort Washita in Indian Territory. The triangular correspondence reveals that soon after arriving at Fort Yuma, Thomas sought to be transferred East by applying for a post as army paymaster. Bragg, who had become "thoroughly disgusted" with the service, wrote that he would like to resign and plant cotton but was willing to arrange an exchange of situations with Thomas first, if he wished. But since Thomas was awaiting a reply to his application, he held the offer in abeyance, hoping for the best.[24] When Bragg was asked to join a new cavalry regiment which Secretary of War Jefferson Davis was organizing, he declined in favor of Thomas. "T—— is not brilliant," Bragg earnestly informed Sherman, "but he is a *solid,* sound man; an honest, high-toned gentleman, above all deception and guile, and I know him to be an excellent and gallant soldier."[25] Bragg's chief reason for declining the appointment was probably his personal dislike for Jefferson Davis, although Davis was to show Bragg the utmost partiality as commander of the Army of Tennessee during the Civil War.

The famous Second Cavalry Regiment came into existence through the Secretary of War's efforts to build an army large enough to guard the expanding western frontier. By Act of March 3, 1855, two new infantry and two cavalry regiments were authorized. Davis envisioned a mounted force of the highest grade. It was to have the very best of equipment and to be staffed on the basis of "merit" rather than by the time-worn seniority system. Davis's appointments, as it happened, nearly all went to officers who were Southern born, which gave rise to the suspicion that he "had regard to a probable war between the Northern and Southern States," as Thomas himself came to believe, although the Secretary flatly denied that politics had

[24] Thomas to Sherman, November 30, 1854, Sherman Papers, 5:588.

[25] Bragg to Sherman, June 3, 1855, North American *Review,* April, 1887, 377. See also Bragg to Sherman, February 5, 1855, Sherman Papers, 5:627.

[26] Van Horne, *Thomas,* 13.

anything to do with his selections.[26] Presumably he was doing what came naturally to a sectionalist and states' rights man in giving preferment to Southern officers. Of the twenty-five who held commissions in the Second Cavalry, seventeen were Southerners and twelve of them later became Confederate generals. The leader of the Second Cavalry was Colonel Albert Sidney Johnston of Kentucky, and Robert E. Lee of Virginia was named second in command. Then came Major William H. Emory of Maryland, Major William J. Hardee of Georgia, Captain Earl Van Dorn of Mississippi, Captain E. Kirby Smith of Florida, and Fitzhugh Lee and John B. Hood among the lieutenants. Only one Northerner, George Stoneman of New York, attained the rank of captain. When Thomas accepted a major's commission in the unit, Emory was transferred to the First Cavalry, the Virginian taking his place. First Cavalry officers of future prominence included Lieutenant Colonel Joseph E. Johnston and Lieutenant J. E. B. Stuart of Virginia, but the more brilliant Second Cavalry was Davis's pride.

Thomas's appointment, which was signed May 25, 1855, took nearly two months to reach him. Leaving Fort Yuma without regrets on July 21, Thomas again crossed Imperial Valley in burning heat and on the last day of the month was at San Diego ready to sail. It took him a little more than a month to reach New Orleans, and boarding a Mississippi River steamboat, he joined his regiment on September 25 at Jefferson Barracks near St. Louis.

The uniforms were strictly gaudy. A silken sash and trim of yellow braid decorated the dark blue jacket which was worn with trousers of pale azure. Brass scales to turn the saber strokes of the enemy covered the shoulders, and the large black Stetson, rakishly looped with an eagle on the right, trailed sweeping ostrich plumes. A gutta-percha raincoat with large, loose sleeves extended to the knees, and the latest-model Colt revolvers, rifle-carbines, and glittering sabers were supplied. The hand-wrought saddles, carrying polished wooden stirrups, gleamed with shining brass. Only the best mounts were purchased—at premium prices, of course—and each company rode horses of an identical color. The squadron of Thomas comprised Company A, the "Mobile Grays," and Company F, a bay-horse troop.[27] Recruiting, outfitting, and the training of new mounts were still the order of the day as Thomas discarded his old artillery officer's uniform for the new. The men were instructed in cavalry tactics fresh from the pen of Major Hardee. Toward the latter part of October, a start was made for Texas, but at Fort Washita Thomas was detached for court-martial duties which kept him occupied until some time in January, 1856. The Major had prepared himself well for this detail, having made a careful study of military law and taken notes on many previous decisions. The docket finally cleared, he was permitted to go to New York City on "recruiting service." More important from the Major's point of view, however, was permission, implicit in the order, to visit his wife, whom he had not seen in nearly three years; and when he returned to the West early in May, he brought her with him. Two capable Negro servants assisted in housekeeping details at Fort Mason, Texas, where the Major and his wife took command. The Second Cavalry had been distributed among a chain of forts extending through central Texas to regimental headquarters at San Antonio and on to Brownsville, a village grown up about the bastion besieged during the early days of the Mexican War.

Lieutenant Colonel Lee was a near neighbor of the Thomas's, at Camp Cooper, 170 miles to the north. Lee made a sweep in search of hostile Comanches that spring but without materials results. Dismissing his squadron, he joined Thomas on a long trek to Ringgold Barracks on the Río Grande. On overnight stops the officers pitched their tents by the roadside, cooking their meals over an open fire. Protracted court-martial duty occupied them for several months, and early in November the steamer *Ranchero* took them to Brownsville for similar indoor service.[28] Save for traveling from one point to another on such duties, Thomas saw little active service in the field for

27 West Texas Historical Association *Yearbook*, October, 1938, 74–75. See also Theo F. Rodenbough (ed.), *The Army of the United States*, 221 f.

28 A complete account of the journeys of Lee and Thomas is found in Carl Coke Rister, *Robert E. Lee in Texas*, 61–84.

some time. March, 1857, found him at San Antonio, where he was joined by Mrs. Thomas and the Negro cook, travelers by stage; and a more abundant bill of fare was assured both the Major and Colonel Lee, who occasionally dined with his friend. Following a tour of some eight months altogether, the two officers returned to their respective commands in April.

Between two fierce northers which roared over the plains, Thomas and his wife joined Lee at Camp Cooper for another court sitting in May. In letters home, Lee reveals himself perplexed and uncertain at that remote station about what he might provide Mrs. Thomas for table fare. "The Major can fare as I do," Lee confided to his wife, "but I fear that she will fare badly as my man Kremer is both awkward and unskilled."[29] Lee freely discussed his difficulties—nothing in the way of meat except an old hen, and scant vegetables, but the actual menu went unreported.

Lawless Texas seemed to provide the two officers with no end of court-martial duty. In July they sat at a hearing at Fort Mason, Colonel Johnston presiding. When the War Department summoned Johnston to Washington and the regimental command devolved upon Lee, who departed for headquarters at San Antonio, Thomas was left to arrive at an opinion. Although the case was a trivial one, the upshot was a fine squabble with General Twiggs, who arrived on the scene as commander of the Department of Texas.

The details of the matter were plain. A young lieutenant named Wood had entered a complaint against some settlers who claimed that he had stolen a drunken man's purse; and after searching the record for malice as was his custom, Thomas decided in Wood's favor and so reported.[30] Twiggs, currying local political favor, set aside the opinion, retried the case himself and arrived at a different decision. Very indignant, Thomas did not hesitate to report the facts to Secretary of War John B. Floyd, a fellow-Virginian, who upheld the Major and reminded Twiggs not to interfere. Twiggs did not wait long before seek-

[29] Lee to his wife, April 26, 1857 in John William Jones, *Life and Letters of Robert E. Lee*, 86; Freeman, *Lee*, I, 371.

[30] Southwestern Historical *Quarterly*, XLI, 169–70.

ing revenge. On October 21, Thomas succeeded to the command
of the regiment when Lee was called home on a personal matter,
the death of his father-in-law. Twiggs straightway attached
Thomas's two squadrons to the command of Earl Van Dorn, recently promoted to major, and ordered the entire force on a
scouting expedition to the Wichita Mountains.[31] This left only
a few noncoms, the regimental band, and the sick at Fort Mason.
Field duty of this importance actually belonged to Thomas.
Breathing hot anger over this latest indignity, the Major dispatched another bill of particulars to Floyd, requesting a formal
inquiry into Twiggs's conduct. While the Secretary of War saw
no need for a court of inquiry, he nevertheless returned orders
directly to Thomas to join and assume command of the eight
companies in the field, whereupon Twiggs sent out riders to
recall Van Dorn and then distributed the extra companies
among several different posts. Early the following summer he
ordered Thomas to report at Fort Belknap, where only one
squadron remained. Although Thomas obeyed the order, he
shot a letter which boldly taunted Twiggs for some grammati-
cal errors in his dispatches, declaring that Colonel Lee would
have respected his rank had he remained on duty at headquarters.[32] Thomas duly reported his transfer to officials at
Washington, who again suggested that Twiggs mind his own
business and leave the Major alone. Second Cavalry officers
were considered to be in a class by themselves and not to be
trifled with by a mere departmental commander.

Thomas's latest assignment was not revoked, however, and
he remained several months at Fort Belknap. He was pleased
to learn of Lee's return to San Antonio in February, 1859. The
Colonel's first letter requested that he take over his old post at
Camp Cooper, where a strong hand was needed to curb rising
troubles between the white settlers and some peaceful Comanches living on the military reservation. But during the early
spring, a dangerous season on the frontier, a band of wild Indians from the plains made matters worse by rounding up some
horses in the vicinity and taking cover overnight on the reserva-

31 West Texas Historical Association *Yearbook*, October, 1938, 76–77.
32 Rister, *Robert E. Lee in Texas*, 141.

tion. Naturally the peaceful tribesmen were blamed. Lacking sufficient men to police several square miles of woods and plain, Thomas was unable to prevent a night battle between a party of mounted settlers and tribesmen which ended in the killing of nine men. Excoriating both parties, Thomas sent a hurry call to Earl Van Dorn to send him two companies forthwith "to prevent the disastrous results of another border war."[33] Reinforcements brought temporary relief, and the reservation policy was officially endorsed following an investigation; but after the settlers held an indignation meeting and sent protests to Washington, the Commissioner of Indian Affairs ordered the reservation abandoned.

Political pressure had decided the issue, since the Indians had no vote. The peaceful Comanches had given Thomas little difficulty, and he regretted their removal from their rightful place. Starting out on July 30, he escorted the tribesmen to new hunting grounds in Indian Territory, setting an easy pace to accommodate the women and children. The Major had a paternal regard for the helpless which was extended to horses, mules, dogs, cats, and even fowls; and every soldier in his command well knew that if any cruelty occurred under his eye, there was no possible way for the offender to escape punishment.

Returning to Camp Cooper on August 21, Thomas served notice that all Kiowas and Comanches discovered off their reservations were to be considered hostile and treated accordingly. To enforce the edict, he mobilized five cavalry companies completely equipped and set out in search of straying Indians. The detachment rode west for some fifty miles past the Double Mountain and then turned north. They picked up an Indian trail near the Cimarron River, but could no longer follow it after a herd of buffalo, stampeded presumably by the redskins, thundered across it. Thomas then circled eastward to the headwaters of the Wichita River, picking up a few mineral specimens but discovering no Indians. It was satisfying, nevertheless, to gratify a more than casual interest in nature. The open country rolled on interminably in its varied dress, and the Major's

[33] Thomas to Van Dorn, May 30, 1859, Dearborn Collection, Rister, *Robert E. Lee in Texas*, 141.

eye caught every hill, hollow, and racing stream. Several new sites for military posts were mapped. Returning homeward across Red River tributaries, the party reached Camp Cooper after fifty-three days in the field.[34]

Aside from the Twiggs episode, the Texas years were the pleasantest of any Thomas spent in active service. His relations with Colonel Lee were always friendly, and as the two men thought alike regarding military matters and Indian affairs, the commander gave him free rein. After remaining quiet throughout the fall and winter, the tribesmen of the plains renewed their depredations with the first approach of warm weather. Late in February, 1860, Thomas notified Lee that a white man had been shot within a few miles of Camp Cooper and that several Indian Agency horses and mules had been stolen or frightened away. Lee, who had his hands full with some elusive Mexican raiders in the Río Grande Valley, advised Thomas to do what he thought best. A letter from the War Department which arrived about this time suggested another tour of field duty as soon as enough grass had grown for forage.

Thomas sent out letters in various directions requesting wagons, guides, reinforcements, and supplies. Some of the men who had accompanied him on the Red River expedition had gone to join Lee, making it necessary for him to redistribute his forces. Every mount had to be newly shod, wagons filled with corn and oats, arms cleaned and made ready, and all equipment inspected. Thomas arranged for two other detachments to meet him en route, and in July he took thirty officers and men, including three Indian guides, and rode south over the stage line to the Colorado River, where he picked up Lieutenant Fitzhugh Lee and another squad of thirty. Turning west, Thomas then rode to Kiowa Creek, where he picked up a squad under Captain Richard W. Johnson and divided his force for a scout through a region covering seven present-day counties. The Indians kept on the alert and out of sight. After four weeks in the field, supplies began to run low; Johnson and Lee were permitted to return to their posts, while Thomas and his original party took up a fresh trail.[35]

[34] West Texas Historical Association *Yearbook*, October, 1938, 81.

One morning the riders in advance gave a shout as they caught sight of eleven mounted Comanches leading some thirty horses. The savages fled into a deep ravine and managed to gain considerable ground while their pursuers were puzzling their way out. The troopers then raced away again, but by the time they got within shooting distance, their horses were nearly exhausted. It is likely that all the Indians might have escaped, but one of them decided to face the whites while the others raced on. This dauntless brave dismounted, stood square in the path of the cavalrymen, and offered to fight them all. He proudly declined to surrender. Arrows began to fly from his bow. One of the shafts glanced off Thomas's chin and lodged in his chest, and three privates were wounded also. It took "twenty or more shots," Thomas reported, to down him.

Although blood was flowing from a score of wounds, the warrior died hard. Private Hugh Clark, who dismounted to use his carbine, "was kicked and stunned by his horse, seeing which the Indian rushed upon him with his lance and tried to kill him but was so weak . . . that he inflicted only a slight wound. . . . By this time the main body of the Indians, who were mounted on their best animals, were at least two miles from us, retiring at a rapid rate."[36]

Thomas pulled the arrow from his chest and permitted the surgeon to dress his wounds. After the three injured privates had been cared for and the dead Indian buried, the detachment rounded up twenty-eight horses and returned to Camp Cooper in rainy and disagreeable weather. The warrior's defiant battle stimulated campfire discussion among doctrinaires of the trail. Captain Johnson summed the matter up by observing that a wounded Indian is more dangerous than four sound warriors, while not only is a wounded white man rendered worthless for fighting but four comrades are required to carry him to the rear and attend to his hurts.[37]

[35] *Ibid.*, October, 1944, 79 f.
[36] Thomas's report, August 31, 1860, Van Horne, *Thomas*, 14–15.
[37] Johnson, *Thomas*, 35.

V

Oath of Allegiance

ON November 12, 1860, a bronze-cheeked cavalry major
wearing side whiskers and a short, well-kept beard left
Texas on a six-months' leave which he planned to spend
in New York City and Troy. Mrs. Thomas, who had endured
her share of frontier life, had preceded her husband eastward
by more than a year and was awaiting his arrival in New York.
Thomas took with him his body servant and his female cook,
neither of whom he wished to sell. The vagaries of the South's
peculiar domestic institution made it difficult for a humane
slaveowner to part with any of his servants if he would preserve
equanimity of conscience, and although it became inconvenient
to retain the cook, Thomas saw to it that she and the family
she acquired were well cared for either at his home in Virginia
or under his own eye until he was ordered to the Pacific Coast
in 1869. He then sent her to his brother Benjamin who was
living at Vicksburg, Mississippi.[1]

The quickest and most direct route north was by stage and
steamboat to New Orleans, by river steamer to Memphis, and
thence by rail to Chattanooga, where it was necessary to change
cars. The railroad then coursed through eastern Tennessee to
another junction at Lynchburg, Virginia, where Thomas suffered the one severe injury of his entire career. One evening as
the engine was taking on water near the town, he stepped down
on what appeared in the moonlight to be a road; but instead of
finding safe footing, he plunged down a steep embankment and
seriously wrenched his spine.[2] Plans to continue to New York
were given up as Thomas resumed an uncomfortable rail jour-

[1] Piatt, *Thomas* 75–76; Van Horne, *Thomas*, 16–17.
[2] *Ibid.*, 19–20; Coppée, *Thomas*, 35–36 n.

ney to Norfolk, where he sought a hotel bed. After summoning Mrs. Thomas by wire, the Major kept to his room until she arrived. On December 15, he was able to leave for the farm in Southampton County, some thirty miles away, and there rested for three weeks. He stored his army baggage at home and left the Negro cook in his sister's care until such time as her services might be required again.[3] Early in January, 1861, he resumed his journey north, stopping overnight in Washington to report to General-in-Chief Winfield Scott. He had a few words to say concerning General Twiggs, who had returned to Texas following several months' leave. Since Twiggs was close to the secessionist faction in Texas, Thomas believed that he "meditated treachery" in the event of conflict between the South and the government.[4] That trouble was near at hand few men could doubt. On December 15, South Carolina had voted to secede from the Union, followed by Mississippi on January 9, 1861, and Florida on the tenth, when Thomas was visiting Washington. The evidence he gave concerning Twiggs resulted in an order for his recall; but unfortunately it was held up by President James Buchanan, who had adopted the policy of inaction. And so Twiggs was left free to surrender troops, property, and equipment to the secessionist Texas Rangers who raised the Lone Star flag over army headquarters at San Antonio on February 18.

Reaching New York at last, Thomas took rooms at the New York Hotel on Broadway near Tenth Street but responded rather slowly to medical treatment. Somewhat discouraged over the prospect, considering himself finished as a cavalry officer, he began to reflect upon the possibility of other future employment. Concern over his personal condition displaced anxiety about the national crisis, which again flared in the newspapers as Alabama seceded. One morning Mrs. Thomas read to her husband a want ad in the *National Intelligencer* that the Virginia Military Institute was seeking a commandant of cadets. Although Thomas still felt unfit for active army service, he be-

3 Wyeth, *With Sabre and Scalpel*, 261 n.

4 Van Horne, *Thomas*, 20–21; also letter of Col. Henry Stone in New York *Tribune*, July 7, 1890.

lieved himself qualified for this position. He was reminded that his friend Sherman, following a severe deflationary period accompanied by bank runs in California, was rehabilitating himself as superintendent at the Military Academy of Louisiana. On January 18, Thomas wrote Superintendent Francis H. Smith of V.M.I.: " . . . I would be under obligation if you will inform me what salary and allowances pertain to the situation, as from present appearances I fear it will soon be necessary for me to be looking up some means of support." A reply was returned within a few days, and Thomas found that the vacancy already had been filled but that Smith had recommended him to Governor John Letcher as chief of ordnance for Virginia, a position quite independent of the regular army.[5]

Thomas gave no sign that he would accept the position if offered. Army officers who discussed the impending crisis with him in his room soon learned that he had no use for extremists on either side and so could not commit himself to either party. A New Yorker who talked with him "many times" during the winter plainly defined his views: "General Thomas was strong and bitter in his denunciation against all parties North and South that seemed to him responsible for the condition of affairs, but while he reprobated, sometimes very strongly, certain men and parties North, in that respect going as far as any of those who afterward joined the rebels, he never, in my hearing, agreed with them respecting the necessity of going with their States, but denounced the idea and denied the necessity of dividing the country or destroying the Government."[6] Of the four opposing political factions active in the recent presidential election which had resulted in the choice of Abraham Lincoln, Thomas belonged with that, headed by John Bell of Tennessee, which advo-

[5] Coppée, *Thomas*, 36n; Cullum, *Biographical Register*, II, 36; Southern Historical Society *Papers*, X, 524–25. Thomas's original letter to Smith is in the War Department Files, National Archives and further explanation by Smith is provided in an endorsement presumably in an attempt to suggest that Thomas was not to be trusted.

[6] Society of the Cumberland, 1870 Reunion, *Report*, 67. The debate was continued in the letter of General Fitzhugh Lee published in the Richmond *Dispatch* and other newspapers, following Thomas's death, and by Colonel Alfred L. Hough in the San Francisco *Alta*, May 9, 1870.

cated adherence to the Constitution, continuing union of the states, and enforcement of the laws.

Alabama had left the Union on January 11, and after a brief pause the tide of secession rushed on. Georgia, Louisiana, and Texas also had voted to withdraw when on February 8 the Confederacy was organized at the Montgomery, Alabama, convention. Although little news came through from Texas, all of it was bad. Following Twiggs's surrender, the American flag was hauled down at all the forts. Loyal troops at Camp Cooper set out on foot for the coast, while Captain Richard W. Johnson and his command said farewell to Fort Mason, leaving the buildings ablaze behind them. No blame for the surrender could be attached to Lieutenant Colonel Lee. Summoned to Washington by General Scott, Lee had boarded ship for New Orleans. It was not yet known which side he would take, and apparently he was somewhat confused in his own mind. Upon taking the stage at Fort Mason, he had exclaimed: "I shall never bear arms against the United States but it may be necessary for me to carry a musket in defense of my native state," a curious contradiction in terms.[7]

Thomas was confronted with an opportunity to make a decision early in March when he received a letter from another officer stationed at V.M.I. The writer stated that he had been requested by Governor John Letcher to ascertain whether Major Thomas would resign from the Federal service and, if so, whether the position of chief of ordnance would be acceptable. Apparently the Major was feeling somewhat improved in health. Choosing his words carefully, he wrote Governor Letcher on March 12: "I have the honor to state, after expressing my most sincere thanks for your very kind offer, that it is not my wish to leave the service of the United States as long as it is honorable for me to remain in it, and therefore as long as my native State remains in the Union it is my purpose to remain in the army, unless required to perform duties alike repulsive to honor and humanity."[8] Thomas had left himself a loophole large enough

[7] Freeman, *Robert E. Lee,* I, 425.

[8] Thomas to Governor John Letcher, March 12, 1861, *Calendar of Virginia State Papers,* XI, 106.

to be considered justifiable evidence that he hesitated before making his decision to join the North in the great conflict, and his expressed sentiment was not far removed from that of Lee. This letter was carefully preserved and reprinted in the published archives of his native state and was occasionally quoted in hotly worded tracts.

A Federal fleet of ten steamboats hurried to Southern ports to bring the loyal troops home. According to the New York *Tribune,* 388 members of the Second Cavalry and 182 First Infantry regulars had boarded the vessel *Coatzacoalcos* at a Texas port, while more were coming on the *Empire City.* The *Coatzacoalcos,* however, had no one higher than the rank of captain aboard. On April 10, Thomas was back in harness again after he had been ordered to take command of the troops upon their arrival. Five months of his leave had been spent with only an occasional twinge to remind him of his once painful injury. The *Coatzacoalcos* was the first ship to anchor in the Hudson River. Groups of tanned and weather-beaten men disembarked declaiming their indignation against "Judas Twiggs" and the other "deserters."[9]

"All well and in good spirits," rejoiced the patriotic New York *Tribune.* "The men were got out of the State with much difficulty, the black sheep being weeded out pretty thoroughly by desertion. Of the officers of the Second Cavalry the men of Northern birth are true and loyal, but Secession has so demoralized those of Southern origin that it would hardly be safe to send them on duty to the South."[10] Major Thomas, in fact, was among those still distrusted, and his presence with the troops aroused renewed speculation concerning his views.

Thomas greeted the men warmly but had little to say concerning himself as he entrained with the remnants of four Second Cavalry companies for Harrisburg, Pennsylvania, and Carlisle Barracks just beyond. But when the echo of the guns which attacked Fort Sumter reached him as he arrived at Harris-

9 New York *Tribune,* April 12, 1861.
10 *Ibid;* see also L. E. Chittenden, *Recollections of President Lincoln,* 361.

burg on April 13, he sent telegrams to his sisters in Virginia and to his wife announcing his decision to continue in Federal service.[11] Although his sisters no longer would consider him a member of the family, Mrs. Thomas quoted her husband's opinion approvingly: "Whichever way he turned the matter over in his mind, his oath of allegiance to his Government always came uppermost."[12] Thomas may or may not have hesitated. But he acted at the proper moment. The fact that he still wore the Federal uniform and was under oath to defend his country's flag brought him to an immediate decision once that flag was fired upon. He had made his decision some days in advance of that of Lee, who, if Thomas hesitated, had hesitated longer. Southern critics have explained away Thomas's decision by arguing that Thomas had been influenced by his Northern-born wife, but Mrs. Thomas asserted that there was never a word passed between them "upon the subject of his remaining loyal to the United States Government." She knew her husband to be independent of mind. "No one," she once wrote, "could persuade him to do what he felt was not right. . . . From the time the actual fact of war was upon us, General Thomas's course was clear . . . without influence of any kind being brought to bear upon him."[13]

The only public reference Thomas ever made to his decision contained a note of gratitude for his education at West Point, the gift of his country. And having taken an oath to defend his country against all enemies, he could not forswear it. After all, there was only one flag. But that a Virginian should be first of all a nationalist was not particularly remarkable. Other examples—George Washington, Lighthorse Harry Lee, James Madison, William Henry Harrison, Winfield Scott, each of them holding the federal government paramount over state powers, may be cited. Thomas, of course, acted quite independently. He had put on his uniform and had taken his oath. Solid and immovable, he would not desert.

To renew his officer's oath and to silence some of the pre-

11 Piatt, *Thomas*, 86.
12 Coppée, *Thomas*, 36 n.
13 Cullum, *Biographical Register*, II, 36.

vailing gossip, the Major presented himself before a local magistrate and again pledged his allegiance to his country and flag. He reported the arrival of the troops at Carlisle Barracks to the commanding general in Pennsylvania, General Robert Patterson whom he had last seen in Mexico. The top-ranking officers with the Army of Pennsylvania were respectable Philadelphians, some of them, like Patterson, relics of the War of 1812. Patterson, now sixty-nine years old, had made a fortune as a cotton-mill owner following his Mexican service but had recently been called from retirement. Second in command was General George Cadwalader, a Philadelphia lawyer by profession. The military experience of General William H. Keim had been restricted to militia service. These men were stationed with the infantry at Harrisburg and Chambersburg.

As ranking officer at Carlisle Barracks, Thomas took up the multitude of details essential to getting soldiers into new uniforms and into the field. On April 20, after 5 officers and 236 men of Second Cavalry Companies B, E, G, and I had been remounted and equipped, Thomas received a hurry call to take them to Washington where fears were entertained for the safety of the public buildings. Rioting in Baltimore on the nineteenth had taken the lives of four Union volunteers and injured many more as the Sixth Massachusetts Regiment marched through the city from one railroad station to another. It was believed that if some regular troops could precede the next detachment of volunteers, further trouble might be avoided. After marching to York, Thomas put his regulars and a volunteer company on the train and glanced about him to see some of the junior officers from border states looking anxious and doubtful. There were still a few who had not yet decided which side to take, and apparently they were looking to the Major as their guide. One of them rather stupidly inquired, "What shall we do?" "We are ordered to go to Washington and there we go," Thomas replied bluntly. "There will be time enough after getting there for you to decide what to do."[14]

Arriving at Cockeysville, Maryland, the detachment found the road blockaded. A detail of Baltimore policemen had de-

[14] Fitz John Porter Papers, I, 34.

GEORGE H. THOMAS

as a major general of Volunteers, in 1862

stroyed all railroad bridges to the north while Mayor George William Brown appealed to President Lincoln to send no more troops through. A dispatch from Secretary of War Simon Cameron was handed the Major: "The President, with a desire to gratify the mayor of Baltimore who fears that bloodshed would immediately result from the passage through that city of the troops from Pennsylvania . . . directs that they shall return to York."[15] The Union Army's first defeat had come at the hands of a mob.

Thomas returned to camp with his men, although after the excitement had quieted down, the Second Regiment troops and the volunteer company got through safely to the capital. He was disappointed to learn that Virginia had seceded and that Lieutenant Colonel Lee had finally decided to carry a musket in defense of his native state. On April 25, Lee's position and rank fell to Thomas, who complied with the rule that every newly appointed officer renew his oath. He took it a third time ten days later when he was made a full colonel to fill a vacancy caused by the resignation of Albert Sidney Johnston. Captain Richard W. Johnson of Kentucky, who had arrived with Second Regiment Companies A, C, F, and K, expressed his surprise. "I don't care a snap of my fingers about it," Thomas admonished him. "If they want me to take the oath before each meal I am ready to comply."[16]

Gaps in Second Regiment rolls had to be filled with volunteer officers and militia of uncertain quality. Some of the aspirants brought letters from their congressmen or from relatives in the service, but after seeing a cavalry candidate tumble from a well-broken nag, Thomas began his interviews with the query: "Can you ride?"[17] Reluctant to discard an old coat or change his insignia, Thomas continued to appear in camp as a major, causing some confusion among the newcomers. He was to make up for the delay at the other end, continuing to wear a colonel's uniform for five months after promotion to brigadier general.

15 *Ibid.*, I, 68. See also *ibid.*, 61, and Hamilton Owens, *Baltimore on the Chesapeake*, 273–75.

16 Johnson, *Thomas*, 38; *A Soldier's Reminiscences*, 161.

17 *Military Service Institution Journal*, LVI, 38.

Green troops felt the influence of a sure hand and encouraging words, but volunteer officers never forgot Thomas's lessons in discipline. One of them, Lieutenant Thomas M. Anderson, ran into trouble when one of his noncoms went on a rampage and threatened to shoot anyone who came near. Anderson trotted over to the Colonel to ask what could be done. "In last resort," murmured Thomas looking out of the window, "death."[18] The harassed officer soon arrived at the conclusion that he might be capable of handling the situation without undue fuss. A day or two later Anderson discovered that the company shoemaker was doling out whiskey to the men and getting them drunk, but this time Thomas asked to see him.

"What have you done about the whiskey," he asked Anderson.

"Knocked in the head of the barrel and emptied it into the street."

"Well, I am glad you did not come to ask this time what you should do."[19]

Some bizarre difficulties were encountered as the cavalry troop began to take shape. There was a grave risk, for example, in placing green men on picket duty. Improvised methods had to be firmly suppressed after two or three pickets had fired their pieces as soldiers were returning to camp late at night and then had called out "What goes there?" at a dead man.

After five weeks in camp, Thomas was instructed to move his command to headquarters at Chambersburg. There he found heavily bearded Colonel Fitz John Porter, his one-time assistant at West Point, and Major Abner Doubleday, who had laid out a baseball diamond at Cooperstown, New York, while on leave from West Point one summer. Generals Patterson, Keim, and Cadwalader were there, as also was United States Senator John Sherman, Cump's younger brother, who was Patterson's chief of staff.

The ablest of these officers, Thomas excepted, was probably Doubleday. Of Huguenot ancestry like Thomas, Doubleday also resembled him in his abstemious habits and logical plans

18 *Ibid.*, 41.
19 *Ibid.*

but he was the more candid and outspoken. Doubleday had fought with Taylor in Mexico and against the Indians in Florida and Arizona and had aimed the first shot directed against the Rebels at Fort Sumter. Therefore, he already knew something of war, although most of the senior officers thought him a queer one. The group dined one evening at the home of Alexander K. McClure, an antislavery newspaper publisher and a power in state politics. After dinner the officers debated the prospect of a short war, conceding that at least one battle would have to be fought before peace resulted on a compromise basis. Thomas, who knew the Southern temper, had little or nothing to say but listened to Doubleday, who aggressively disputed the theory. According to McClure's account of the meeting:

"Thomas, with that modesty which always characterized him, was silent. Doubleday had met the Southerners in battle at Sumter and he knew how desperately earnest they were, and Thomas was a son of Virginia who knew that the Southern people were as heroic as any in the North. . . . Doubleday surprised his fellow officers by declaring it would be one of the most desperate and bloody wars of modern history . . . and that they (the Rebels) meant to make it a fight to the death. He was the first to leave after the dinner, and when he was gone several leading officers ridiculed his ideas of a long and terrible war, and I well remember the remark of one of them that Doubleday was a Spiritualist and a little gone in the head."[20]

McClure, who saw Thomas several times in camp, found him always reluctant to discuss the situation, but, he added, "he knew." Although the Colonel had no control over the ideas held by his superiors, he kept on the alert against loose talk in his own First Brigade. One of his captains, hearing that part of General Ben Butler's army had been routed at Big Bethel, Virginia, remarked, "I'm glad the damned old abolitionist was whipped." From a junior officer came the reply, "It seems to me, sir, that you are fighting on the wrong side." A challenge to

20 Alexander K. McClure, *Lincoln and Men of War Times*, 341; *Recollections of Half a Century*, 341–42; Sherman, *Personal Memoirs*, I, 205–206.

a duel was passed, but before any shooting could take place, Thomas took the matter up at mess. This was no personal issue, he reminded the officers and men standing at attention, but one that concerned the whole regiment. If the captain really meant what he said, it was indeed true that he was fighting on the wrong side. There was to be no more talk from anyone about its being "a damned abolition war."[21]

Thomas stood on the north bank of the Potomac at Williamsport, Maryland, looking across the river into his native state of Virginia. The cavalry drew up in line, then waded in. It was the beginning of an invasion almost wholly defensive in character and secondary to action pending near Washington. Orders to Patterson were to hold in check a Rebel force commanded by General Joseph E. Johnston while a Federal army sallied out of Washington to meet General Pierre G. T. de Beauregard, who had been threatening the city. The position at Williamsport in western Maryland was not well chosen since it was some distance the other side of Johnston's army rather than between it and Beauregard. Relative positions made little difference, however, when orders from Scott brought the cavalry and volunteers back to the north bank before they could strike a blow. Since the Administration's chief concern was the safety of Washington, the aged General-in-Chief asked Patterson to send him the regulars and artillery to reinforce General Irvin McDowell, second in command. A move of this kind, naturally, would leave Patterson badly weakened in addition to curbing the ardor of the volunteers. Patterson debated his next course with Thomas and the other officers and then selected Senator John Sherman to write a letter of protest to Secretary of War Cameron. Scott's orders were then modified to read: "Retain two companies of Thomas's horse and send him with the other two here"; but on learning that Johnston had retreated from Harper's Ferry to near-by Martinsburg, Patterson stalled.[22] Although he let some of his artillery go, he was persuaded to retain

21 *Military Service Institution Journal*, LVI, 39.

22 U. S. War Department, *Official Records of the War of the Rebellion*, 1st Series, II, 679 f.

Thomas and the Second Cavalry men. He was worried over the fact that most of his 12,000 men were three-months' volunteers whose terms would expire by July 24. Since it was now June 18, they had only six more weeks to go.

Cump Sherman, whom Thomas had not seen for some years, greeted the Colonel on the day of the crossing. While Scott and Patterson continued their quarrel by telegraph, Thomas and Sherman took a long look into the future. Sherman, who had rejoined the army as a colonel, had ridden over from Washington ostensibly on inspection duty, but he believed it part of his mission to satisfy himself concerning Thomas's views. He was somewhat reassured when he heard Thomas say, "I have thought it all over and I shall stand firm in the service of the Government."[23] Following dinner in a near-by inn, the two officers bent over a large map spread on the floor. They placed a dot on Richmond, then marked the cities of Knoxville, Chattanooga, Nashville, and Vicksburg. This was sharpshooting. Senator John Sherman, who was standing by, expressed his surprise in his *Memoirs*. "To me," he wrote, "it has always appeared strange that they were able confidently and correctly to designate the lines of operations and strategic points of a war not yet commenced, and more strange still that they should be leading actors in great battles at the places designated by them at this country tavern."[24]

Two weeks of idleness consumed most of the initial eagerness of the volunteers. Patterson was authorized to cross the Potomac again on July 2. General Johnston's main force, numbering about 9,000 availables, had retired by this time to Winchester, some forty miles south, and it became Patterson's duty to hold the Confederates there. An enemy detachment of 3,500 cavalry troops under Colonel Thomas J. (later "Stonewall") Jackson and Colonel Jeb Stuart was flung out to delay the Federals. Leading Patterson's advance, Colonel John J. Abercrombie ran into Jackson's men near Falling Waters, a country hamlet five miles across the river. When he was stopped by rifle fire from a stretch of timber in front, Abercrombie called for

23 Society of the Army of the Cumberland, 1870 Reunion, *Report*, 68.
24 John Sherman, *Recollections*, 250.

help and deployed his men. Commanding the next brigade in line, Thomas signaled that he would attempt to flank the enemy right while the brigade in front took the other side of the road. The artillery battery was hurried forward and sent into action. Bursting shells and iron balls which ricocheted among the trees drove the enemy slowly backward. Since the Confederate force was well outnumbered, Jackson declined to press the fight. Thomas slackened his fire in turn, although Abercrombie's men were still firing away. When one of the officers called out, "The brigade on the right seems to be hotly engaged," Thomas listened for a moment. "I hear no return shots," he remarked severely.[25]

Both sides took several prisoners in the skirmish behind fence rails and brush. The Federals rambled on for three miles and encamped. "My brigade went into camp upon part of the ground previously occupied by the enemy," Thomas reported; "150 tents were found and destroyed."[26] Patterson marched without further delay into Martinsburg where Union flags were draped from windows as drums rolled and fifes shrilled "Yankee Doodle" on a gala Fourth of July holiday. The next move was discussed at mess that evening. Thomas was all for routing the enemy out of Winchester, although Fitz John Porter feared that the volunteers were too inefficient for a stand-up fight. "Why Fitz John," rejoined Thomas, "you forget that Johnston's men are nothing but militia."[27] Although Patterson was persuaded to agree to an advance, he countermanded the order next day when some late arrivals showed up weary and footsore. Some of the volunteers lacked trousers, and many had no shoes. Meanwhile, valuable time was slipping away.

Since Patterson had not been instructed to attack the enemy main force, he decided to make a flank movement toward Winchester to occupy Johnston by a demonstration. On July 15, Thomas approached within nine miles of the enemy camp, brushing aside 600 Confederate troops at Bunker Hill and taking a few prisoners. But instead of permitting him to remain

25 George Price, *Across the Continent with the Fifth Cavalry*, 200.
26 *Official Records*, 1st Series, II, 180.
27 *Military Service Institution Journal*, LVI, 40.

there or advance upon Winchester as Thomas himself suggested, Patterson cut back to Charlestown, twenty-two miles from the enemy camp. He was disturbed by an imperative order from Scott asking that the troops already requested be sent to Washington at once. Another telegram disclosed that McDowell had made his first stroke on July 17, driving Beauregard to the rear of Fairfax Court House. "Do not let the enemy amuse and delay you with a small force in front while he reenforces the [Manassas] Junction with his main body," Scott wired Patterson.[28] If the Pennsylvanian had possessed a little more confidence, which was difficult under the circumstances, he might have blocked a railway line which Johnston was likely to use in quitting the Shenandoah Valley for Manassas. But although Patterson still clung to Thomas and a Second Cavalry squadron, the volunteers were of no help at this stage. Disappointed over being deprived of a fight earlier in the campaign, they insisted that they would go home the very day their terms expired.

Again recounting his difficulties to Scott, Patterson inquired, "Shall I attack?" Scott's reply put the General on the defensive: "I have certainly been expecting you to beat the enemy . . . [or] at least had occupied him by threats and demonstrations." Patterson insisted that he had been doing that right along, wiring the War Department at 1:00 p.m. on the eighteenth: "I have succeeded in keeping General Johnston's force at Winchester." But shortly after midday, Thomas's scouts saw clouds of dust rising over the road leading from Winchester to a gap in the mountains. Racing to camp with the news, Lieutenant Anderson saw Thomas rush over to Patterson's tent without stopping to put on his hat or button his coat. "I know from hearsay that he told Patterson there was time even then to intercept Johnston," the Lieutenant asserted.[29] But Patterson was of the opinion that enough time had been allowed for McDowell to defeat Beauregard and that Johnston would be too late. Thus the detachment of 6,000 Confederates continued

[28] *Battles and Leaders of the Civil War*, I, 182.

[29] *Military Service Institution Journal*, LVI, 40. Speech of Colonel Thomas M. Anderson before the Oregon Commandery, Military Order of the Loyal Legion of the U. S., 7.

on their way unmolested, boarding waiting trains at Piedmont and arriving at Manassas just in time to stem a Confederate retreat and beat back the confused Federal battalions under McDowell. The Battle of Bull Run turned into a humiliating panic and rout. General-in-Chief Scott could hardly believe it.

Winning some success among the recruits, Thomas began to wish he could organize and train an army of his own. He watched the three-months' men promptly take their leave on July 24. None seemed willing to serve a day over their time. Even the Philadelphia generals went home. Thomas led the two troops left in service to Point of Rocks on the Potomac River below Frederick, keeping a lookout for enemy movements on the opposite shore. Amid the general hubbub in Washington, the military high command was being reorganized. Much to their own surprise, the colonels who had fought and fled at Bull Run were named brigadiers as of August 3, while General Mc-Dowell, as well as Patterson, was dismissed. The list of new appointments contained thirty-eight names, including Sherman, Fitz John Porter, George Gordon Meade, and Erasmus Darwin Keyes. Thomas was still regarded as a Southerner and had no one to speak for him at Washington. So it remained for a man in the ranks, Sergeant Samuel J. Randall, speaker of the Pennsylvania House, to mention his name. Unfortunately, Randall was just a little too late, although he sent a warm letter to Thomas A. Scott of his state, the new assistant secretary of war.

Opportunity had not been lacking, explained Randall, to compare men in the field. He confessed he had seen enough of inefficiency. "In the name of God," he implored, "[let the new officers] be men fully competent to discharge the duties of the positions to which they may be assigned. . . . Colonel George H. Thomas . . . is thoroughly competent to be a brigadier general, and has the confidence of every man in his command for the reason that they recognize and appreciate capacity. . . . This appointment would give renewed vigor and courage to this section of the Army."[30] Randall had no other name to recommend in his letter. An army man occupying higher rank also was inquiring about Thomas. This was Thomas's old West

30 Van Horne, *Thomas*, 37.

Point teacher, General Robert Anderson, who had defended Fort Sumter. Placed in command of the Department of the Cumberland, Anderson had been authorized to recommend the brigadiers he wished to serve under him. It was his intention to suggest Sherman of Ohio, Don Carlos Buell of Kentucky, and Thomas, who had not yet been named a general. He asked Sherman to help and also sent for his nephew, Lieutenant Thomas Anderson, then at Point of Rocks. When Anderson examined the Lieutenant concerning Thomas's sympathies, he was told "there was no doubt about his loyalty" and the Ben Butler incident was described.[31]

This decided Anderson, but he had yet to convince a group of stern-faced politicians who gathered at Willard's Hotel to discuss the appointments. Present were Senator Andrew Johnson of Tennessee, a courageous and combative Unionist; Congressman Horace Maynard, who recently had arrived in the capital following a tumultuous election campaign in East Tennessee; and Congressman Carey A. Trimble of Ohio and another member of the House from Kentucky. These gentlemen had been urging the necessity for military action in the West. East Tennessee, Unionist home ground of Johnson and Maynard, was already under the Confederate heel. A force of Rebel invaders had been burning barns and dwellings, destroying stores of food, driving off cattle, and spreading terror everywhere. Hundreds of destitute refugees had fled for safety to Federal military camps in central and eastern Kentucky. Congressman Thomas Nelson, elected on the same ticket with Maynard, had been arrested by Confederate partisans while on his way to Washington and thrown into jail. The Rebels were pressing vigorously everywhere.

Concerned over the safety of both Tennessee and Kentucky, the Westerners were in no mood for temporizing measures. They approved the nomination of Sherman, who was present, and of Buell, but summarily rejected Thomas. The name of Simon Bolivar Buckner, commander of the Kentucky State Guard was suggested. If Buckner were made a brigadier in the Federal Army, the argument ran, he would bring the

[31] *Military Service Institution Journal,* LVI, 39.

State Guard over to the Union side. This gave young Tom Anderson a turn. "I stated I had been offered by Buckner a commission in the Kentucky State Guard and that it was known to be a rebel organization," he testified boldly.[32] Sherman left an account of a similar hotel meeting, possibly the same one, at which he spoke up for Thomas, although he seemed to believe that President Lincoln was there. He declared he would not hear of Thomas's being passed over. "I was still more emphatic in my indorsement of him by reason of my talk with him at the time he crossed the Potomac with Patterson's army."[33] Anderson, he related, had some difficulty in prevailing upon the President to appoint Thomas "because so many Southern officers had already played false."

But after Lincoln was seen, Thomas was duly appointed and confirmed. Lieutenant Anderson was pleased to take the commission back to Point of Rocks and place it in the General's hand. A letter from Lincoln to Secretary of War Cameron deferred to the officer who had made the recommendation: "At the request of Brigadier General Anderson, I have concluded to appoint George H. Thomas of the 2nd cavalry a Brigadier."[34] Dated August 17, the commission placed Thomas in fifty-fifth place on the entire list of brigadiers, many of them his juniors at West Point. One week later an official order assigned Sherman, Buell, and Thomas to the Department of the Cumberland, General Anderson commanding, with headquarters at Louisville.

Thomas moved his brigade to Hyattsville, near Washington, and relinquished the command to General Nathaniel P. Banks, a Massachusetts man. He was allowed time for a hasty visit to his wife, who happened to be in New Haven, Connecticut; and after six days on the road, going and coming, the General kept a Cincinnati appointment with Anderson and Sherman at the mansion home of the commander's brother Larz. A group of Union stalwarts from Kentucky came to the Anderson

---

[32] *Ibid.*, 40.

[33] Sherman, *Personal Memoirs*, I, 221.

[34] Lincoln to Secretary of War Cameron, August 19, 1861, Dearborn Collection; Thomas to Anderson, August 26, 1861, U. S. Military Academy Library.

home—men such as John Marshall Harlan, a volunteer officer and a future chief justice, and James Speed, personal friend of President Lincoln.[35] An editorial in the Cincinnati *Daily Gazette* next day bespoke matters discussed at the council: "The possession of the Louisville & Nashville RR. is deemed of the greatest importance. Kentucky once precipitated, Louisville and not Nashville would be the interior rendezvous of treason, and war would be at the door of Ohio, Indiana and Illinois."[36]

Kentucky had been kept neutral through the efforts of a strong Unionist faction led by Harlan and Speed, although Governor Beriah Magoffin was a known Confederate partisan and Simon Bolivar Buckner was conspiring with the State Guard. Young Kentuckians were riding their horses in opposite directions, some north, and some south to a recruiting station just over the line in Tennessee. The Federals had made a start with 4,000 volunteers in training at Camp Dick Robinson in the Blue Grass country near Danville, where some 2,200 refugees from East Tennessee, including two full regiments of volunteers, were accommodated. General William Nelson, a navy lieutenant on furlough, was trying to organize the troops at the camp, but had made himself intensely disliked by his quarterdeck bearing. General Lovell H. Rousseau, Federal leader in the Kentucky legislature, was enlisting recruits at Camp Jo Holt, just across the Ohio River from Louisville, while Buckeye State troops were mobilizing at Camp Dennison near Cincinnati. Danger of invasion was not far distant with three Confederate columns threatening the border state. General Leonidas Polk, a West Pointer turned Episcopal bishop, had laid aside the cloth for the sword and was approaching the Mississippi River towns in the west. General Albert Sidney Johnston and Simon Buckner were gathering Confederate volunteers at Nashville and preparing for a thrust at the center, while the invaders of East Tennessee were headed by General Felix Zollicoffer, resolute soldier and popular citizen and a former member of Congress.

Anderson conceded that the primary need was for men. An immediate recruiting task was decided upon for Sherman, who

35 Sherman, *Personal Memoirs,* I, 222.
36 September 2, 1861.

hurried off to consult with the governors of Indiana and Illinois at the respective state capitals and with General John Frémont who was in command at St. Louis. Thomas was assigned the post which he asked for, the vital training center at Camp Dick Robinson. Regarding future strategy, he volunteered the opinion that given a force of 20,000 men properly armed and equipped, he could invade East Tennessee and cut the Virginia and Tennessee Railroad linking Chattanooga and Knoxville with the East.[37] Once East Tennessee were liberated and Knoxville taken, a wide and firm wedge could be driven into Jefferson Davis's Confederacy.

[37] Although the leading article in *The Collector*, January, 1942, says that Thomas talked with Lincoln, other scattered references indicate that he saw only General-in-Chief Scott.

VI

Victory at Mill Springs

WHILE Sherman was absent on his recruiting mission, Anderson and Thomas set up headquarters at Louisville. Kentucky's neutrality was swept into the discard when General Leonidas Polk marched into Columbus on the Mississippi River and erected fortifications. While the invasion was a little too remote for Anderson to handle, the Confederates were blocked by General Ulysses S. Grant, one of the new brigadiers, who moved into Paducah from his post at Cairo, Illinois. There was no longer any reason to protest, as some Kentuckians had been doing, the presence of Federal troops at Camp Dick Robinson. General Nelson answered one carping letter by pointing out that the camp had been established "to defend Kentucky . . . preserve its tranquility, and protect the rights of all the citizens."[1] Apparently this was the purpose for which Dick Robinson, Esq., wealthy owner of the camp's 3,200 acres, had loaned the government the land. Risking some personal danger, since plans had been laid to capture him, Thomas reached his post by a roundabout route on September 15.

Lacking clothing and arms for the two Tennessee and four Kentucky regiments at the camp, Nelson had been marking time. Thomas loaded the mails with appeals for rifles, ammunition, artillery, wagons, uniforms, overcoats, shoes, and necessary cash to pay for hired teams. He angrily protested the dumping of shoddy materials on his men and reported the dishonest contractors by name. Not only was the clothing a profiteer's dream but many of the rifles sent into Kentucky were Belgian and had been rejected elsewhere. Local suppliers and teamsters were not averse to making a dollar or two over the

[1] Cincinnati *Daily Gazette*, September 3, 1861.

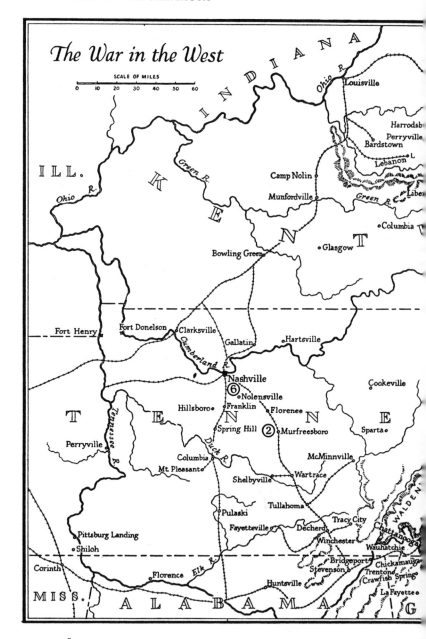

The War in the West

SCALE OF MILES

0   10   20   30   40   50   60

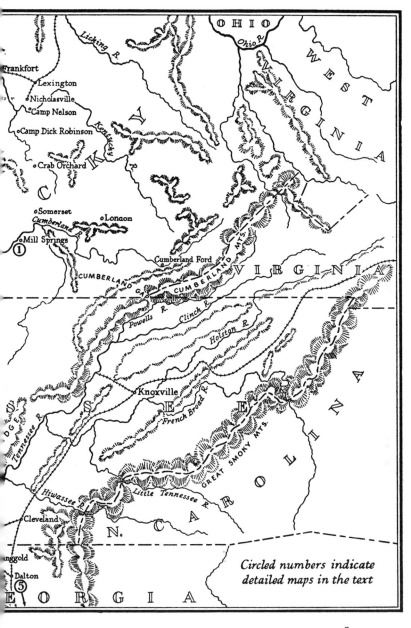

Circled numbers indicate
detailed maps in the text

honest one, and Thomas was compelled to borrow funds from the bank at Lexington to pay them. Tents and barracks were drafty, and with the approach of cool weather the sick list began to lengthen. Thomas covered the fields with recruits at drill and kept a close eye on their progress. "I am beginning to work some order out of the confusion which I found existed in every part of the camp when I arrived," he notified headquarters on September 21.[2]

More talk of enemy invasion ran through the camp. General Zollicoffer, it was learned, had established himself in a strong position on Kentucky soil near Cumberland Gap while Simon Buckner had advanced from Nashville to Bowling Green. When public notice was given that the Kentucky State Guard would mobilize on the Fair Grounds at Lexington, it became apparent that Buckner planned to unite his forces, seize the banks and the arsenal at near-by Frankfort, and disperse the legislature then in session. The alarmed delegates prepared to leave the capital but found it safe to remain when Thomas marched a Kentucky regiment to Lexington, where it camped on the Fair Grounds the night before the State Guard was due to take over. Although Confederate sympathizers had purchased or stolen all the powder and lead available, even tearing up lead pipes, it was decided to postpone the contemplated subjugation of that area.[3] Sherman guarded Louisville against Buckner's army of 4,000 by making a stand with General Rousseau on a steep hill thirty miles south of the city. After burning a bridge and causing wild excitement, the Rebels retraced the road to Bowling Green with no casualties anywhere reported.

Camp Dick Robinson soon became conscious of the character of its leader. More recruits flocked into the camp, which was winning new prestige. Partial to farm boys who could ride, Thomas hand-picked a regiment of Kentucky cavalry and daily watched its progress. A Kentucky battery was mustered in with four Ohio infantry regiments and two of light artillery, while

2 Thomas to Capt. O. D. Green, September 21, 1861, Johnson Papers, 13:2889.

3 Army of the Cumberland, 1888 Reunion, *Report*, 98; Official Records, 1st Series, IV, 262–66.

BATTLE OF MILL SPRINGS
January 19, 1862

"Terrific bayonet charge of the 9th Ohio Volunteers (Col. Mc-Cook) and total defeat of the Rebel army under Genl Zollicoffer by the Gallant Soldiers of the West."

Indiana and Minnesota were sending a regiment each for an army which would number some 8,000 men by the middle of October. "Thomas still wore his colonel's uniform with the buff shoulder straps of a colonel of cavalry," wrote an officer who watched him at work. "The most patient of men . . . he attended the dress parades of each regiment, inspected clothing, arms, accoutrements. He instructed the quartermaster and commissary, ordnance officer and provost marshal in their duties. . . . All his staff officers were young men whose hearts were easily won by kindness and appreciation of difficulties. . . . Step by step the process went on. Ploughboys exchanged their slouching gait for an erect carriage, officers found more interest in studying tactics than in reading newspapers and talking politics. On every side improvement was visible."[4] Still the boys were having quite a time breaking in the mules.

To watch Zollicoffer's movements, Thomas posted a Kentucky infantry regiment under Colonel Kenner Garrard on a road to the southeast. He suggested to Anderson that more regiments be organized at various points along the frontier and submitted his plan to invade East Tennessee. "As soon as prepared, I propose to enter Tennessee by way of Somerset, march on Knoxville, seize the RR., push towards Nashville & Granville & distroy the bridges as near to Nashville & Granville as possible . . . then turn on Zollicoffer whilst he is in the passes of the Cumberland Mountains."[5] Once between Zollicoffer and his base of supplies, Thomas believed he could soon disperse his army. Nashville, he notified Anderson, had been made a depot for the Army of Virginia.

Since Lincoln himself has recommended that East Tennessee be invaded in October, the movement could become quite a military plum for the successful commanding general. That the midwest faction still coveted the command became apparent on October 11 when Senator Andrew Johnson and Congressman Maynard arrived in camp with a letter from General O. M. Mitchel of Cincinnati who had been ordered to replace

4 Military Order of the Loyal Legion of the United States, District of Columbia Commandery, *War Papers*, II, 15–16.

5 Johnson Papers, 13:2889.

Thomas. Loath to yield control of his Ohio troops, Mitchel had urged upon the War Department "the necessity of placing in supreme command of this expedition . . . an experienced general, who will command the entire confidence of the Government."[6] Mitchel, a former West Pointer, had been out of uniform for some years teaching science and astronomy at Cincinnati College and was fifty-eight years old. His suggestion stuck, nevertheless, and by some means not made plain he received the coveted appointment.

Since General Anderson had recently resigned on account of ill health, Thomas had lost his principal champion. The situation was made more awkward because the letter brought by Johnson was from Mitchel, not the War Department. Flushed with anger, Thomas wasted no time in stating his views to the General. "I ask to be relieved from duty with these troops since the Secretary of War thought it necessary to supersede me in command without, as I conceive, any just cause for so doing," he notified Mitchel.[7] Another stiff note went off to Sherman, who had succeeded Anderson at headquarters: "General: I received an official communication today from Brigadier General O. M. Mitchel informing me that he had been notified by the Secretary of War to repair to this camp and prepare the troops for a forward movement. . . . As I have been doing all in my power to effect this very thing, to have the execution of it taken from me when nearly prepared . . . is extremely mortifying. I have therefore respectfully to ask to be relieved from duty with the troops on the arrival of General Mitchel."[8]

Sherman, who was too much of a rampant Californian to suit the easy-going Kentuckians, was decidedly out of his element at Louisville and was getting himself disliked. He was willing to sacrifice Thomas if his hand could be strengthened in other ways. Although Sherman often related how he had helped make Thomas a brigadier, he was silent concerning the Mitchel appointment. His reply dated October 13 "authorized" Thomas to continue preparing his command for active service.

6 *Official Records*, 1st Series, IV, 266.
7 Van Horne, *Thomas*, 43–44.
8 *Ibid.*, 44.

"I will, if possible, give you the opportunity to complete what you have begun," Sherman's message ran. "Of course I would do all I can to carry out your wishes but feel that the affairs of Kentucky call for the united action of all engaged." Thomas knew this to be temporization, but the effect of his threat was not lost. Some days later, Sherman received a note on the same subject from General Anderson, who was then in New York. "I am very anxious that Thomas shall have charge of the advance upon Cumberland Gap and hope that Genl. Mitchel will not be allowed to supersede him," declared Anderson.[9] Andrew Johnson made a vague claim sometime later that he had selected Thomas for the advance on Cumberland Gap, and it is possible that he made such a recommendation after learning the views of the Tennesseans in camp. In any event, General Mitchel never reached Camp Dick Robinson, and apparently the appointment was set down as a tactical mistake.

Getting down to cases, Johnson asked Thomas for a written statement "of what is needed for an advance on Tennessee." While Sherman was bawling loudly for an overwhelming force for wholly defensive measures—30,000 men from Kentucky and 30,000 from other states—Thomas restricted his immediate necessities to:

"Four [more] well drilled Regiments supplied with means of transportation & ammunition.

"Two [more] batteries of Arty. completely equipped for the field.

"50,000 dollars Qr. Master's funds to purchase forage and defray incidental expenses.

"50,000 dollars Com'ry funds to purchase Fresh beef, Bacon, flour, corn meal & vegetables."

"As I have no funds on hand," he added, "I have been compelled to contract large outstanding debts & at the last moment have had to borrow money from the Bank in Lexington to pay for clothing which is absolutely necessary to have for issue to the men for Winter, but which the contractors refused to deliver

9 Sherman Papers, 9:1603.

unless they receiv'd cash for the lots as they are delivered."[10] The General was leaving nothing undone to obtain adequate food and clothing while hoping for the best in the way of ordnance and ammunition from the War Department. Both Thomas and the East Tennesseans were grateful for Johnson's help in steering a shipment of breech-loading Sharps rifles their way.

The road from East Tennessee into Kentucky wound through the wooded fastness of Cumberland Gap and across the lower reaches of the Cumberland River. Fortifying the mountain passes as he advanced, General Zollicoffer was making this route a royal highway for invasion, hoping for a concerted movement with Buckner, who had been joined by General Albert Sidney Johnston, commanding Confederate forces in the west, at Bowling Green. A Federal army under Generals Alexander McDowell McCook and Lovell H. Rousseau stood in Buckner's way at Camp Nolin, some twenty miles north of Green River. Thomas, who had too few men at hand for his task, sent forward an Ohio and an Indiana regiment on October 14 when he heard that Zollicoffer was again on the way. Colonel T. T. Garrard's Seventh Regiment of Kentucky Volunteers had fallen back to the selected rendezvous at Rock Castle Hills, a two days' march south of Dick Robinson. General Albin Schoepf, commanding operations, threw up barricades about "Camp Wildcat" on the north bank of Rock Castle River and prepared to meet the invaders. On October 19, Thomas ordered the Fourteenth Ohio Regiment and six pieces of artillery to join Schoepf. He preferred to keep the East Tennesseans in hand for a little longer lest too many lives be lost through sheer ardor.

Concern over the fortunes of Schoepf was uppermost in Thomas's mind when, on the twentieth, General Sherman showed up in company with former Senator John J. Crittenden of Kentucky whose two sons, both of them generals, had chosen opposite sides. Johnson and Maynard were still in camp supervising the welfare of their constituents. After supper that evening the army band assembled before headquarters and played

[10] Thomas to Johnson, October 12, 1861, Johnson Papers, 13:2902.

a program of patriotic airs. Cries of "speech" went up, winning a warm response from Johnson, Maynard, the aged Crittenden, and finally Sherman. Having had enough of this, Thomas excused himself and withdrew to the little room which he used as an office. One of his aides working unobserved behind a desk saw him stride up and down in growing impatience. As Sherman finished his speech, shouts arose for Thomas. "Damn this speech-making," the General exploded. "I won't speak. What does a man want to make a speech for?" Catching sight of his aide, he ducked into an inner room, slamming the door behind him and keeping to his quarters until the next day.[11] Civilian interference and oratorical froth had fed his growing irritation. Sherman reported that the camp still lacked clothing and other essentials and that Thomas was "also troubled for want of money," finding it impossible to engage needed transportation or even to buy the simplest items for want of ready cash.[12]

Approaching lonely Camp Wildcat on October 21, the Fourteenth Ohio Regiment and the artillery battery quickened their steps at the sound of rifle fire, taking position in time to engage in a battle already commenced. The enemy attack died down after the guns had been wheeled to the front and unlimbered but was later renewed for about an hour, though to no purpose. "The loss among the rebels is said to be awful," wrote a soldier with pardonable exaggeration.[13] According to Federal reports, 30 of the enemy were killed among a force which Confederate prisoners reported to comprise 6,000 infantry and 1,500 cavalry but which actually was closer to 4,000. Zollicoffer renewed the attack next day; but after losing rather more heavily, he took the road back to Cumberland Gap. Delighted by this "decided victory," Thomas hurried to join Schoepf and advanced him to a point near London, thirty miles farther on, where he could watch a fork of the roads.[14] Since the East Tennesseans could no longer be restrained, two more regiments were permitted to join him.

11 *Battles and Leaders of the Civil War*, I, 382.

12 *Official Records*, 1st Series, IV, 312.

13 Cincinnati *Daily Gazette*, October 25, 1861.

14 *Official Records*, 1st Series, IV, 321; Joint Committee on the Conduct of the War, *Supplemental Report*, I, 4.

Thomas gathered up the rest of his army and left Camp Dick Robinson on the twenty-sixth to organize an advance post at Crab Orchard. Strong feeling prevailed among the exiles that Zollicoffer should be pursued right into East Tennessee, but Sherman was putting on the brakes. Thomas did his best to explain the situation to his commander: "With four more good regiments we could seize the railroad yet," he wrote. "With my headquarters at Somerset, I can easily seize the most favorable time for invading East Tennessee which ought to be done this winter."[15]

But Sherman's mood was entirely defensive. Although McCook and Rousseau were well manned and were closely watching Johnston at Bowling Green, a few well-laid rumors had aroused trepidation that an overwhelming Confederate force was poised for a thrust toward Louisville, Lexington, and Cincinnati. The responsibility of departmental command was proving too much for the volatile Sherman, who was still clamoring for 60,000 men for defensive duty. He acknowledged his own shortcomings when he confessed to Thomas on November 6, writing from Louisville, "It would be better if some more sanguine mind were here, for I am forced to order according to my convictions."[16] Thus forewarned, Thomas was not greatly surprised to receive a message dated November 11 ordering him to consolidate his forces and retreat. In view of the circumstances, this was about the worst action Sherman could have directed, particularly since he had just been deposed from the command and was then awaiting the arrival of General Don Carlos Buell, his successor.

Although Thomas had no other choice than to obey, he attempted to put some heart into his old friend and schoolmate: "I am sure the enemy is not moving between us. All my information is that they are moving south." His cool estimate of the situation was passed over. Still Johnston made no move to leave Bowling Green, and the army in his front was left undisturbed. Sherman's order plunged the Tennesseans into "an agony of

15 *Official Records,* 1st Series, IV, 339.

16 *Ibid.,* 341; J. G. Nicolay and John Hay, *Complete Works of Abraham Lincoln,* V, 65.

despair." Highly elated over the first success, they had been bent on relieving their homeland before Christmas; but when word came for Schoepf to abandon London, epithets and curses were flung at everyone in authority from the President down. "Tears were flowing down bearded cheeks, and many . . . declared they would not return," wrote an eyewitness.[17] One of the Tennessee-born officers, Brigadier General Samuel P. Carter, tall, handsome, and dignified, moved among the troops on foot and promised an early renewal of the campaign. The retreat, he assured his men, was only a temporary measure. The mutiny subsided somewhat. Clad in rags, their shoes almost gone and their stomachs empty, the disheartened soldiers gripped their rifles and faced about for a hurried and painful night march over mud-filled roads to Crab Orchard. The Fourteenth Ohio Regiment band was playing the "Dead March" from *Saul*. "In a march of 14 miles we must have passed 200 Stragglers," related a Buckeye soldier. "Some were lying prone on the ground sobbing, some stood on the highway swearing defiantly; others leaned against the fences sullenly, undetermined to move one way or the other."[18] It was the night of November 13.

"Are we to stay here always—must we forever stay and guard Kentucky? Will we never be allowed to go back to East Tennessee—to our homes and our destitute, unprotected families?" This soldier's letter found its way into the Cincinnati *Daily Commercial,* which was moved to protest that the "absurd and ruinous retreat is enough to sicken the whole country."[19] Thomas shooed the war correspondents out of his camp. His forces united at Crab Orchard, he retired under orders as far north as Lebanon, which was about midway between Lexington and Bowling Green. He read some strictures directed against him in the Cincinnati newspapers which hinted that he had purposely failed to pursue and capture Zollicoffer. Not only did such criticism reflect upon his loyalty, but a reproving letter also came from Congressman Maynard: "You are still farther

[17] Military Order of the Loyal Legion of the U. S., D. C. Commandery, *War Papers,* XIX, 5.

[18] Cincinnati *Daily Commercial,* November 19, 1861.

[19] *Ibid.,* November 16, 18, 1861.

from East Tennessee than when I left you nearly six weeks ago. There is a shameful wrong somewhere. I have not yet satisfied myself where."[20] Among the saddened troops in the field the dismal feeling was growing that the federal government would be unable to sustain itself.

If the Administration had known all the facts and wished to replace Sherman with the officer who had demonstrated the most interest in an offensive campaign, then Thomas would have been selected as Army of the Cumberland leader. The fact that Don Carlos Buell was a native Kentuckian and therefore was acceptable to the political leaders of his state was obviously the deciding factor. Buell, West Point graduate of 1841, had experienced the same military schooling as Thomas in Florida and Mexico, but as a leader of volunteers he possessed little personal appeal. Short-statured, slight of figure, and cold in bearing, he was intensely soldierly, and yet no military ramrod such as he ever possessed the heart-warming qualities essential to raise an occasional cheer. Although Buell was on entirely friendly terms with the dashing George B. McClellan, who had replaced Winfield Scott as general-in-chief, he was to demonstrate little interest in winning back East Tennessee.

For while McClellan urged Buell to lose no time in pushing on toward Cumberland Gap, the Kentuckian's personal friendship with his chief made his excuses go a long way. Letters to his "Dear Friend" in Washington stressed difficulties of organization and supply. On December 7 he heard from Johnson and Maynard, who prodded him by telegraph: "Our people are oppressed and pursued as beasts of the forest; the Government must come to their relief."[21] But rather than succor the poor whites in the mountain districts to the east, Buell pursued the idea of mobilizing for a thrust at Bowling Green and then Nashville. Throughout the month of December he continued to collect fresh troops and supplies, sending some to Thomas at Lebanon, although the greater part seemed to find their way to Louisville or to General McCook, who was still facing Johnston

[20] Military Order of the Loyal Legion of the U. S., District of Columbia Commandery, *War Papers*, XLIV, 21–22.

[21] Hall, Clifton R., *Andrew Johnson*, 17.

across Green River. McClellan, who was playing the same bureaucratic game with the Army of the Potomac, forever declaring that he was undermanned, agreed with his friend concerning the need for better organization. For armchair perfectionists, a model army is needed, complete in every detail. Christmas Day passed, and all was quiet along the Potomac and on the Kentucky and Tennessee front. Ultimately, on January 5, 1862, in response to Lincoln's pointed inquiry, "Have arms gone forward for East Tennessee?" Buell confessed that his judgment had been against such a move from the first.[22]

A forward thrust was then being made, however, since Thomas happened to be on his way to the Cumberland River. During November, as soon as permitted, he advanced a brigade to Columbia, some forty miles beyond Lebanon, and returned the East Tennesseans to London to guard the roads. Midway between these two points, General Schoepf had been stationed at Somerset. No open means were permitted Zollicoffer for a quick stroke. The new recruits were assigned daily duties in instruction and drill, although likewise important, according to Captain Judson W. Bishop of the Second Minnesota Volunteers, "the coeducation of the wagoners and mules was begun and some progress was made. The earlier lessons," the Captain continued, "afforded a great deal of entertainment to those not engaged in them but were sadly demoralizing to the wagoners. It has been stated that no man ever broke a team of six green army mules without breaking his Christian character, and the army chaplain who offered the long-standing reward of $100 to the man who should drive such a team for 30 days without the use of profane language did not have to part with his money."[23]

General Zollicoffer, traveling light, re-entered Kentucky early in December. A public proclamation which reached Thomas's hands conveyed more than a hint that the Confederates were living off the land, a privilege officially forbidden Union troops. "People of Southeastern Kentucky," the message trumpeted. "The brigade I have the honor to command is here

22 *Official Records*, 1st Series, VII, 530.
23 Judson W. Bishop, *Story of a Regiment*, 32.

for no other purpose but war upon those Northern hordes who with arms in their hands are attempting the subjugation of a sister Southern State."[24] Thomas passed the word along to Buell, who sanctioned the advance to the Cumberland although adding a caution against crossing the river "unless absolutely necessary." Zollicoffer was heedlessly saving Thomas the trouble by making his camp on the north bank at a point about eighteen miles southwest of Schoepf's position at Somerset. To encamp on the Union side of the river was obviously unwise, and General George B. Crittenden of Johnston's forces was delegated to remedy the situation; but by the time he had joined Zollicoffer, it was too late to make any change.[25]

Under Buell's new organization, Thomas's detachment of five brigades was known as the First Division, Army of the Ohio. On the last day of the year the volunteers folded their tents, loaded the baggage trains and filled their haversacks with three days' rations. Well-loaded packs containing blankets, overcoat, knapsack, and haversack with rifle and forty rounds of ball cartridges weighed down the men by nearly fifty pounds, but nevertheless a good pace was maintained for the first three days. After leaving Columbia, the volunteers were pelted by snow and a cold, stinging rain. The push through the mud grew tedious and slow. Nearly half the day, according to Captain Bishop, was spent in the woods and fields waiting for the wagons to catch up. Entire companies lent a hand to extricate sinking vehicles and helpless mules stuck in the mud; "men and beasts suffered terribly." A long-standing rule forbade the troops even to tear down fences for firewood, although it finally was amended slightly to permit use of the top rail. Soon cheerful fires were blazing, warming the troops at night, and it was useless for any company commander to try to find any soldier who had taken any but the top rail. All private property was generally supposed to be sacrosanct although now and then a soldier would stretch out a hand. "The people were not seriously foraged upon or molested, but pigs and geese occasionally did come into the camp and were duly mustered into the army," Captain Bishop

24 *Official Records*, 1st Series, VII, 787.
25 Stanley B. Horn, *The Army of Tennessee*, 68.

observed.[26] One night the soldiers discovered an applejack still near their camp site, and after duly declaring the product a contraband of war, they spent a hilarious evening warming their insides.

After two weeks on the road, Thomas made camp at Beech Grove near Somerset and ordered Schoepf's brigade to follow along. General Carter's brigade, with two Tennessee companies, the Twelfth Kentucky and an Ohio battery, had come from London, falling in well ahead of Schoepf. Undisturbed except for a minor picket skirmish, Thomas reached a position variously known as "Logan's Crossroads" and "Mill Springs" on January 18, 1862, taking position about ten miles north of Zollicoffer's entrenched camp on the river. The Fourteenth Ohio Infantry and the Tenth Kentucky were ordered out to watch for any enemy reinforcements which might be approaching from Bowling Green. A heavy downpour of rain that flooded the banks of near-by Fishing Creek prevented Schoepf from getting up on time. "It was the darkest night and the coldest and most pitiless and persistent rain we ever knew," recorded Captain Bishop, who already had seen much bad weather on the march. Thomas posted Carter's men on an adjacent road and arranged his own columns to guard against surprise. Not including the commands of Schoepf and Carter, he had only four infantry regiments near at hand, with the First Kentucky Cavalry and another Ohio battery, or less than 4,000 availables to pit against 6,250 in the Confederate camp.[27]

Discovering Schoepf to be blocked behind Fishing Creek, Crittenden and Zollicoffer planned to catch Thomas by surprise early on Sunday morning, January 19. Six Tennessee regiments, the Fifteenth Mississippi, and the Sixteenth Alabama were assembled just before midnight, with an artillery company and a battalion of cavalry which was to fight dismounted. During the early morning hours they stumbled blindly through the mud, marching in pitch darkness through the cold rain. The foul weather proved more of a handicap than an aid. Guns and wagons sank deep in the slimy soil, delaying the advance so as

26 *Story of a Regiment,* 35.
27 *United Service Journal,* October, 1885, 387–88.

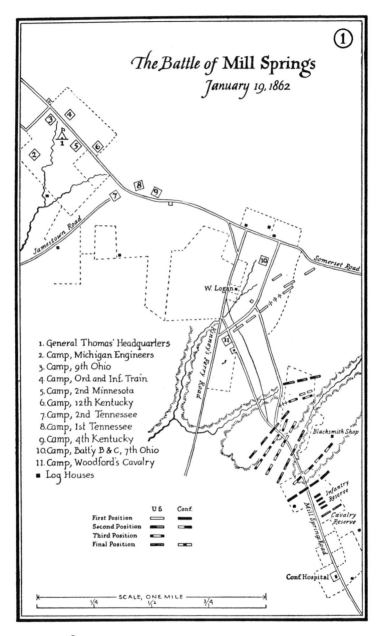

The Battle of Mill Springs
January 19, 1862

1

1. General Thomas' Headquarters
2. Camp, Michigan Engineers
3. Camp, 9th Ohio
4. Camp, Ord and Inf. Train
5. Camp, 2nd Minnesota
6. Camp, 12th Kentucky
7. Camp, 2nd Tennessee
8. Camp, 1st Tennessee
9. Camp, 4th Kentucky
10. Camp, Batt'y B & C, 7th Ohio
11. Camp, Woodford's Cavalry
■ Log Houses

	U.S.	Conf.
First Position		
Second Position		
Third Position		
Final Position		

SCALE, ONE MILE
1/4   1/2   3/4

to defeat the possibility of a surprise. At about six-thirty o'clock the alarm was signaled by the First Kentucky Cavalry, which Thomas had posted in front, and the pickets slowly retreated making a great noise. An exchange of musketry sprinked the gloom with pin points of light. The distant sound of rifle fire and the long roll aroused the slumbering camp. Men groped for their weapons and began forming "in hot haste" as one of the General's aides galloped off to summon Carter's brigade. Immaculately dressed, wearing brigadier's uniform for the very first time, Thomas faced his men drawn up in double line and spoke a few calm words as each regiment filed into position. His only fear was that they might become panic stricken. He kept a rigid eye on the volunteer officers and felt his temper rise when Colonel Mahlon D. Manson, an excitable Hoosier, rode up to report his Tenth Indiana in position. Manson had lost his hat, his uniform was all mussed, his hair disheveled, and his face unwashed. He had no sooner begun to announce his position than Thomas interrupted him with: "Damn you, sir, go back to your command and fight it." Manson caught the point, borrowed a hat, and fought well.[28]

Posted behind trees and brush, the Tenth Indiana and Colonel Speed S. Fry's Fourth Kentucky Infantry occupied the front line, which at once began to blaze and smoke. Riding forward to watch the action, Thomas saw enemy figures slipping through a cornfield to gain the Kentucky left. The Ohio battery was summoned to pepper this Alabama regiment, as it proved, which was skirting the field. The Ninth Ohio and Second Minnesota exchanged front-line positions with the Kentuckians and the Hoosiers as they retired to refill their cartridge boxes. The begrimed fighters drew nearer together in the murk; at one place the lines were so close that Federals and Rebels were poking their rifles through the same fence.[29] Mist and smoke thickened the air at daybreak. Mistaking foe for friend in the gloom, General Zollicoffer ordered one of his regiments to hold its fire, fearing that they were attacking his own men. Wearing a white rubber raincoat, the Confederate leader rode

28 Shanks, *Personal Recollections*, 66.
29 Bishop, *Story of a Regiment*, 39.

blindly ahead with an aide just as the Fourth Kentucky returned to the line. He then called to the Kentuckians to stop firing, exclaiming to their colonel, Speed Fry, "We must not shoot our own men." Fry stood speechless for a moment, then Zollicoffer's aide came to life, taking a quick shot at him and wounding his horse. The Union officer grabbed his gun and let fly.[30] The first bullet wounded the inaccurate aide, the second furrowed a path through the Confederate general's heart. And since Crittenden had fortified himself too well against the damp and cold, the Rebels now lacked a competent leader.

Old-fashioned flintlock muskets, dampened and made useless, proved of little use to a Confederate Tennessee brigade. Angered and disheartened after their wearisome night march, the secessionists smashed them against the rail fence and tossed them aside.[31] Lieutenant Baillie Peyton of Gallatin stood calmly alone; and after shooting a Union officer through the body, he defied the whole army to take him. Parley was useless, so he was shot where he stood.[32] Although the enemy had some hundreds of men in reserve, when green troops broke in front, the panic was caught by those in the rear, the also-rans. With no reserve to speak of, Thomas was hammering away with all available men in one line. Determined Confederates armed with breech-loaders prolonged the fight. "Trees were flecked with bullets, underbrush cut away as with a scythe," a Union soldier narrated. "Dead and wounded lay along the fence, on the one side the Blue, on the other the Gray; enemy dead were everywhere scattered across the open field."[33] Seeing their commander ride unhurriedly among them, the volunteers clung to the ground and fired away. After nearly one hour, General Carter's brigade managed to arrive and inched into the cornfield on the left. The Confederates took shelter behind some log huts and privies in their rear, but after Thomas ordered a bayonet charge, the whole enemy line gave way, "retreating in the utmost disorder."[34]

30 W. Preston Johnston, *Albert Sidney Johnston*, 402.
31 Bell Irvin Wiley, *The Life of Johnny Reb*, 288.
32 Bishop, *Story of a Regiment*, 40–41.
33 *Ibid.*, 42.
34 Thomas's Report, January 31, 1862; Coppée, *Thomas*, 66.

Thomas re-formed his lines in the cornfield. Time was allowed to refill cartridge boxes, but the soldiers had nothing to eat. About eight o'clock the Federals took up the chase. A few scattered shots were exchanged and some exhausted stragglers and enemy wounded picked up during the ten-mile pursuit to the fortified camp on the river. Shortly after midday Thomas formed his men in double line and stormed a high ridge which blocked the approach. This barrier removed, he called upon the artillery to get the range of a stern-wheel steamboat which was ferrying enemy officers across the river; but gaining the other side, the Rebels burned the boat. The artillery now practiced on a few flatboats which were taking off but without notable success. After examining the stout fortifications in front, Thomas decided against storming the camp. Since enough already had been gained without sacrificing any more men, he ordered the troops to bivouack where they stood. Somehow it never occurred to him to send in a demand for a surrender. "Hang it all, Fry, I never once thought of it," he exclaimed when reminded.[35]

Rations in haversacks had been spoiled by the rain, and the men were very hungry. Not until late in the evening when the wagon trains rolled up were the tired troops fed. The Confederates evacuated their trenches during the night and crossed the river on the flatboats. Marching into the enemy camp next morning, Thomas's men filed down company streets neatly laid out between shelter tents still standing. All was silent as the grave. A few wounded men and skulkers had resigned themselves to capture. The enemy had left all their provisions, wagons, and extra clothing in camp, and an artillery train of twelve guns was discovered bogged down in the mud, useless for any fight. A thousand or more horses and mules, a grand prize, were milling about in the valley below. General Schoepf's brigade, which arrived some hours later, was sent on a chase after the stampeded Rebels; but, thoroughly used up, they had scattered far and wide over the border, deserting in large numbers. Enemy casualties, according to Thomas's estimate, outnumbered his own by nearly three to one. While his official

[35] *Battles and Leaders of the Civil War,* I, 391.

return showed only 29 killed and 208 wounded, 192 of the enemy had been killed, 309 wounded, and 157 taken prisoner. The body of General Zollicoffer, marked by an expression of deep dejection, was cared for tenderly and returned to his Tennessee home under a flag. The remains of Lieutenant Baillie Peyton were also taken home to his father, a known Union sympathizer.

News of the victory was greeted with the thunder of guns fired in celebration in a score of Union camps. Aroused from its dejection following Bull Run, the North suddenly began to cheer. Thomas not only had nullified the Confederate threat from East Tennessee but had terminated the careers of two Southern generals. Not only was Zollicoffer dead, but George B. Crittenden would never recover from the disgrace. But, although four Federal colonels were named brigadier generals after the fight, the War Department recommended no award for the commanding general; nor was Thomas even mentioned by name in the official order of thanks "to the gallant officers and soldiers who won that victory," a galling omission. Thomas had only a letter from Congressman Maynard to show: "You have undoubtedly fought the great battle of the war . . . ."[36]

36 *Official Records,* 1st Series, VII, 582.

VII
Shiloh, Corinth, Perryville

S ATISFIED that the enemy had been completely dispersed, Thomas turned back to Somerset, where beds were commandeered for the wounded. A message from Buell suggested that he occupy Monticello, the next town beyond Mill Springs, but Thomas declined to do this after Schoepf brought word that the village had been stripped bare of supplies. Thomas could see no military necessity now for using a sizable force to invade East Tennessee. He told Buell that General Carter's brigade would suffice for the movement against Cumberland Gap while he hoped to co-operate with the main army against General Albert Sidney Johnston at Bowling Green.

Buell, however, had been instructed to invade East Tennessee. "How soon could you march and how long do you suppose it would take you to reach Knoxville?" he asked Thomas on February 2.[1] A great deal depended upon the weather. Thomas ordered his men to fell trees and corduroy the mud-filled roads leading southward, but the work was halted a few days later when another message from Buell asked him to combine in a stroke against Johnston and agreed that Carter should attempt to force Cumberland Gap. Another Union victory had brought about the change in plan. On February 6, General Grant had taken the Confederate bastion of Fort Henry, a strong earthwork fortification on the Tennessee River. Aided by Commodore Andrew H. Foote's gunboats, Grant was now pounding at the defenses of Fort Donelson, not many miles away on the Cumberland River. Meantime Federal forces converging on Bowling Green would either trap Johnston or force him to retreat. Thomas was well satisfied with this strategy. As

[1] *Official Records*, 1st Series, VII, 580.

his army pushed slowly northward through alternating snow and rain, it was cheered by the news of the fall of Fort Donelson on February 16. Defeated on the right at Mill Springs and with his left flank now in air, Johnston decided that Bowling Green was untenable and retreated to Nashville.

Kentucky, at least, was cleared of Rebels. Orders to Thomas kept him on the straight road to Louisville. According to a new scheme concocted by McClellan, Buell, and General Henry W. Halleck at St. Louis, the western forces were to combine with the Army of the Tennessee led by Grant. After Buell's Army of the Ohio had taken Nashville, the combined forces were to strike at the railroads running across Alabama and Mississippi. Thomas ploughed along through the mud. His worst enemy throughout the campaign seemed to be the weather. As he approached Bardstown on February 21 "it rained as I never saw it rain before," he notified Buell on Washington's Birthday. "It has done the same today."[2] But as the army entered Louisville three days later, it was warmed by an enthusiastic welcome. "Sidewalks were full of loyal men and flags were waved to us from windows and porches as we gaily marched through the principal streets toward the river," related Captain Judson W. Bishop, whose Second Minnesota Regiment displayed a beautiful silk banner from the hands of the "Loyal Ladies of Louisville."[3]

Thomas spent a few minutes at headquarters catching up with the news. General Grant had taken some 12,000 enemy troops in capturing the two river forts. On the heels of Johnston's retreat, a Federal division under General Mitchel had encountered only rear-guard action in entering Bowling Green. Mitchel was proceeding overland to Nashville while the rest of the army was descending the Ohio River and coming up the Cumberland by flatboat. Four divisions—those of William Nelson, Alexander McD. McCook, Thomas L. Crittenden, and Thomas J. Wood—were already on the way; and just as Thomas was about to embark, word came that Nelson had seized Nashville undisturbed. Since the Tennessee capital never had been

[2] *Ibid.*, 653.
[3] Bishop, *Story of a Regiment*, 50.

fortified, General Johnston considered it indefensible; and he was now heading south to unite with General Beauregard's army in Mississippi.

Because Thomas's division already had fought a battle, it was assigned to the rear of the advancing columns and was the last to reach Nashville. Trailed by a swarm of Negroes eager to do any service, the First Division entered the city on a spring-like March 4. Andrew Johnson, who had come with the army, was inducted into office as military governor and assigned a suitable guard. Buell remained in the city for about three weeks, a little too long as it proved, erecting fortifications about the high-towered capitol building and organizing his supply lines. On March 16, General Nelson started for the appointed rendezvous with Grant's army at Pittsburg Landing on the Tennessee River, a site which General Sherman, leading the advance, had selected. The landing on the west bank was only twenty miles north of Corinth, Mississippi, where Johnston had joined Beauregard; but instead of entrenching and fortifying their position, Grant and Sherman simply waited. The West Pointers in the army never had been instructed in the use of shovels, and it was considered bad psychology to make the soldiers dig.

Following Nelson on the road from Nashville came Mc-Cook, then Crittenden, Wood, and Thomas, marching one day apart. General Mitchel headed for Murfreesboro to repair the railroad and later entered Alabama in an effort to cut Johnston's supply line to the east. He managed to destroy several bridges and trestles which Thomas later had to repair in moving eastward along the line during the summer but encountered more trouble from lack of discipline in his own camp than from the Confederates. Buell's army made good progress for the first few days, but enemy destruction of a bridge over Duck River forced a long halt at Columbia. The river was then in flood, the water rich with mud. With no pontoons or boats available, Buell had to wait for the flood to subside. Ultimately a bridge was improvised for the wagons, and about the same time a ford, "deep and rapid," was located and the crossing begun. Thomas waited three days more in the rear while the troops in advance crossed over. Once on the way again, the army splashed through a heavy rain which brought further delay as the wagons defied the combined efforts of mules and men to move them in the mud. On April 4, while the road ahead was being cleared, the First Division remained all day in camp, but not long afterward the army discovered that time was running out. On Sunday, April 6, whenever Thomas's men halted, the rumbling of cannon met their ears. "We knew a great battle was in progress," penciled a diarist. Hurrying after the divisions ahead, they began to overtake and pass the wagon trains in advance, marching twenty-two miles before dark. After only a brief rest, they went on again, and at eleven o'clock threw themselves down on a soft, plowed cotton field. Fence rails were laid in the mud to stand or sleep on. The order was passed: "Be ready to march at 4 o'clock A. M."[4]

Only three of the five divisions on the road—those of Nelson, McCook, and Crittenden—reached Pittsburg Landing in time to reinforce the battered Union Army at Shiloh. Grant, with 33,000 men, had been attacked that Sunday by Johnston and Beauregard with 40,000, who only failed from want of discipline. As evening came on, the Confederates seemed to lose all interest in the fight, raiding the Union camps and filling themselves with commissary whiskey. Encountering 8,000 Federal fugitives at the wharf, Buell hesitated to bring his men across the river; but after satisfying himself that Grant and Sherman were still in control of the situation, he transferred the three divisions to the west bank during the night. General Lew Wallace, commanding an Army of the Tennessee division, had lost his way on Sunday but managed to arrive in time for the fight the next day. Even with these fresh reinforcements the Federals did not breach the Confederate line until three o'clock in the afternoon on April 7. Two days later Thomas's First Division crossed the river and stacked arms on a bloody field. Of the Confederate Army nearly 11,000 men were reported killed, wounded, and missing, although most grievous to the South was the loss of Albert Sidney Johnston, who had bled to death from a small bullet wound in the leg. The South was learning the truth of the saying, "Nobody ever wins who starts

4 *Ibid.*, 53.

a battle on a Sunday." First it had been Mill Springs and now Shiloh. Federal casualties exceeded 13,000, including 2,100 from the Army of the Ohio. In respect to numbers engaged it had been the most terrible battle of the war. The task of burying thousands of mangled and decaying dead from both sides and the rescue of the wounded consumed nearly five days. "None who participated in it or witnessed it will ever forget it," a volunteer officer observed soberly.[5]

The subject of promotions, after the battle, was being weighed by General Henry W. Halleck who arrived tardily to take command of the combined armies. Senior commander among those on the field, Halleck was to direct operations for the next few weeks. Apparently he had lost confidence in Grant, who, he complained, had "resumed his former bad habits," that is, drinking. General Sherman, who had commanded the Union right, was recommended for promotion to major general of volunteers and a similar commission was suggested for Thomas even though he had taken no part in the fighting. Halleck later explained that he urged the appointment in order to place Thomas over the right wing of a newly organized army. Another theory concerning the recommendation was that the promotion was obtained as a sort of disciplinary measure for Grant, who was relegated to "second in command," a post carrying little or no authority. Grant was in a mood to resign on hearing the news, only to be dissuaded by his friend Sherman. While Sherman was placed under Thomas in the right wing, the incident would not be forgotten by Grant after he became commander-in-chief, and so Sherman unintentionally had scored over Thomas.

No one could claim, however, that the huge army of 120,-000 men under Halleck was brilliantly led. Buell, with two divisions of the Army of the Ohio, commanded the center, while the left wing was headed by General John Pope of the Army of the Mississippi, neither of whom would last out the war. Commanding the reserve was John A. McClernand, an Illinois lawyer and member of Congress whom Grant soon got rid of after regaining leadership in June. "Old Brains" Halleck, au-

[5] *Ibid.*, 54.

thor of a standard military textbook at thirty-one, gave the impression of being a stupid field general. Thus again, as at the start of the war, Thomas found himself in bad company. The capture of Corinth called for a slashing movement by the two wings and an energetic thrust by the center, but Halleck was hesitant to the point of timidity. Delaying the advance until May 6, he ordered Thomas forward with a warning to be prepared for a sudden enemy movement in advance and impressed this note of caution on every corps. Vast entrenchments were dug and extensive fortifications thrown up along the way. All together, nearly three weeks of valuable time were lost in getting within shooting distance of Corinth. An officer of the Sixth Ohio Volunteers disgustedly watched Halleck "jogging along the lines with a tall army hat on, minus cord and tassel, his head thrown forward, his shoulders up and jerking about; if he had only had a pair of saddle bags, 'Old Brains' would have been the *beau ideal* of a country doctor."[6]

The Confederate leaders watched Halleck's every move, worrying him almost daily with detachments of skirmishers. As the ponderous Federal Army drew near Corinth, they prepared their last stroke, mounting wooden "Quaker" guns and dummy "paddies" for gunners upon the redoubts.[7] On May 29, Sherman's division repulsed a savage counterattack and stormed the enemy line near the town but was ordered to wait while the rest of the army came up. The Confederates made a great noise in camp that night, with bugles sounding retreat, tattoo, and taps all along the lines while an empty train of cars was run back and forth on the railroad and loud cheers were given as if in greeting fresh reinforcements. Light dawned upon the puzzled Federals the next morning when a series of explosions and a dense cloud of smoke signaled the departure of the Confederates from Corinth. Thomas immediately advanced his line, meeting some resistance from a row of enemy pickets who had been left in position. After nearly all had been taken prisoner, they were disgusted to learn that the Confederate Army had abandoned them. The Federals were hardly less chagrined as they marched

6 E. Hannaford, *Story of a Regiment,* 346.
7 Alexis Cope, *The 15th Ohio Volunteers,* 155.

through the vacant streets of the town and found little left even in the way of booty. While northern newspapers heaped ridicule on Halleck for his barren triumph, a show of pursuit was made as far as Boonville.

Federal strategy never appeared so weak as after Corinth, when the North possessed the strength but declined to use it. Instead of pursuing the Confederates in force and bringing them to battle, Halleck erected more fortifications in the grand manner, extending the works so far that they were useless except to an army of about 100,000 men. A message from Lincoln asked that Buell be detached and sent against Chattanooga and Knoxville in East Tennessee. Buell's departure aroused a fresh storm of criticism against Halleck, who only transmitted the order as it happened, but the Confederate high command kept one jump ahead by sending General Braxton Bragg and the Army of Tennessee to Chattanooga. Taking the divisions which had been transferred to Thomas during the march on Corinth, Buell hurried after the foe, although never fast enough to catch up. Halleck, meanwhile, was kicked upstairs to the post of general-in-chief, succeeding McClellan who later was relieved of his duties as head of the Army of the Potomac by General Ambrose Burnside. Left in charge of operations at Corinth, Thomas did not relish his post. On June 10, at his own request, he yielded command of the Army of the Tennessee to its former commander, Grant.[8] Major General Edward O. C. Ord of Maryland succeeded Pope as Army of the Mississippi chief.

Within a fortnight Thomas had left Corinth and was marching to join Buell with his favorite First Division which he had trained himself. Tuscumbia, Alabama, was fortified and the Memphis and Charleston Railroad slowly but diligently repaired. For nearly a month Thomas labored to keep tracks and trestles intact while roving bands of guerrillas undid at night what had been accomplished by day. Ultimately, trains of supplies began rolling over the railroad to Grant. Late in July one of General Ord's divisions relieved him of his railroad duties, and the march was resumed. Crossing the Tennessee River at Florence, Alabama, Thomas advanced over dusty roads

[8] Van Horne, *Thomas,* 65–66.

to Athens and Huntsville, then turned north to Decherd, Tennessee, where he greeted General Buell on the seventh of August, a hot and fatiguing day.

General Buell, "cool, smooth-toned and silent," found several matters to distract him as he waited for Thomas to arrive. Confederate E. Kirby Smith, a one-time Second Cavalry officer, was pursuing an aggressive campaign in East Tennessee and was hammering against Carter at Cumberland Gap. General Nelson, whom Buell had sent ahead to help protect Nashville, was threatened by the cavalry leaders Nathan Bedford Forrest and John H. Morgan, who had destroyed two bridges in his rear, while General Richard W. Johnson, assigned a squadron of horse, had been ignominiously trapped and taken prisoner at Hartsville. Buell's placid demeanor also masked his worry over the possibility that Earl Van Dorn, Confederate commander in Alabama, might be disposed to attack his rear. Although it was Buell's primary task to strike a hard blow at Bragg, who had reached Chattanooga, he lingered several weeks at Decherd as if uncertain what to do.

Governor Andrew Johnson, indeed, had lost all faith in Buell. When Thomas arrived at Decherd, his chief handed him a letter in which the Governor expressed his grave concern over "dilatory steps," as he expressed it, to drive out the enemy. Addressing himself directly to Thomas, Johnson expressed the hope that he might be assigned the task of defeating Bragg. Thomas did not concur. Always loyal to his commander whenever he scented civilian interference in army plans, Thomas reached for some South-Western Telegraph Company blanks and made his reply: " . . . I most earnestly hope I may not be placed in the position, for several reasons. One particular reason is that we have never yet had a commander of any expedition who has been allowed to work out his own policy, and it is utterly impossible for the most able General in the World to conduct a campaign with success when his hands are tied, as it were by the constant apprehension that his plans may be interfered with at any moment. . . . I can confidently assure you," Thomas went on, "that Genl. Buell's dispositions will eventual-

9 Thomas to Johnson, August 16, 1862, Henry E. Huntington Library.

MAJOR GENERAL DON CARLOS BUELL

ly free all Tennessee and go very far to crush the rebellion entirely."[9]

These were bold words, but Thomas could not foresee that Buell would shrink from forcing Bragg to an encounter. Army maneuvers of the next three weeks made little sense. To strengthen the right flank, Buell advanced Thomas to McMinnville, a four-day march over rough country roads toward a position from which Bragg might have been intercepted as he advanced north from Chattanooga. Buell believed that the Confederate leader intended to strike at Nashville, but after questioning some friendly citizens and Negroes at McMinnville, Thomas thought he had the truth of it. "The demonstration in this direction is to cover the advance of the enemy toward Kentucky," he warned his chief.[10] Back came a reply that Bragg might possibly strike toward Alabama, or at least toward Decherd. Thomas, whose intelligence system was working well, replied that no junction of Confederate forces was intended in Alabama and that General Van Dorn was moving west. Inasmuch as the left flank was not in danger, he advised that the entire army concentrate in the vicinity of McMinnville, obviously the best position from which to stop Bragg. Thomas had explored all the roads and knew it to be the only route Bragg could possibly take.

But Buell was incapable of accepting any suggestions. Still preoccupied over a possible enemy thrust from Alabama while Bragg threatened from the right, he asked Thomas to inspect conditions at Altamont, a mountain village nearly thirty miles south of McMinnville. "Water scarce, only one spring here, and not forage enough in the neighborhood to last for one day," Thomas replied from that place. "I deem it next to impossible [for Bragg] to march a large army across the mountains by Altamont." The most important position for the army to occupy, he reiterated, was McMinnville. "The occupation of McMinnville, Sparta & Murfreesboro will in my opinion secure the Nashville & Chattanooga Railroad," he informed Buell. The

[10] Buell-Thomas correspondence, *Official Records*, 1st Series, XVI, Part 1, 150f., reprinted in part in Van Horne, *Thomas*, 68–73, and in Piatt, *Thomas*, 62–65.

towns designated formed a triangular area directly in Bragg's path, and as Thomas later avowed, the Confederate leader "could not possibly have passed Sparta without fighting. He would have arrived in an exhausted condition both from fatigue and want of supplies, and in my opinion could not have fought more than one day."[11]

One of the volunteer officers ascribed to Buell "the dancing-master policy: 'By your leave, my dear sir, we will have a fight; that is, if you are sufficiently fortified; no hurry, take your own time.'" The debate over tactics continued as Thomas returned to his base at McMinnville. Buell now excused himself on the ground that insufficient supplies would not permit the army to linger longer in the vicinity. On August 30, orders were issued for all the divisions to proceed to Murfreesboro, which lay on the direct road to Nashville and a little way out of Bragg's direct route to the Kentucky border. Still maintaining that the enemy would occupy McMinnville, Thomas tried to make the best of the situation: "By concentrating at Murfreesboro we shall be within striking distance of this place," he patiently reminded Buell. "By convenient roads the main force can be thrown upon the enemy . . . overcome him and drive him towards Sparta, his longest line of retreat."[12]

Such was Thomas's call to battle, but Buell would not be convinced. An unseasoned commander fearful of making the wrong move, he was willing to accept any alternative to tangling with the enemy. No sooner had Thomas entered Murfreesboro than fresh orders directed him to hurry on to Nashville whither Buell was also hastening to calm the fears of Governor Johnson. Again, as in Kentucky, where his plans for an offensive had been upset by an order from Sherman, Thomas had no choice but to obey. Evacuation of the towns on the right flank now left the way open for Bragg to invade Kentucky by the shortest possible route, which he took after making a demonstration toward McMinnville.[13]

11 John Beatty, *Memoirs of a Volunteer (The Citizen Soldier)*, 117.

12 Joint Committee on the Conduct of the War, *Supplemental Report*, I, 21.

13 *Battles and Leaders of the Civil War*, III, 7–8; S. S. Canfield, *History of the 21st Ohio*, 59–60.

The only battle left to Buell in Tennessee was a verbal one with Governor Johnson, and after only a brief stay at Nashville he hurried on to Gallatin and the Kentucky line, leaving Thomas to face the irate Governor. While it was embarrassing to admit that his commander's plans had gone amiss, Thomas provided Johnson with some material comfort during his stay of two weeks by strengthening the fortifications about the capitol, leaving a division of 6,000 men under General James S. Negley as a garrison while he went on to join Buell. Both armies were now advancing into Kentucky, Bragg by way of Sparta, Cookeville, and Red Boiling Springs, and Buell on his left by way of Gallatin, then heading directly north toward Bowling Green. On September 14, the Federal vanguard reached that place while Bragg was only a two days' march away at Glasgow; and although a fight appeared imminent, Bragg now excused himself on the ground that he lacked supplies. He had only thrown away his best chance to meet his enemy on even terms. Ten days later Thomas caught up with Buell at Prewitt's Knob below Munfordville where he formed the divisions in advance in line of battle; but although Bragg already had taken the Munfordville garrison in a surprise movement, he again declined to fight. His unwillingness disgusted and angered his own officers; but they, too, had to obey orders. The excuse he later gave was lack of supplies, and yet he was marching through a rich agricultural area during the harvest season and was living off the country in advance of Buell's troops. A few days later he turned off the road leading to Louisville and took a northeasterly route for Bardstown. His actual goal, as events proved, was not Louisville but Frankfort, where he intended to install a Confederate governor and contribute to the history of the state.[14]

Save for almost constant thirst, for the enemy was enriching springs and pools with dead mules, the Union Army was in good spirits. The discovery of a cool underground stream near Cave City kept men and horses going. As long as Bragg kept on the road ahead, Buell's pickets found occupation in skirmishing for apple orchards, but the direct route to Louisville lay wide

[14] Horn, *Army of Tennessee*, 177.

open after Bragg turned aside at Sonora. Hurrying along in the rear of the Federals, Thomas reached the city on September 27 and found it in an uproar against his commander. Governor Levi Morton of Indiana, who was in town with several companies of new recruits, was heard to declare that Buell would never command his Hoosier volunteers. Sentiment and feeling against Buell were fed by the remarks of volunteer officers. "We never did cheer him, even when we had perfect confidence in him as we had until a few weeks ago," one of them asserted.[15] Congressmen at Washington set him down as an imbecile or worse, an opinion also shared by Secretary of War Stanton. A fatal climax resulted when two of Buell's brigadiers, hot-tempered William Nelson of Kentucky and Jefferson C. Davis of Indiana, used their pistols to settle the argument and Nelson was shot. Since Governor Morton possessed too much influence to allow Buell to press charges, that officer remained helpless in his hotel room as Nelson lay dead.

That same day, September 29, 1862, orders from Washington directed Buell to yield the command to George Thomas. Summoned to headquarters from his camp just outside the city, Thomas found the streets and hotel lobbies buzzing with excitement. Well aware of which side of the argument he would take, Thomas went to Buell's room at the Galt House and announced his decision to decline the command.

"I answered," Buell later explained, "that I could not consent to his doing so on any ground that was personal to me, and that if his determination was fixed, I must be allowed to see the message he prepared to send. He then prepared the following dispatch: 'General Buell's preparations have been completed to move against the enemy and I respectfully ask that he may be retained in command. My position is very embarrassing, not being as well informed as I should be as the commander of this army and in the assumption of such responsibility.'"[16]

Despite the extraordinary lack of self-interest, even though Thomas pleaded unfairness to himself, it was a poor excuse for

[15] Hannaford, *Story of a Regiment*, 346.
[16] *Battles and Leaders of the Civil War*, III, 44; Van Horne, *Thomas*, 75–76.

a man of his caliber. Surely Thomas could have commanded on short notice had he wished. Buell maintained that he even encouraged him to accept the post, saying that "nothing remained to be done but to put the army in motion, and that I would cheerfully explain my plans to him and give him all the information I possessed." Still Thomas would not budge. Buell had completed all his preparations and was ready to march; therefore, "his removal and my assignment were alike unjust to him and to me. It was unjust to him to relieve him on the eve of battle, and unjust to myself to impose on me the command of the army at such a time."[17] Still the army's departure from Louisville could have been postponed for a day or two while Thomas acquainted himself with his commander's arrangements and altered them if necessary. Thomas explained his attitude some years later when he remarked that he would not permit himself to be made use of "to do Buell an injury."[18] Whether consciously or not, he was siding with the West Pointer and regular army officer against what might be construed as uncalled-for civilian interference.

Receiving Thomas's message, the surprised War Department (surfeited, hitherto, with ambitious generals) suspended the order displacing Buell. "Will await further orders but [will] go on assisting Buell in putting troops in the field," Thomas telegraphed in reply. "He desires placing me second in command should he be retained." This suggestion also was accepted at Washington; but while the *status quo* was temporarily preserved, the woods were combed for a willing successor to the general who had failed to check the enemy in two months of campaigning. During the exchange of messages with army headquarters, Thomas engaged a room at the Galt House where he could be near the telegraph office. He tried to make himself comfortable on the soft hotel bed but was unable to sleep. When midnight found him still wide awake, he sent an aide to field headquarters to bring his army cot, which was set up in the middle of the room and on which he slept soundly. Hotel maids were barred from the General's room and only his body servant, "Old Phil," was allowed to attend him.[19]

17 *Ibid.*, 76.   18 *Ibid.*, 425.
19 Shanks, *Recollections*, 63.

Again Thomas had obligated Buell to whip Bragg, a responsibility which he himself shared. Reinforced by several fresh volunteer brigades, Buell had no lack of men in a command which numbered about 70,000 availables organized into three provisional corps, each comprising three divisions. Major General McCook headed the First, Major General Thomas L. Crittenden the Second, and C. C. Gilbert, whose brigadier's commission never was confirmed, was in temporary charge of the Third. General Bragg also had been reinforced. E. Kirby Smith, who joined him after occupying Lexington and Frankfort, swelled his numbers to some 52,000. Against the counsel and advice of Smith, who wished to get on with the war, Bragg took part of his command to Frankfort, where he was bent on witnessing ceremonies inaugurating Richard Hawes as Confederate governor.

The event was scheduled for October 2. Buell's three corps had marched from Louisville on the previous day, the men falling out by scores from too much whiskey consumed during a recreational three-day leave. The arrangement of his command probably could have been improved. General McCook, who was to earn a reputation for rashness, commanded the left wing nearest the enemy. In the center was Gilbert, while Crittenden, accompanied by Thomas, occupied the right. Although Thomas could tell Crittenden what to do, he had no jurisdiction over either Gilbert or McCook. However, Bragg's inaugural plans were spoiled by General Joshua W. Sill of McCook's corps, who, marching in advance, sprinkled some artillery shells over the city. Compelled to break off in the middle of his formal address, the embarrassed Hawes hustled back to the main Confederate Army with Bragg. The latter yielded to the general confusion at this point, taking 36,000 men on an abortive chase after Sill and leaving only 16,000 with General Polk at Bardstown.

Polk naturally retreated as the superior Federal force approached Bardstown, Thomas's cavalry driving out the rear guard with little loss. On October 7, the opposing forces picked their positions carefully since that part of the state had been suffering from drought. Inclining southeasterly toward Perryville, Thomas made a long search for water for his parched men and animals, not finding suitable ground until late at night, when he encamped two miles from his appointed position.

Believing that Bragg was in his front with his entire force, Buell was actually preparing for a fight the next day, but he had ill luck in aligning his corps. By the time a courier with marching orders had located Thomas, it was 3:00 A.M. the next day, although this made little difference. Thomas started a bit late, and after reaching his assigned position three miles southwest of Perryville, he reconnoitered his front as ordered and drove some enemy pickets toward town. It was McCook who advanced too far, and it was a high wind and the peculiar topography of the country which kept the noise of battle from Buell and Gilbert. About one o'clock Thomas and Crittenden began to hear an occasional rumble of artillery but surmised it might be some Federals shelling the woods. When the fire became prolonged, Thomas sent his chief of artillery to Buell, who was in the rear of Gilbert, to request further orders. But Buell had heard no artillery fire, and he was not imaginative enough to guess what might be happening to McCook on the left and in front. He merely again asked for a reconnaissance along Thomas's front, although one had already been made. About three o'clock "very heavy cannonading" prompted Thomas to communicate with Gilbert, who replied that he had encountered only slight resistance in taking his position and was now encamping for the night. He believed that General Rousseau of McCook's corps had been driven back by the enemy but had regained the lost ground.

The unhappy truth, however, was that the search for water on October 8 had lured on Rousseau of McCook's corps to a branch of Chaplin's River, which three enemy divisions had reserved for themselves. A furious artillery fire opened on Rousseau as he was about to descend into the valley; then General Polk swooped down, driving the Federals back a full mile. Although only the lesser Rebel force had occupied Perryville, three enemy divisions had managed to cut off two of McCook's and inflict some 4,000 casualties before nightfall. General Buell, in his official report, blamed McCook for overconfidence "which made him believe he could manage the difficulty without aid or control"; but had there been no wind to smother the sound of battle, the unfortunate General surely would have been reinforced in time. Buell inserted a compliment for Thomas "for the most valuable assistance during the campaign," although little credit could accrue either to the first or the second in command for an unnecessary loss at Perryville. The Federals were deprived of their last chance to fight in Kentucky three days later when Bragg shunned an obvious opening at Harrodsburg and trailed off dismally into Tennessee. It had been a polite and mutually deferential campaign.[20]

[20] Joint Committee on the Conduct of the War, *Supplemental Report*, I, 24 f; *Battles and Leaders of the Civil War*, III, 48–49; Horn, *Army of Tennessee*, 179–89; Van Horne, *Thomas*, 77–83.

VIII

Stone's River

DISCUSSION in Washington over the choice of a commander to succeed Buell now centered about Thomas and William Starke Rosecrans of Ohio, who had dubbed Thomas "George Washington" during student days at West Point. Following graduation from the Military Academy in 1842, Rosecrans served for twelve years in the army, then reentered civil life as a Cincinnati architect and engineer. He rejoined the colors at the outbreak of war, was appointed one of the senior brigadiers on May 16, 1861, and thereafter won some minor victories in western Virginia against Robert E. Lee's left wing. Transferred to the Army of the Mississippi, he led a brigade during Halleck's advance against Corinth, and on August 21, 1862, was commissioned a major general of volunteers. He defeated General Sterling Price at Iuka on October 4 and thereafter helped Grant defend Corinth against a combined assault by Price and Earl Van Dorn. But when Grant criticized him sharply for an indecisive pursuit of the enemy, the War Office decided upon his availability elsewhere. During a Cabinet meeting at the White House, President Lincoln heard Secretary Stanton urge the merits of Thomas, while Treasury Secretary Chase, a Cincinnati man, spoke up for Rosecrans.[1]

A brother of the Catholic curate Sylvester Horton Rosecrans and a devout churchman, the Ohioan was an obvious choice in this election season. Most Catholics viewed the conflict as "a Yankee war, originating with Puritans," and the attitude of the church was something less than lukewarm. A point which weighed heavily against Thomas was the fact that he had recently declined to assume the command when given opportunity,

[1] *Official Records*, 1st Series, XVI, Part 2, 657; Piatt, *Thomas*, 198–99.

or at least had requested that Buell be retained a while longer. Moreover, it was unwise in Lincoln's view to replace one Southern-born general with another. There remained certain objections in seniority, which the President removed by changing the date of Rosecrans' commission from August 21 to March 31. "Let the Virginian wait, we will try Rosecrans," the President decided, and a trial it would be. About the middle of October, Rosecrans was ordered to return to Cincinnati, where he broke the seal on an order naming him leader of the reorganized Army of the Cumberland.

Perryville had knocked all the fight out of Buell. Troubled also by an injured leg, the result of a fall from his horse, he had returned to Louisville for treatment, leaving Thomas in charge of the army. Thomas, many soldiers hoped, would now receive the command. But while the Virginian marched the troops to Bowling Green on the road back to Nashville, a tall, hook-nose officer looked up Buell at the Galt House. Commenting sometime later upon his visit to Buell's headquarters, General Rosecrans said it was more like that of a constable bearing a writ for the ejection of a tenant than a general coming to relieve a brother officer in command of an army.[2] The source of the "writ" was General-in-Chief Halleck, who was never noted for diplomacy or tactfulness and who had not taken the trouble to notify Buell that he was being replaced but simply had asked Rosecrans to carry the message.

The news came as a shock to Thomas, who mulled the question over for an hour or two and then committed himself to paper. He had not been notified of the revised date on Rosecrans' commission when he protested to Halleck on October 30:

"On the 29th of last September I received an order . . . placing me in command of the Department of the Ohio and directing General Buell to turn over his troops to me. This order reached me just as General Buell had by most extraordinary exertions prepared his army to pursue and drive the rebels from Kentucky. Feeling convinced that great injustice would be don⊇ him if not permitted to carry out his plans, I requested that he

[2] Military Order of the Loyal Legion of the U. S., District of Columbia Commandery, *War Papers*, LXVIII, 5–6.

might be retained in command. The order relieving him was suspended, but today I am officially informed that he is relieved by General Rosecrans, my junior. Although I do not claim for myself any superior ability, yet feeling conscious that no just cause exists for overslaughing me by placing me under my junior, I feel deeply mortified and aggrieved at the action taken in this matter. . . . P. S. I do not desire the command of the Department of the Tennessee but that an officer senior in rank should be sent here if I am retained on duty in it."[3]

Thomas had no personal objection to Rosecrans, whom he believed competent. He made no secret of his feelings, however, when he talked with Rosecrans upon the new commander's arrival at Bowling Green. He informed him of the reason for his protest and in the same breath declared that he would like to return to the service in Texas, where, knowing the country well, he could make himself useful. Naturally Rosecrans would have none of this, as he had counted upon Thomas to help him. His new command, he once recalled, was all the more desirable because Thomas was the senior major general. He reminded that officer that the command had come to him wholly unsought and spoke in the right way to retain him: "You and I have been friends for many years and I shall especially need your support and advice."[4] Thomas, who was not inclined to sulk, could not resist further. When offered his choice of commands in the new organization, he said he would prefer to lead a corps to the somewhat empty honor of second-in-command. At his request he was assigned the center. McCook and Crittenden respectively led the right and left wings.

Thomas had based his protest largely on technical grounds, but learning from Halleck that Rosecrans' commission was dated prior to his, he replied that had he known this in the first place, the protest would not have been made. However, when Rosecrans belatedly admitted that the date of his commission had been changed, Thomas's temper rose again; and he angrily wrote Halleck: "I have made my last protest while the war lasts. You may hereafter put a stick over me if you choose to do so. I

3 Piatt, *Thomas*, 199–200.
4 Army of the Cumberland, 1887 Reunion, *Report*, 48.

will take care, however, to so manage my command, whatever it may be, as not to be involved in the mistakes of the stick."[5] These were rather bitter words, but it was not the best of all possible worlds, nor did military life present for every general suitable rewards. Just as one failure after another had been nominated in the East—McDowell, McClellan, and now the hopeless Ambrose Everett Burnside—so they were matched in the West by Halleck, Buell, and Rosecrans, who was to last a little less than one year.

Rosecrans started out well by demonstrating endless energy and industry and by conferring long and often with Thomas. The first officer to leap from his cot in the morning, according to a subordinate, he was the last to dismount from his horse at night. As the result of some suggestions from Thomas, Rosecrans ridded himself of the more obviously drunken and incompetent officers. General Ebenezer Dumont, an Indiana politician attached to Thomas's corps for a time, and a few others soon dropped from sight. Nothing appeared to escape the new commander's scrutiny. Every shoe, every canteen and cartridge belt seemed important to the new Commander-in-Chief who jovially bullied the men into complaining to their captain whenever an essential item was found lacking. "Bore him for it:" he urged them repeatedly. "He'll do," remarked a soldier.[6] The genial Rosecrans was rated higher among the troops than any other officer except Thomas because they were satisfied that the top man also took an interest in their welfare, and his activity fairly matched the diligence of Thomas, whose remark to an artillery officer was quoted: "Keep everything in order. The fate of a battle may turn on a buckle or a linch-pin."[7]

Thomas, it was generally understood, was Rosecrans' actual chief of staff. The two men were a contrast in temperament—the one careful, cautious, watchful, and deliberate; the other ebullient, pugnacious, impulsive, and subject to alternate moods of elation and depression. Recalling his West Point days, Rosecrans once remarked that he had been in the habit there of

5 Van Horne, *Thomas*, 88.
6 Bickham, W. D., *Rosecrans' Campaign With the 14th Army Corps*, 29.
7 Army of the Cumberland, 1870 Reunion, *Report*, 80–81.

calling Thomas "George Washington," as much in seriousness as in fun. Apropos of this remark, another officer observed of Thomas: "His grave aspect, dignified deportment and imposing presence justified this conceit."[8] But Thomas sometimes found himself in conflict with his own nature, contending that he would like to be able to laugh and joke with the soldiers and expressing envy for those who could. "I am naturally reserved and have found it difficult to be on familiar, easy terms with my men," he admitted to a friend, and went on to say: "While stern and exacting in the line of service when on duty, the officer can be the comrade when off without any loss to the service or the official dignity."[9] The General's dignity never troubled the veterans and youngsters of his command, however. They not only found him always accessible but knew him familiarly as "Old Pap," "Old Slow Trot," or "Uncle George." A historian of the corps opined that "his steadiness rather attracted the lads" who had dubbed him "Pap" because of his fatherly regard for their comfort and morale.[10]

Commanding the right wing of the Army of the Cumberland was Alexander McDowell McCook, an irrepressible and occasionally blundering youth of thirty-one. McCook had graduated from the Military Academy in 1852, had served in some Indian campaigns, and was instructor in infantry tactics at West Point when the war broke out. Six McCook brothers had been commissioned—six "fighting McCooks." Short-statured, full-faced, and stalwart, McCook had a ready smile but commanded respect in the ranks—more, in fact, than from his fellow officers. General Thomas Crittenden, commanding the left wing, was a contrast in physique—tall, trim, and slender, with a full black beard and long hair falling nearly to his shoulders. Polished and graceful in manner, he easily won the affection of his men. The sons of the Whig Senator John J. Crittenden of Kentucky were divided in allegiance; Thomas's brother George had commanded the defeated Confederate army at Mill Springs.

The Army of the Cumberland was at full strength with

8 Bickham, *Rosecrans' Campaign*, 32.
9 Piatt, *Thomas*, 333–34.
10 Bickham, *Rosecrans' Campaign*, 30.

nearly 70,000 men, including the various garrisons. Division commanders Lovell H. Rousseau, J. J. Reynolds, Robert B. Mitchell, J. S. Negley, and S. S. Fry were assigned to Thomas's corps. McCook had three divisions under Jefferson C. Davis, Philip H. Sheridan, and Richard W. Johnson. Commanding under Crittenden at this time were only two divisions led by Thomas J. Wood and H. P. Van Cleve, but another was to be organized under John M. Palmer of Illinois in time for the campaign against Murfreesboro. The army was healthy and confident; saving Kentucky from Bragg had given it little trouble. Reorganization complete, the advance corps left Bowling Green, and on November 17 relieved Nashville, which had been virtually under siege; only the protests of the residents that their homes and property would be destroyed by shells had saved the city from a general assault by the Confederates.

Left behind to guard the railroad link with Louisville, Thomas suffered some aggravation from night attacks on railroad trestles and tunnels but managed to keep supplies moving. Farm boys who could ride were organized into a cavalry unit under General David S. Stanley, but still there never were enough riders or horses to contend with the famed Confederate cavalry. On November 23, Thomas crossed the Tennessee line on his delayed march to Nashville. A chaplain called for three cheers and the band played "Dixie." The weather grew colder as the men marched south; soon after they reached Nashville, it began to snow. Soldiers gathered fence rails for fuel; but not content with ordinary foraging, two army sergeants removed a brass dome from a locomotive, hung it on a rail, and started back to camp with a view to converting it into a stove. Apprehended by a guard, they were marched "protesting and pleading" to General Thomas, whose language, it was reported, "was anything but mild." What did they think they were made of, the General inquired, that they needed a five-hundred-dollar stove to warm themselves?[11] The noncoms trudged back a full mile with their weighty burden suspended between them while delighted privates cheered. Freshly killed hogs and corn bread served as standard fare, but the soldiers induced the poor whites

[11] Samuel Merrill, *The 70th Indiana Volunteer Infantry*, 46.

in the vicinity to exchange chickens, eggs, and sweet potatoes for ordinary clothing tags and used stamps. When this type of currency gave out, new stamps were offered, but the citizens declined to accept them and be cheated.

News of political activity among the Copperheads on home soil aroused the soldiers who flocked to mass meetings to hear patriotic speeches. A colonel of the Seventieth Indiana Volunteers held their close attention for an hour at the end of a long program and was "vociferously cheered." The presiding officer slapped Captain Samuel Merrill of the Seventieth Indiana Volunteers on the back: "By George, Captain, that Colonel of yours will be President of the United States some day." The men of the Seventieth held Colonel Benjamin Harrison in high esteem.[12]

Pressure from Washington was being brought on Rosecrans to advance against Bragg at Murfreesboro without delay; but, counseled by Thomas, he declined to move until ready. The greatest need of the army was more cavalry. The enemy excelled with mounted troops under Generals Nathan Bedford Forrest, John Hunt Morgan, and Joseph Wheeler, but the War Office declined to permit any extension of Federal cavalry to greater strength than the 3,000 newly organized under General Stanley. Principal troublemaker in the Nashville sector was the dreaded raider Morgan, who had been responsible for considerable damage to Thomas's railroad. On December 7, Morgan swooped down upon Hartsville, eleven miles west of Gallatin, and captured 1,834 men, leaving 262 killed and wounded behind him. Meanwhile the tireless Forrest was on the loose in western Tennessee, burning fifty trestles of the Mobile and Ohio Railroad and wrecking miles of track. General Grant's line of communication with the North and East suffered accordingly.

Thomas's corps was nearly ready to move out of Gallatin when on December 18 the General visited Nashville to testify before the so-called Buell Commission which was collecting information concerning the campaign of the previous summer and early fall. Remaining on the stand for nearly two days, Thomas

12 *Ibid.*, 39.

explicitly remarked that he had recommended a stand against Bragg at McMinnville and Sparta before the army fell back to Nashville. This gave Buell a turn. When he demanded a reading of the record, Thomas obliged by digging up copies of his telegrams. There was the evidence, and yet Thomas had not permitted Buell's disregard of his advice to weigh in his partiality for his commander at Louisville.

Returning to Gallatin, Thomas brought most of his command back to Nashville on the twenty-second. All except one brigade of Fry's division and all of Reynolds' men were left behind to guard the railroad against further depredations. General R. B. Mitchell from Thomas's corps relieved Negley as the guardian of Nashville. This left Thomas with only two full divisions—Rousseau's and Negley's—and a detached brigade, 13,400 men all told. McCook, with 16,000, was at Mill Springs, a few miles south; Crittenden had 13,200, including the divisions of Wood, Van Cleve, and Palmer. Stanley's cavalry made up the remainder of a mobile force of around 47,000 who were to march against Bragg at Murfreesboro. Many soldiers wrote their last letters home on Christmas Day. Commissary officers issued three days' rations for haversacks and placed enough for five more in wagons; quartermasters toiled through the night getting the wagons in position and ready to move. Last instructions to corps commanders came from Rosecrans: "We shall begin to skirmish probably as soon as we pass the outposts. Press them hard. Drive them out of their nests. Make them fight or run."[13] Horses' hooves struck fire as couriers raced about the darkened city setting things straight.

December 26 was a rainy Friday, one of many drenching days, but the troops were obviously eager and in good trim. Stanley's cavalry swept down Nolensville pike, driving the enemy pickets before them. Below Nashville, the army fanned out. Crittenden's corps advanced on Murfreesboro pike, Thomas on Franklin pike as far as Brentwood, crossing over to Nolensville. McCook was on his way to Triune to discover whether General Hardee would offer battle there or retreat. Enemy cavalry felt

[13] Military Order of the Loyal Legion of the U. S., District of Columbia Commandery, *War Papers*, LXVIII, 12–13.

out the advance at La Vergne, but the Federals were in no mood to linger. The big guns were brought out, and after an artillery duel in the rain a bayonet charge carried the left wing in a swift rush across the creek. Here at La Vergne the luckless McCook parked three hundred supply wagons, only to lose them a few days later when General Joseph Wheeler's cavalry raced behind the Federal Army and applied the torch. Circling the Federal rear, Wheeler burned more wagons at Nolensville, captured several guns, and made off with a generous supply of fresh horses. Ahead, as the men marched, there was skirmishing every day. On the twenty-ninth and thirtieth the various Federal units halted, closed in, and encamped about three miles from Murfreesboro, where Stone's River coursed through partially wooded country intersected by a railway and several roads.

The men in blue were still debating: Would Bragg fight? The hard-featured Confederate leader was an enigma even to his own troops. None too promptly, Bragg signified to his generals—Polk, Breckinridge, and Hardee—that he was going to fight. He had no excuse not to. His army numbered 37,800 men, his position between Stone's River and Murfreesboro was well chosen, and his officers were anxious to launch a concerted blow at the cocky Federals. A dense cedar thicket masked Bragg's center and good country roads radiated from his headquarters to both flanks. His plans were to strike McCook on the right and roll up the Federal Army while his cavalry arm isolated weakened segments and annihilated them. Rosecrans, discussing the prospects in his lively manner, happened upon a similar idea— to strike Bragg on *his* right. This meant that the heavier Confederate force would advance clockwise from the southwest while Rosecrans drove toward Breckinridge on the opposite flank. If both assaults were successful, the armies would then turn as a wheel, but success was likely to depend on which side moved first.

The soldiers polished their gun barrels and lined up for fresh ammunition. Skirmishers felt out and located opposing lines. They were not far apart; enemy bugle calls were clearly heard in both camps. At four o'clock on the thirtieth the big guns began to pound more vigorously. "This means a fight tomorrow," said Thomas, busy with preparations for the night.[14] Rosecrans discovered the enemy line to be extended beyond McCook's and ordered the campfires strung out. Unfortunately this strategy backfired; Bragg simply concentrated more men on that flank, which he planned to strike in the morning. After mess the artillery fire ceased and the bands began to play. Well-known and beloved tunes—"Yankee Doodle," "Dixie," "Hail, Columbia," and "The Bonnie Blue Flag"—alternated in each camp as measured echoes traced the wooded glades. Then one band struck up "Home, Sweet Home," the other took it up, and the men began to sing. Thousands of voices followed the familiar tune.[15] The plaintive strains still rang in the soldiers' ears as they curled up in their blankets to sleep and dream or lie tossing until the clatter of arms dispelled the calm of night.

General Bragg struck first when only one brigade of General Richard W. Johnson's division on the right was ready. At 6:00 A.M. on December 31 General Edward Kirk's men spied the gray-clads creeping forward and sighted their guns. But General August Willich's troops were still eating breakfast, their arms neatly stacked, when the grand rush started. Flanked by the enemy concentration in front of the extended campfires, the line buckled and broke. General August Willich was made a prisoner, and some of his men hardly stopped running until they reached Nashville nearly thirty miles away. Others had to be stopped by a line of bayonets held fast by a Union regiment in the rear. Most of the extreme right flank was swept back and away; those closer to the center raced to take new positions. Davis and Sheridan were thrown against Negley, thus placing the weight of battle on Thomas. New lines had to be formed under fire.

If Negley and Rousseau could maneuver and fight, the center might be saved; but Negley, in the woods, was flanked and almost surrounded. "Cut your way out," snapped Thomas. Sheridan raced up to ask for help. Thomas declined to detach any of his men until he heard from Rosecrans, but as soon as

---

14 Piatt, *Thomas*, 205.
15 Wiley, *Life of Johnny Reb*, 317–18.

the order came, he backed him up with two brigades he hurried over to Rousseau and helped get the men in place. The lines took curious shapes in stop-gap movements—concave, convex, triangular; what was left of Sheridan and Negley's commands, plus Rousseau's brigades, formed three sides of a shaky rectangle with Negley in front, Sheridan on the right, and Rousseau on the left. Advancing through open woods, the Rebels were the more exposed, but their fire did not slacken. The field was in a turmoil, the troops sometimes difficult to control. When Colonel Foreman of the Fifteenth Kentucky Volunteers toppled from his horse, his entire regiment gave way.

"Our comrades were falling as wheat falls before the cradling machines at harvest time," recorded an officer of the Nineteenth Illinois. "We could hear the hoarse shriek of shell, the swift rattle of musketry, the sound of buzzing bullets, the impact of solid shot, the 'chug' when human forms were hit hard, the yells of pain, the cries of agony, the fearful groans, the encouraging words of man to man and the death gasps of those who reported to the God of Battles. . . . Struck horses, no longer neighing or whinnying, were agonizing in their frantic cries. Cannon balls cut down trees around and over us, which falling crushed living and dead alike. . . . We hugged old Mother Earth, meanwhile firing low."[16]

Sheridan had been thrown back to his third position. Rousseau and Negley were both badly shaken when it became necessary to permit the latter to retire to more favorable ground. To cover the movement, Thomas ordered Rousseau to fall back out of the cedars and form a temporary line on open ground. "Take your brigade over there and stop the Rebels," Thomas gestured to Colonel O. L. Shepherd, who raced with his brigade of regulars along the Nashville pike and the railroad track to the edge of the cedar forest.[17] The maneuver was accomplished "under a most murderous fire," according to the General's report. Shepherd and two other brigades lost nearly half their men, but the new line now faced southwest on rising ground.

---

[16] J. H. Haynie, *The Nineteenth Illinois*, 186–87.

[17] Frederick Phisterer, *The Regular Brigade of the 14th Corps* (pamphlet), 9.

The remnants of McCook's corps dug in; Thomas massed his men in positions most suitable for a stubborn defense while Van Cleve and Wood formed a close reserve. The Federal Army was indeed rolled up, but the more it was compressed, the stronger and more threatening it became. Every available gun was massed about a thick clump of trees variously known as "Round Forest" and "Hell's Half-Acre." A survivor of the carnage reported the noonday scene. "Along this line rode Rosecrans; Thomas, calm, inflexible, from whose gaze skulkers shrank abashed; Crittenden, cheerful and full of hope, complimenting his men; Rousseau, whose impetuosity no disaster could quell; . . . Wood, suffering from a wound in his heel. . . . 'All right, fire low,' said Rosecrans as he dashed by."[18] From his uniform dripped the blood and brains of his chief aide, the Cuban-born Colonel Julius Peter Garesche, beheaded by a shell.

The massed artillery shook the earth. "Men plucked the cotton from bolls at their feet and stuffed it into their ears." Double-shotted with canister, the guns hurled their masses of iron at the charging, plunging enemy. Showers of Minié balls swept the field as the Confederates charged the line once, twice, and again. Men went down in windrows; heads, arms, legs and entire bodies would disappear suddenly; exploding shells blasted mangled flesh through the branches of trees and over the topmost. The final charge gained the Rebels nothing. General Rousseau now asked Thomas if he could advance his line. Testified Rousseau: "He directed me to do so; we made a charge upon the enemy and drove him into the woods, my staff and orderlies capturing some 11 prisoners. Thus ended the fighting of that day." Considering themselves robbed of victory, the defiant Confederates hovered among the cedars or withdrew to their tents.

Faulty intelligence had saved the Union Army. The fault lay with the Confederates, who, despite their superior numbers of cavalry, had missed one of Rosecrans' vital moves. Early that morning, just before Bragg struck, Van Cleve's division of

18 Military Order of the Loyal Legion of the U. S., District of Columbia Commandery, *War Papers,* XLIII, 2; *Battles and Leaders of the Civil War,* III, 627.

Crittenden's corps had moved across Stone's River only to be recalled when the fighting started on the right. But although a body of enemy cavalry witnessed and reported the advance, Van Cleve's withdrawal went unnoticed and Breckinridge kept four brigades in their places to meet an expected assault. Breckinridge, so Bragg later reported, was drunk—at least it seems to have been an off day for this former presidential candidate and future Confederate secretary of war. When he finally got into action, it was much too late.

The wounded were gathered up and placed in ambulances or on stretchers. Taken to field hospitals, they were relieved of shattered legs, arms, hands, and sundry bullets. Outside the cabins, beneath convenient windows, the dripping pile was heaped wide and high. Campfires started to blaze all along the lines, but, to conceal his position, Rosecrans ordered them extinguished soon after supper. The commander's wish was not universally observed on this cold, wet night. Men and officers supped on coffee, hard bread, and steaks cut from the flanks of dead artillery horses.[19] Letters were written by the firelight to be sent home. Penciled one soldier in a brief note to his wife: "Martha I Cant tell you how many ded men I did see. . . . thay were piled up . . . all over the Battel feel."[20]

Still more rain fell on this New Year's Eve. The soldiers felled trees and dug into the sodden and bloodstained earth to fortify their positions. Rosecrans, his mind a turmoil, called a council of war to meet in the cabin headquarters of General McCook. Late that evening, Thomas, Crittenden, Stanley of the cavalry, Chief Surgeon Eben Swift, division commanders, and several staff officers crowded in. Rosecrans was seated on a camp stool, drying his clothes before a fireplace ablaze with crackling cedar limbs. The crutch of Thomas J. Wood, who had been wounded, clicked on the floor; Rosecrans quickly got up and offered him his seat, the only one in the cabin, but Wood continued to stand, leaning his tall frame against a wall. The officers were dirty, powder stained, and weary and depressed in mood. McCook, ordinarily debonair, seemed thoroughly down-

---

[19] Beatty, *Memoirs of a Volunteer*, 157.
[20] Wiley, *Life of Johnny Reb*, 33.

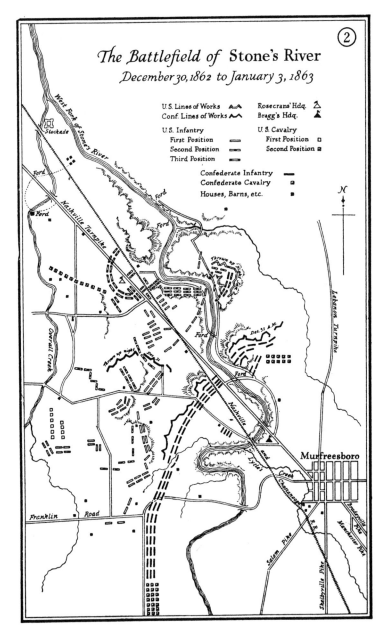

The Battlefield of Stone's River
December 30, 1862 to January 3, 1863

cast, but it was he who had been worst beaten that day. Observed
Adjutant John L. Yaryan: "If there was a cheerful-expressioned
face present I did not see it." But turning to Thomas he saw him
"as always . . . calm, stern, determined, silent and perfectly self-
possessed, his hat set squarely on his head. It was a tonic to look
at the man."[21]

A grim half-hour of silence passed as raindrops continued
to pelt the clapboard roof. Finally Rosecrans stood tensely erect.
He put the question to each of his generals in turn: Attack or
retreat? McCook, related Yaryan, had no suggestion except "I
would like for Bragg to pay me for my two horses lost today."
But according to another account, both McCook and Stanley,
who had witnessed the worst phases of the early retreat, counseled retirement to Nashville. Oppressed by the seeming necessity of retreat, Rosecrans continued to talk nervously, weighing
division returns of dead and wounded. "Have you enough
wagons to remove the wounded," he suddenly asked Swift. Of
the 5,000 or 6,000 disabled, replied the surgeon, there were
many who could walk. Enough wagons and ambulances were on
hand, he added, to accommodate those worst hurt. So, related
Adjutant Yaryan:

"From man to man Rosecrans went around the room, the
answer of each, in substance, the same as the first. Thomas was
held for the last. I had watched him closely, but he never had
changed a muscle; his eye never left the bed of red coals that
were now aglow on the old hearth; he did not appear to hear
any of the replies; the same set, determined look I had seen when
I came in was still there.

"Rosecrans hesitated a little when he came to him, and said,
'General Thomas, what have you to say?'

"Without a word of reply, Thomas slowly rose to his feet,
buttoned his greatcoat from bottom to top, faced his comrades
and stood there, a statue of courage chiseled out of the black
marble of midnight, by the firelight, and said, 'Gentlemen, I

[21] Military Order of the Loyal Legion of the U. S., Indiana Commandery, *War Papers*, I, 174.

know of no better place to die than right here,' and walked out of the room into the dripping night.

"The council was over. No one else moved for a moment, when Rosecrans, quick as a flash, and with the dash that was a part of him, said, 'If you are not attacked by six o'clock this morning, you will open the fight promptly, posted as you are, and move on to Murfreesboro. Clear the field yet tonight of all wounded and see to it that your ammunition is well up; we will whip this fight tomorrow.'"[22]

The several accounts of the midnight council vary widely in detail. Other officers relate that Rosecrans, while still undecided about his course, left the cabin in company with McCook and rode to Overall's Creek, a mile and a half in the rear, to inspect a new position to be taken on retreat. Reaching the south bank of the stream, McCook objected to taking position beyond it since the south side, where the enemy might mass, was the higher. The men started back to the cabin, but along the way Rosecrans caught sight of some lighted torches in motion west of the road. Since the Federals had been ordered to show no lights, he immediately decided that Bragg had gained his rear and was forming his lines by torchlight. Actually, some mounted Union stragglers were carrying firebrands here and there to light one pile of fuel from another.

Again entering the cabin, Rosecrans related what he had seen. "Go to your commands . . . we must fight or die," he remarked sententiously.[23] This seemed satisfactory enough to Thomas and Crittenden. The corps commanders were ordered to put their divisions in readiness and to issue all spare ammunition. McCook resumed his customary jauntiness and ended the council with a song. Although eyewitness accounts of the council vary in detail, they agree that Rosecrans had seriously considered retreat, an idea opposed by only Thomas and Crittenden.

[22] *Ibid.*, 174–75. Secondhand accounts of the council are to be found in Alexander F. Stevenson, *Battle of Stone's River*, 120, and Van Horne, *Thomas*, 97.

[23] *Battles and Leaders of the Civil War*, III, 634.

BATTLE OF STONE'S RIVER (MURFREESBORO)

Several useful changes in the army's tactical position were opportunely made while the enemy was sleeping. First, the advanced salient was withdrawn from Round Forest, straightening the line. The divisions of Negley on the right and Van Cleve on the left swung out to strengthen the wings. Two fresh brigades joined Thomas from the reserve and were placed between Rousseau and Sheridan. Again advancing across the river, Van Cleve occupied an elevated position which Bragg had neglected to seize while there was time. Several batteries of artillery were moved to the height. Meanwhile Bragg did nothing more than hold the ground already gained. It had been his fatuous hope that the Federals would retreat and leave him undisturbed in possession.

The armies were too tired to fight a battle the next day. New Year's morning found the Confederate soldiers exploring Thomas's side of the line. Here the men were well entrenched; brisk rifle fire prevented the gray-clads from getting clear of the woods. Rival batteries renewed acquaintance while opposing skirmish lines continued to spit lead, but until near the day's close there was no very heavy fighting. "Both armies want rest, both have suffered terribly," explained Colonel John Beatty of the Third Ohio Volunteers. "Here and there little parties are engaged in burying the dead which lie thick around us. . . . Generals Rosecrans and Thomas are riding over the field, now halting to speak words of encouragement to the troops, then going on to inspect the line. . . . A little before sundown all hell seems to break loose again and for about an hour the thunder of artillery and volleys of musketry are deafening; but it is simply the evening salutation of the combatants. The darkness deepens; the weather is raw and disagreeable. . . . Fortunately I have a piece of raw pork and a few crackers in my pocket. No food ever tasted sweeter." Opening his pocket Bible, the Colonel read the comforting Ninety-first Psalm.[24]

So far little had been accomplished during two days of fighting save the killing and wounding of many thousands. The Federals had been forced into new positions for the most part, their lines compressed, while the enemy occupied ground for-

[24] Beatty, *Memoirs of a Volunteer*, 155–56.

merly held by McCook and Thomas. But Rosecrans and his captains had demonstrated a combination of tenacity and flexibility; far from chastened, they stood ready to repel any assault. The Confederates had been unable to discover any weak spot on January 1.

Showers of shot and shell greeted the sunrise next morning. Cannon balls rolled down the Murfreesboro pike, killing and maiming horses. Thomas discovered both a direct and a cross fire coming from enemy artillery across the river. He inspected his lines, and when an infantry assault was launched, he was ready. The Rebels did not gain, but still no serious attack was made. For several hours there was quiet. What were the Confederates up to? Bragg, in truth, was arriving at a fateful decision which Thomas, whose military abilities he respected, helped him to make. Discovering the center, which backed up the right flank, to be impregnable, Bragg ordered an assault against the ridge occupied by Van Cleve on the left. If the ridge were taken, guns could be placed there to enfilade the enemy line.

That this happened to be Rosecrans' strongest position meant nothing to Bragg. Both Polk and Breckinridge protested, but the inflexible Bragg had given the order and there was no other choice but to carry it out. Breckinridge, dejected, rode over to General William Preston of his corps on the Confederate right and put his views on record: "General, this attack is made against my judgment and by special orders of General Bragg. . . . If it should result in disaster and I be among the killed, I want you to do justice to my memory and tell the people that I believed this attack to be very unwise and tried to prevent it."[25] The doubting General, who had his share of pride, turned away to do his duty.

Somehow the Federal Army had caught an inkling of what was in the wind. Consulting with Rosecrans, Thomas moved Negley's brigade to the left as a reserve for Van Cleve. At 4:00 P.M. the thunder of enemy guns and a deafening crash of musketry found the Federals ready. An Ohio volunteer regiment lay on the ground waiting for orders as Rosecrans rode by.

[25] Horn, *Army of Tennessee*, 207.

"Boys," inquired the General, "do you see that strip of woods?"

"Yes, sir."

"Well in about five minutes the Rebels will pour out of it and come right toward you. Lie still until you can easily see the buttons on their coats, then drive them back. Do you understand?"

"Yes, sir."

"Well, it's just as easy as rolling off a log, isn't it?"[26]

But when three enemy divisions dashed against Van Cleve, superior man power and Southern fury could not be withstood. Two Federal brigades were badly mauled. While another still held its ground, Negley dashed over and called for volunteers "to save the left." The Nineteenth Illinois responded and raced to the river's edge, plunging through to the other side with water "over the hips of the tallest and up to the ears of the shortest."[27] Up the muddy bank they climbed with the rest of the division at their heels. Fifty-eight massed guns belched flame and iron, shaking the earth and plowing great holes in the enemy line. Stanley's cavalry splashed across the river to support Van Cleve, but the Confederates let go only one more volley. An Indiana regiment broke out in wild yells as a Confederate flag was shot down. "The miserable rag is torn to pieces to be sent home in the next letters."[28]

Breckinridge's loss was 1,700 men all together. The tactics of Bragg had been hesitant and piecemeal and thus had failed. His subordinate officers, uttering their disgust, were no longer willing to fight under him, considering him temperamentally unfit for battle. That night, Generals B. Franklin Cheatham and Jones M. Withers drew up a letter advising retreat. General Polk read it, endorsed it, and sent it to headquarters at 2:00 A.M. Bragg dismissed the petition in a huff, but by ten o'clock, fortified by a hot breakfast, he agreed to retreat.[29] Some vigorous skirmishing occupied the attention of several Union

26 A. D. Richardson, *The Secret Service*, 33.

27 Haynie, *The Nineteenth Illinois*, 191.

28 William R. Hartpence, *The 51st Indiana*, 111.

29 Horn, *Army of Tennessee*, 209–10.

brigades that morning; the Confederates seemed as full of fight as ever. Although the Forty-second Indiana, on picket about eight hundred yards in advance of Thomas's main line, was driven in "with considerable loss," Bragg was merely covering his retreat. Bragg, meantime, was packing up to depart for Winchester, fifty miles to the southeast. The excuse he now gave was that captured papers showed the enemy to be stronger than he thought. Fresh reinforcements, he said, were on their way to join Rosecrans. Studying some captured returns, Bragg concerned himself with the totals of Rosecrans' entire command, including the divisions at Nashville and along the railroad to the north. But neither these forces nor any others were on their way to join Rosecrans.

Thomas organized a final sortie about six o'clock that evening, sending four regiments against the troops which had attacked his front line. The Rebels were driven from their wooded cover and their entrenchments. Thus ended the four-day battle.[30] That night Hardee marched his dejected corps through the rain and sleet toward Wartrace while Polk fell back to Shelbyville.

More daring tactics might have won the field for the Confederacy. Rosecrans had suffered the more severely, losing about 13,230 officers and men or 31.5 per cent of his force. Confederate killed, wounded, and missing totaled 10,306 or 28 per cent of Bragg's 37,800. The losses at Stone's River were nearly as great as those at Shiloh, the bloodiest battle in the war up to this time. While the Confederates suffered 400 fewer casualties than at Shiloh, Rosecrans had about 200 more. And yet nothing had been decided at Stone's River. No knockout blow had yet been delivered by either Rosecrans or Bragg. After an interval of some months, the two armies would meet again, and in stronger force.

[30] Thomas's Report, Coppée, *Thomas*, 115–16.

IX

The Road to Chickamauga

THE Union soldiers took shovels and buried their dead comrades and the stiffened bodies of horses. Nearly all about them trenches and breastworks pitted the landscape; the trunks of great oaks were badly scarred, the ground littered with their tops and branches, but where the fields were smooth, soldiers' graves were thickly planted. Donors of the land made a grim jest: "We wish there might be more of it."[1] The task of burial completed, the army, on January 5, 1863, moved into Murfreesboro, an elaborately fortified town. "We were satisfied with fighting and were glad to rest," an officer noted in his diary. "We had had a hard time since Christmas."[2]

The war bore worse upon the enemy. While Union spirits were soaring, Confederate morale continued to sag. Officers and men openly railed against their sullen, inept leader. What was the use of winning a battle, as at Perryville and Stone's River, if retreat had to follow? Early accounts of the fight at Stone's River had carried a high note of triumph, but taking into account the dispatches of the last day, a Richmond newspaper was plain spoken: "We have to perform an unwelcome task this morning and to chill the glow of triumph which the intelligence hitherto received from Murfreesborough has imparted to every patriotic heart. A reverse, the causes and extent unknown, has been suffered . . . by General Bragg."[3] Clippings of the item were collected and circulated by Union officers.

Bragg's soldiers, never very well fed, plodded dejectedly

1 Statement of W. Sheridan Kane, a former Nashville resident, now of New York City, to the writer.

2 Hartpence, *The 51st Indiana*, 111.

3 *Official Records*, 1st Series, XX, Part 2, 308.

for two or three days southward. Hardee dug in at Wartrace on the right and Polk at Shelbyville on the left. Occupying the center, the Confederate chief fell back another day's march to make Tullahoma and "Fort Bragg" his headquarters. Hardee and Polk in their turn threw up strong protective earthworks, erecting a network of sharpened stakes and fallen trees for a distance of six hundred yards; cavalry detachments posted well in front extended the lines east to McMinnville and west to Columbia, a span of seventy-five miles. Although Bragg had holed up in a purely defensive position, the cavalry would be called upon to raise mischief with the Federals.

Bragg, firmly stationed, considered himself well nigh immovable, nor was he forced to budge until late the following June. The Federal army, meanwhile, dug in where it stood. There was a long pause after Stone's River. Rosecrans began to clamor for more cavalry, artillery, fresh troops, and necessary arms. Now at the height of his prestige, the Union commander set to work to efface a bad scare by raising the Army of the Cumberland to the peak of efficiency. An early request, following Stone's River, was that his center and two right wings be designated army corps, as in the Army of the Potomac, Rosecrans pointed out. War Secretary Stanton replied with promptness on January 7: "The order for army corps will be issued today. There is nothing within my power to grant to yourself or your heroic command that will not be cheerfully given."[4] The center under Thomas was designated the Fourteenth Army Corps, the right wing the Twentieth Corps, the left the Twenty-first.

Some 14,000 fresh troops were supplied when the "Army of the Kentucky," a temporary designation, under Major General Gordon Granger, moved in. Certain problems of organization still remained, for instead of filling up the regiments reduced by recent battle losses, these troops were placed in reserve, thus retaining their own volunteer officers in accordance with political necessity. Rosecrans, however, began to clean house by dismissing "a large number" of officers for various offenses and filling their places with carefully picked men.

4 *Ibid.*, 306.

138

Thomas, it appears, had a hand in their selection, for several battle-tested West Pointers were soon numbered among the Fourteenth Corps. Newcomers included Brigadier General Milton Brannan of Indiana—West Point, 1841; Chapultepec, 1847; and recently in service in Florida—also Major General Joseph J. Reynolds of Kentucky, who had been left behind to guard the railroad lines around Nashville.

In promising Rosecrans everything within his power, Secretary Stanton had laid himself open to requests of every kind. While Rosecrans was quite justified in asking for 1,000 horses and 2,000 short rifles for the cavalry (a request which the tactless Halleck appeared to regard as a complaint), he had little excuse to beg that his major general's commission be antedated again from March 21, 1862, to December 21, 1861. This, if granted, would have made him the senior of every general in the field. A number of other small requests were ignored on the general ground that it was the business of the War Department to get on with the war. Ultimately, on April 20, Halleck reminded the temperamental Ohioan of the "enormous expense to the Government of your telegrams; more than that of all the other generals in the field."[5]

Halleck, meantime, was seeking to persuade Rosecrans to move on, and when he displayed impatience, although the army was not yet equipped, Thomas avoided sharing his senior officer's irritation. "Our government," he was quoted as saying, "is struggling under a heavy weight that we in the field have no knowledge of," but Thomas believed also that the War Office should send some responsible person to learn and report the army's actual position regarding cavalry and other needs.[6]

With spring already in the air, Thomas kept a watchful eye on the recruits who came his way. His favorite method of training soldiers was to send them into the field as skirmishers, and there seemed to be no lack of enemy cavalry on which to practice. Training for the Fourteenth Army Corps was limited to the demands of actual warfare, with showy tactics outlawed. While Thomas shunned the parade ground, no general kept as

[5] *Ibid.*, XXIII, Part 2, 255–56.
[6] Piatt, *Thomas*, 329–30.

close a watch on the supply department as "Old Pap." Apparently he had Rosecrans' blessing in all that he did as the Fourteenth Army Corps was growing in size somewhat faster than the others; by late spring it numbered around 26,000 officers and men and was larger by far than any of the other three, including the Reserve Corps.

Many leaves and furloughs were granted during the spring season; from both armies, the essential business of planting crops called many men away. But although Thomas obtained permission to go East to visit his wife, he later reconsidered and stuck to his task. He would not take a chance, he explained, of being absent while there was the least danger of an enemy attack. Certain other soldiers could not withstand the urge. One hopeful private, whittling a stick, brought a request for a furlough directly to his General.

"I ain't seen my old woman, general, for four months," he explained as he whittled.

"And I have not seen mine for two years," Thomas responded. "If your general can submit to such privation, certainly a private can."

"Don't know about that general, you see me and my wife ain't made that way," returned the private, as Thomas and his aides rocked with laughter.[7]

Wives of Western officers who had not far to travel came to camp. "Many officers have their wives here," recorded Brigadier General John Beatty as early as March 14. "The roads are becoming good and everybody is on horseback. The army . . . looks better than it ever did before."[8] Beatty, an observer of character, set down some candid views of his superior officers: "Crittenden . . . is a good drinker, and the same can be said of Rousseau. Rosecrans is an educated officer who has rubbed much against the world and has had experience. Rousseau is brave, but knows little of military science. McCook is a chucklehead. Wood and Crittenden know how to blow their own horns exceedingly well. Major-General Thomas is tall, heavy, sedate; whiskers and head grayish. Puts on less style than any of those

7 *Ibid.*, 334; Shanks, *Personal Recollections*, 72.
8 Beatty, *Memoirs of a Volunteer*, 172.

named and is a gentlemanly, modest, reliable soldier . . . shaves the upper lip."[9]

Although outnumbered by enemy cavalry, Rosecrans considered that he needed more elbow room and so ordered a general reconnaissance during March. Certain small successes were entirely outweighed by the loss of 1,300 men under General John Coburn, who attempted a skirmish with the cavalry of Forrest and Van Dorn near Franklin, only eighteen miles south of Nashville. The triumphant Forrest then rode off to seize some valuable Union equipment, stores, and some 800 men at near-by Brentwood. Even worse than this was the loss of 1,800 men under Colonel Abel D. Streight, who was making a foray behind Bragg's lines in northern Alabama. Lacking horses, Rosecrans had mounted the men on mules, but Forrest caught up with them on May 3. It was plainly evident that the Union detachments could never match the swift tactics of gifted Rebel fighters on horseback. There was some excuse for Streight, whose force, both men and animals, was "in a desperate condition" from fatigue and loss of sleep when captured by a stratagem. If Rosecrans was to move at all and hope for success, it must be with the whole army, it became apparent. The Union force was far superior in infantry.

General Bragg, suffering from boils and the animosity of his officers, continued to remain on the defensive. His right was protected by rugged mountains and poor roads, his left flank was thrown out so as to compel the Federals to make a wide detour should Rosecrans choose to march in open, fertile country to reach the railroad in his rear. Intensive conscription had furnished many new men for Bragg's army. Although he had lost the services of General Breckinridge after a quarrel, the Kentuckian marching west with 10,000 men to reinforce Joseph E. Johnston who was endeavoring to match Grant's tactics at Vicksburg, Bragg had actually increased his force to about 44,-000 officers and men. And for the time being, apparently, he had little to fear from Rosecrans.

Like Bragg, although not in the same class with Grant,

[9] *Ibid.*, 176.

Rosecrans was prepared to fight it out on his present line if it took all summer. By early June his army was at maximum strength—97,000 officers and men present and fit for duty, with a cavalry force increased to 12,000, and nearly all mounted. Deducting the necessary garrisons, the Reserve Corps, and 2,-400 convalescents, Rosecrans still possessed superior numbers for an offensive campaign. Yet he still hesitated, although a better example was shown him. To the west, in Mississippi, Grant and Sherman were striking hammer blows against Vicksburg, blandly disregarding fixed bases of supplies and living off the country; in short, taking chances. Rosecrans, at this juncture, played safe by circulating three questions among his various corps and division commanders, dating his inquiry June 8, 1863:

"1. From the fullest information in your possession do you think the enemy in front of us has been so materially weakened by detachments to Johnston or elsewhere that this army could advance . . . at this time with strong reasonable chances of fighting a great and successful battle?

"2. Do you think an advance of our army at present likely to prevent additional re-enforcements being sent against General Grant by the enemy in our front?

"3. Do you think an immediate or early advance of our army advisable?"[10]

Apparently Rosecrans was not willing to lead but only to be pushed. While the War Office had ordered an advance, his officers declined to push him. Some of the replies correctly implied that inasmuch as the Secret Service was managed from headquarters, Rosecrans himself should have the answer to the first question. But the majority of the responses to the three questions were in the negative, which again posed the question of leadership. Thomas, McCook, Crittenden, and Philip Henry Sheridan all answered "no," although Crittenden had a "yes" for question number two. The officers united in negative responses to the third inquiry. Nearly all seemed to assume that

[10] *Official Records,* 1st Series, XXIII, Part 2, 395.

the battle to be fought would take the shape of a direct assault on the enemy entrenchments at Shelbyville, where the approach was more open but better protected. Even if the Confederates retreated, Thomas declared in his letter, they still would "draw us away from our base, attack and destroy our communications, or threaten them so strongly as to greatly weaken our main force, and then send re-enforcements of artillery and infantry to Johnston."[11] But the trouble with Thomas and most of the other officers who sat in their tents late at night formulating answers to their commander's questions was that they pondered too much the perils of a campaign against General Bragg. Recalled to mind was the old saying, "Councils of war never fight."[12]

Credit must be given one volunteer officer, Brigadier General James A. Garfield, Rosecrans' principal aide, for setting down an independent opinion. Garfield, then only thirty-one years old, was naturally ambitious; it was his task simply to summarize the answers, but he went further by adding some pertinent observations. He estimated that if the campaign were launched, Rosecrans would have "65,136 bayonets and sabers" (exclusive of officers) to pit against an estimated 41,680 for the enemy, and that the forward movement ordered by the War Office would surely prevent Bragg from sending any more re-inforcements to Johnston. "Your general movement has been wisely delayed until now till your army could be massed and cavalry mounted," Garfield boldly reminded Rosecrans.[13] Now, with Johnston immobilized in the West, was the time.

Disregarding Garfield's letter, Rosecrans forwarded to Halleck a summary of the views he had received. The General-in-Chief responded on June 16: "Is is your intention to make an immediate movement forward? A definite answer, yes or no, is required."

"If 'immediate' means tonight or tomorrow, No," Rosecrans replied defensively. "If it means as soon as all things are ready, say five days, yes." He hardly needed a poll of opinion

[11] *Ibid.*, 413–15.
[12] Cox, *Reminiscences*, 480f.
[13] *Official Records*, 1st Series, XXIII, Part 2, 423.

to decide that. Why ask questions? Why write letters? The government had put Rosecrans in Buell's place for only one reason—to fight.

The responses to his questions had given Rosecrans a hint of what his officers believed to be poor strategy—an advance against Bragg's left wing. So it was decided to take the more difficult course—through the mountain gaps and around Bragg's right. If the move were successful, the enemy would find itself outflanked. Once the decision was made, the camp began to stir. Thomas ordered his men to pack eight days' rations in their knapsacks, forty rounds in their cartridge boxes, and be prepared to march. A company, fully equipped, with cartridge box and gun, knapsack, haversack, shelter tent, and blanket, marched to corps headquarters for Thomas to inspect the loads. Lifting the packs, the General remarked in quaint phrase that he did not think the whole world would make so heavy a load, and the order was modified. At 9:00 A.M. on June 24 came the order to strike tents. The Fourteenth Corps marched out on the Manchester pike in a drenching rain.[14]

Federal strategy was well planned. Stanley's cavalry feinted toward Shelbyville, extending their campfires some distance out. This gesture immobilized Polk. Meanwhile the rest of the army poured through three mountain gorges—McCook's Twentieth Corps through Liberty Gap where the Confederates held on stubbornly; Thomas through Hoover's Gap, and Crittenden around the left end through Guy's Gap. Six miles in front of Thomas rode Colonel John T. Wilder's mounted infantry brigade which was ordered to trot through Hoover's Gap, an order literally obeyed. Taking position on the south side, Wilder held on until reinforced by a Fourteenth Corps brigade led by Brigadier General George Crook. This officer described the ensuing contest in few words: "Our troops were lying behind a small elevation, alongside a fence, while the enemy occupied the other side. They kept up a desultory fire all night, the bullets going over our heads. The rain still continued to pour in torrents. The troops had trod up the mud into a thin mush of

[14] *Battles and Leaders of the Civil War*, III, 635. Canfield, *The 21st Ohio*, 98.

two or three inches deep. I ordered the men to stack arms, and to cook supper if they had any. But they were tired, stacked their arms, and flopped down in the mud and went sound asleep, many of them without blankets."[15] Behind them, on the rapid march, the road was strewn with quilts, blankets, and everything else that could be dispensed with in sultry weather.

The Confederates were forced from the gap next day. Still it rained. Mules and men tugged at artillery in roads which had turned into quagmire. Feinting at the enemy at Fairfield village, where a smart skirmish took place, Thomas cut through Matt's Hollow and pulled up at Manchester on the twenty-seventh, his men quite fagged out. Hardee, who had left his base at Wartrace to help defend Liberty Gap, was outflanked. Thomas's present position was fifteen miles southeast of Wartrace and about twenty-two miles due east of Polk's headquarters at Shelbyville.

Bragg, who had asked Polk to reinforce Hardee at Liberty, now began to realize what had occurred. With Forrest's cavalry slowed by heavy rains and flooded creeks, Bragg ordered Polk to evacuate Shelbyville, and the Confederate Army began its retreat. Fortified Shelbyville, after some stubborn rear-guard action, fell before a cavalry charge. Thomas hurried a mounted force to destroy the railroad south of that town. Rain still poured. Soldiers gathered brush and fence rails to keep them out of the water at night. Despite chafed legs and some saddle galls, the Federal cavalry was working well. Discovering that the bridges on the railroad leading to Chattanooga were threatened, Bragg evacuated Tullahoma late on June 30. In a skirmish on the Manchester road, Forrest's command had been beaten that day.

McCook had come up behind Thomas nearly on time and if Crittenden had not been delayed on the left, Bragg might have been caught, the rejoicing Federals contended. The Twenty-first Corps commander had floundered so long in the mud over his difficult course that twenty miles became a four-day march. Helpless mules, losing themselves in morasses, painfully

15 Martin F. Schmitt (ed.), *General George Crook—His Autobiography*, 102–103.

perished, and some of the men had narrow escapes. Delayed two full days altogether, the Twenty-first Corps arrived too late to cut off Bragg's escape on the Chattanooga road, which turned left, toward Crittenden's route. During the first week of July, however, the sun began to shine. After crossing swollen Elk River on the road between Tullahoma and Decherd, Thomas halted his corps and formed the men in solid ranks. A general order was read announcing the defeat of Lee's army at Gettysburg and the surrender of Vicksburg to General Grant. "The bands played. Exultant thousands cheered."[16]

Congratulations were in order. Despite preliminary forebodings, the strongly held enemy positions had been gained at small expense—only 570 killed and wounded and 13 captured or missing in the entire campaign. This was far better, in Thomas's view, than winning a famous but hard-fought battle. Returning to Tullahoma, he seized Rosecrans' hand and exclaimed in a rare burst of enthusiasm, "This is the grandest campaign of your life!"[17] With dry clothes on, everyone seemed to be in good humor. One evening some Fourteenth Corps men turned out with a band to serenade General Thomas. "We called him out and cheered him until he had to talk," wrote a Kentucky volunteer officer. "He raised his hand. . . and said: 'Soldiers, when I saw the gallant charges and assaults you made that drove the enemy out of Hoover's Gap, I felt proud of my corps,' and we cheered him till it echoed through the woods."[18]

Now it began to be realized that the Tullahoma campaign was but the preliminary to a much more difficult task. Although Rosecrans had managed to chase Bragg almost unmolested, he still had not caught up with him. One day he submitted to Thomas a plan to outflank Bragg at Chattanooga, and to his surprise that officer uttered a firm dissent. The two men looked again at their maps. Chattanooga was protected by high mountain ranges and the Tennessee River. To the north, the steep cliffs of Walden's Ridge rose 1,300 feet; to the southwest lay

16 Edwin W. High, *The 68th Indiana*, 47.

17 Military Order of the Loyal Legion of the U. S., District of Columbia Commandery, *War Papers*, 74, 19.

18 *Ibid.*, 95; 6.

Raccoon Mountain and Sand Mountain, two long ridges extending far into Alabama; Lookout Mountain in Georgia, and Missionary Ridge. The gorge of the Tennessee River narrowed sharply as it passed through the mountains and was easily commanded from the heights. Everywhere the country was rugged and precipitous. Dark, gloomy valleys, glens, and canyons comprised a wild and romantic setting for a game of military hide-and-seek on a grand scale.

To Rosecrans, the situation presented a challenge. Again there were three passes through the mountains, three routes by which the three corps could cross the ranges. These lay respectively two miles, twenty-six miles, and forty-two miles south or southwest of Chattanooga. But to march the Army of the Cumberland through these passes, according to Rosecrans' plan, would mean separating the three corps so that each was without support from the others. Were Bragg on the alert, he could meet and defeat each in turn. Thomas suggested a flanking movement much farther south, cutting the East Tennessee and Georgia Railroad between Rome and Atlanta. Meanwhile, the Army of the Ohio, led by General Ambrose Everett Burnside, who had just marched into Knoxville, should threaten Chattanooga from the north. By this means, Rosecrans' army could be kept intact and could surely intercept Bragg, on his retreat, at a place of its own choosing.

Rosecrans may have considered this plan briefly, but in the end he abided by his own. Although he sent repeated appeals to Burnside to move, that officer declined to leave his comfortable quarters at Knoxville, where he had been greeted as a Heaven-sent rescuer by the Unionists of East Tennessee. A blundering campaigner, Burnside had lost the disastrous Battle of Fredericksburg when Lee outsmarted him on December 13, 1862, and thereafter had been relieved by General Joseph Hooker as Army of the Potomac commander. Rather than risk another battle, Burnside preferred to remain snugly at Knoxville, which had fallen into his hands following the Tullahoma campaign.

Rosecrans now began to shape his preparations meticulously, collecting large supplies of food and ammunition, building boats and rafts, opening mountain roads, and searching out information about the best routes to be followed. While General-in-Chief Halleck at Washington continued to call for an immediate advance on Chattanooga, Rosecrans was forced to spend nearly three weeks in repairing the 113-mile railroad link with Nashville, his primary base of supplies. He wrote Halleck to urge that part of Grant's army, now practically idle since Vicksburg, be sent to help protect his long supply line. Halleck declined to concede the soundness of this view. He took a conciliatory attitude toward Burnside at Knoxville and continued to forward carping telegrams.

But the Army of the Cumberland had to collect at least twenty days' rations and ammunition, enough for two great battles, before crossing the Tennessee River into a wild and unfertile country. The growing corn, wherever it might be found, would have to be ripe to afford feed for horses and mules. A trestle bridge, 2,700 feet long, was not yet completed over the Tennessee River at Bridgeport, Alabama. When Halleck, on August 5, peremptorily ordered an advance, Rosecrans called his corps commanders together and read a telegram he had written in reply. " . . . It is necessary to have our means of crossing the river completed and our supplies provided to cross 60 miles of mountains and sustain ourselves . . . before we move," it read. "To obey your order literally would be to push our troops into the mountains, on narrow and difficult roads, destitute of pasture and forage, and short of water, where they would not be able to maneuver as exigencies may demand, and would certainly cause ultimate delay and probable disaster. If, therefore, the movement which I propose can not be regarded as obedience to your order, I respectfully request a modification of it or to be relieved from the command."

"That's right," exclaimed Thomas with sudden energy. "Stand by that and we will stand by you."[19] The other corps leaders concurred, the telegram was sent, and General Halleck drew in his horns: "I have communicated to you the wishes of the Government," he replied resignedly. "The means you are to employ and the roads you are to follow are left to your dis-

[19] Society of the Army of the Cumberland, 1879 Reunion, *Report*, 175.

GENERAL BRAXTON BRAGG

From an engraving by H. B. Hall, Jr.
Courtesy The New York Public Library

cretion. If you wish to promptly carry out the wishes of the Government you will not stop to discuss mere details."[20] Such details could be boresome indeed when in conflict with official opinion.

Preparations took ten days more. Then, on August 16, 1863, the advance movement began, first across the wide and rapid Tennessee River where it coursed across northeastern Alabama. To deceive the enemy about places of crossing and to exhibit a great show of force, Federal campfires were extended far along the banks; bugle calls were sounded everywhere. Thomas led four divisions across the river. The First Division of Brigadier General Absalom S. Baird, a young Pennsylvanian replacing Rousseau, now commanding the District of Tennessee, went over the Bridgeport trestle. Negley's Second Division went by Caperton's bridge some distance farther down; Brannan's Third crossed on newly constructed rafts, and Reynolds' on captured boats at Shellmount. Sand Mountain, an enormous ridge extending many miles to the southwest, was the next barrier. All the roads had been washed away; in some places, as the men marched, none existed. Teams were doubled up to haul the artillery and supply wagons. Horses and mules strained at their loads; men placed their shoulders to the wheels and shoved. While McCook advanced far around the right end to Alpine, and Crittenden took the most direct course to Chattanooga, Thomas, in the center, arduously descended Sand Mountain, crossed Will's Valley, and pushed along dusty roads toward Lookout Mountain, rising 2,200 feet in the sky. On September 8, Fourteenth Corps troops in advance gained the summit and saw far ahead in the valley long lines of dust trending slowly southward. These dust clouds could come only from Bragg's retreating army, Thomas correctly deduced. Crittenden's advance had forced Bragg to evacuate Chattanooga that very day, and on September 9 the Union flag flew over the city. Bragg had no choice but to retreat. His left flank had been turned.

The Federals now grasped Chattanooga, prime object of

[20] Chickamauga and Chattanooga National Park Commission, *The Campaign for Chattanooga* (pamphlet), 13.

their campaign. Rosecrans was at Trenton, twenty miles southwest of Chattanooga, when he received the news. He summoned his intelligence officers. What were Bragg's present intentions? Everyone seemed to believe that Bragg was making a
disorderly retreat to Rome, Georgia, they replied. One volunteer informant, a supposed loyal citizen of Chattanooga, reported at headquarters that the enemy was "badly demoralized,
. . . all feel that they are whipped . . . one-seventh of the troops
mostly naked, . . . rations for three days would make one good
meal," and that if Bragg were pursued vigorously, he would
"not stop short of Atlanta."[21] Unfortunately, this was just the
kind of news that Rosecrans wished to hear. He dictated this
message to Thomas: "A dispatch is just received. . . . Chattanooga is evacuated by the rebels. The general commanding
desires you to call on him at once to consult in regard to arrangements for the pursuit. . . . Order your whole command in
readiness to move at once."

Thomas remarked upon reading this order that apparently Rosecrans already had made up his mind to pursue. He,
therefore, was being invited to consult only in regard to the
means of pursuit. Thomas inquired upon reaching Trenton:
Why chase Bragg further now? Why not first establish the whole
army at Chattanooga and perfect communications with Bridgeport and Nashville, two somewhat remote bases of supplies?
This done, the offensive could be resumed with Chattanooga as
a base.[22]

Rosecrans, in high fettle, would not hear of it. His plan had
won again. Obviously he did not require much if any further
counsel in pursuing the enemy pell-mell into the heart of
Georgia. It is true that the three corps of his army were still
widely separated—Crittenden at Chattanooga, Thomas's corps
crossing Lookout Mountain, and McCook far to the south near
Alpine, sixty laborious miles from wing to wing. But Thomas
could save the situation, he decided, by marching promptly on
Lafayette, which lay across Pigeon Mountain about fifteen miles

21 *Official Records*, 1st Series, XXX, Part 3, 481; Cope, *15th Ohio
Volunteers*, 305.
22 Van Horne, *Thomas*, 104–106.

southeast of Stevens's Gap. There he could menace the enemy's right wing and McCook could do the same.

This much was possible, provided Bragg was in full retreat. But Rosecrans did not then know that Bragg was about to be reinforced by Buckner from East Tennessee and by two divisions which Johnston was sending from Mississippi, while the renowned corps of General James Longstreet was about to entrain in Virginia for the West. Beaten on all fronts, the Confederates were leaving nothing undone to win this campaign. Meantime, the armies of Grant and Burnside remained intact. Following his council of war, Rosecrans dictated another order at 10:00 A.M., September 9:

"Major-General Thomas,

"Commanding Fourteenth Army Corps:

"The General commanding has ordered a general pursuit of the enemy by the whole army. General Crittenden has started to occupy Chattanooga and pursue the line of Bragg's retreat. . . . General McCook has been ordered to move at once on Alpine and Summerville. The General commanding directs you to move your command as rapidly as possible to Lafayette and make every exertion to strike the enemy in flank, and if possible to cut off his escape."[23]

What was Bragg actually doing? His army, which, combined with Forrest's corps, numbered 59,000, with 14,300 more under Buckner, was making a leisurely march southward and concentrating on Lafayette, in position to strike each Union corps at will and crush them all, a wonderful opportunity. Disregarding a fundamental rule of warfare, Rosecrans had divided his forces in the face of the enemy, or, rather, he had permitted them to remain divided.

Consider a hand widely spread and placed with the forefinger pointing northwest upon the map. McCook is near Alpine, off the tip of the thumb; Thomas at Lookout Mountain and Stevens's Gap, end of the forefinger. To the north, Chattanooga is at the point of the middle finger. Halfway down the

[23] *Ibid.*, 107–108.

forefinger, Bragg is in force at Lafayette, a position much nearer Thomas than either of the other Federal corps. The three finger tips, extending far into the mountains, could not close and grasp Bragg. To advance Thomas into the open country without support from the other corps was to place him in actual danger. Crittenden, who also credited the story of disorderly enemy retreat, was to make his course southeast rather than south, the direct route to effect a junction with Thomas and McCook.

Thomas returned down the valley. The divisions of Negley and Baird were leading the Fourteenth Corps across Lookout Mountain, clearing away fallen trees and huge rocks placed in their way by the enemy. These divisions comprised only foot soldiers; Thomas had no cavalry to help clear the way or to reconnoiter the enemy or to verify information. His corps, furthermore, was heavily burdened by 400 precious wagons. On September 10, while two divisions were still coming over Lookout, Negley reached Dug Gap, a pass through the next range, Pigeon Mountains, and began clearing away an extra-heavy obstruction. Thomas rode forward to inspect the work. Negley, he found, had been questioning an officer of the Thirty-second Mississippi Regiment, who, losing his way on picket duty, had wandered into the Federal lines. "He was not very communicative," Thomas reported, "but he was generous enough to advise General Negley not to advance or he would get severely whipped. It was also reported . . . by citizens that a large force of the enemy were endeavoring to flank his position by moving through Catlett's Gap."[24] Catlett's was some miles north of Dug Gap; obviously some Confederate forces still lingered between Thomas's position and Chattanooga.

But Thomas could obtain no knowledge of Bragg's actual whereabouts. Replying to a message from Rosecrans chiding him for not sending Negley forward a day earlier, he pointed out that, considering the many obstructions, "I do not see how it was possible for him to advance further or more rapidly than he has. If I had had Wilder's cavalry I am satisfied LaFayette would have been in our possession as with it [the cavalry] I

24 *Official Records*, 1st Series, XXX, Part 3, 510.

could have prevented the enemy from blockading this road."[25]

Thomas was still willing to proceed, but he should have been grateful to an unseen Providence for the road blocks which kept him from moving forward too fast. Bragg, with 35,000 men posted north of Lafayette, had ordered an attack on the Federal advance on September 9 and again the following day. Neither order, fortunately, was carried out. The first, to General Thomas C. Hindman, had been delayed, and when it arrived, it found that officer not ready. The second, to General Buckner, was discussed by that officer in a council of war with the inevitable result—no fight. Learning that Crittenden was circling down from Chattanooga with three divisions, Bragg needlessly took alarm and notified Hindman that the enemy "estimated 12 or 15 thousand, is forming in line." Hindman ordered a retreat and then reversed himself, but the alarm had been given, and it was too late. General Negley, discovering "an overwhelming force" just ahead at Davis's crossroads, escaped in good order after some sharp fighting and retreated to inaccessible Stevens's Gap. Bragg had shown his hand to no advantage and had lost his chance.[26] "All information goes to confirm that a large part of Bragg's army is opposed to Negley," Thomas notified Rosecrans on September 12, confirming a dispatch of the previous evening which reported withdrawal "without losing a single wagon."[27]

But Rosecrans shrugged off this wise suggestion. Bragg, in his opinion, was much farther away. He replied airily to Thomas: "Your desperate dispatches of 10:30 last night and of 4 this morning have been received. After maturely weighing the notes, the General commanding is induced to think that General Negley withdrew more through prudence than compulsion. He trusts his loss is not serious."[28] While this message was on the way, Thomas had been busy ferreting out more information. Reports from citizens, he warned Rosecrans, confirmed his im-

25 *Ibid.*, 534.

26 Horn, *Army of Tennessee*, 250–52.

27 *Official Records*, 1st Series, XXX, Part 3, 247–64.

28 *Ibid.*, 564–65. The word "desperate" appears in the original dispatch, so quoted in Joseph Hergesheimer, *Sheridan*, 62.

pression that the enemy was concentrated at Lafayette in force; a dispatch from McCook "says it is reported that Bragg's whole army with Johnston's" was there. Although Johnston had sent less than 10,000 men, combined reinforcements for the Confederates would total about 24,000 at Chickamauga.

Crittenden also had encountered the enemy south of Chattanooga, J. T. Wilder's cavalry turning back a part of Forrest's command. On that same evening, September 12, after questioning a few Negroes and citizens and reviewing Thomas's dispatches, Rosecrans began to see the truth of the matter. No longer could tactics be shaped for pursuit—immediate concentration of the army, as Rosecrans himself now contended, had become "a matter of life and death."[29] He sent a message through Thomas ordering McCook to join the Fourteenth Corps with all speed. Learning that the enemy was hovering on his front, McCook consulted by courier with Thomas, who told him he should go back across the southern end of Lookout Mountain, march up Lookout Valley, and across the mountain through Stevens's Gap where the Fourteenth Corps would remain. For the sake of safety, this meant a march of sixty miles instead of twenty-five, but, although Rosecrans was irritated by what he regarded as a waste of time in the present emergency, McCook kept his army and wagon train intact, reaching Spring Gap safely on September 17.

Had McCook marched by the direct route, he would have run straight into Bragg's waiting troops; but by taking the mountain road, he managed to keep out of reach while Thomas was well holed up as usual and Crittenden was protected by cavalry. Frustrated by the invader's cautious defensive moves, Bragg had failed to strike one solid blow. "The resistance of the enemy's cavalry and bad and narrow country roads caused unexpected delay in the execution of my orders," the Confederate leader reported gloomily.

General Halleck, at Washington, had been demonstrating his complete ignorance of the situation concerning enemy reinforcements. One-time "Old Brains," now known as "Woodenhead," had notified Rosecrans on September 11 that a portion

[29] Henry Villard, *Memoirs*, II, 97.

of Bragg's army, as he had been informed, was reinforcing Robert E. Lee in Virginia. Precisely the opposite was true; General James Longstreet and John B. Hood were even now on their way from Virginia with 8,000 men, a fact which Halleck reluctantly conceded on the fourteenth. His reversal of mind was as complete as Rosecrans'. He hurriedly telegraphed Burnside at Knoxville, Grant at Vicksburg, and General Stephen A. Hurlbut at Memphis to hurry reinforcements to Rosecrans' relief—one month too late.

Thomas arose at 3:30 A.M. on September 17, 1863, and dressed himself with his usual care within the ten minutes allotted for this purpose. An order from Rosecrans to advance to the Chickamauga River, where Crittenden was posted, was the first item of business. Although still in the mountains, McCook was less than a day's march away, so it was considered safe for the Fourteenth Corps to close up on Crittenden, who was moving toward him from Lee and Gordon's Mills. Summoning his chief of staff, Colonel George E. Flynt, Thomas dictated orders, marked 3:40 A.M., to each of his division commanders. "See that the men are provided with 20 rounds of ammunition in their pockets in addition to the cartridge boxes being full," each message read.[30] No one then knew just where the enemy might be or where cavalry might be encountered.

Now came breakfast. Old Phil, a dignified contraband, had a hot meal ready under the fly of the tent. War Correspondent William Shanks, who breakfasted with Thomas twice during the campaign, was brought "an excellent punch with Col. Flynt's compliments as an appetizer," of which little was needed in the crisp morning air. On the table, recalled Shanks, "smoked fresh beef, ham and strong black coffee. At each silver plate was a napkin of the purest white, artistically folded, a silver water goblet, a china cup, and the usual knives and silver forks. Better beef and better coffee would not have been found in the country in which the army was campaigning, while the hot rolls and potatoes, baked in the hot ashes of a neighboring fire, would have made many a French cook blush."[31] The setting was na-

30 *Official Records*, XXX, Part 1, 111.
31 Shanks, *Personal Recollections*, 76.

turally rude, the mountain wilderness loomed above, and fog still blanketed the dark valley below, but breakfast atop Stevens's Gap, in Shanks' opinion, was as luxurious as in any city hotel.

The corps got underway early and marched all day. At 10:20 A.M. on September 18, Thomas had reached Alley's Spring on the Chattanooga road, where he busied himself getting three divisions into position adjoining Crittenden's troops. Reynolds had been left in the rear until McCook could get down to cover Dug Gap. Because some of Crittenden's men happened to be in the way, further advance was delayed somewhat, but catching up with that officer early in the afternoon, Thomas saw that the necessary adjustments were made. About six o'clock, when the head of his column had reached Crawfish Springs, a note from Rosecrans brought him to army field headquarters. Evening found the two officers discussing orders which apparently never were committed to paper, but from Thomas's movements that night it is clear that he was being placed between Bragg and Chattanooga to outflank the enemy if possible and to make the city safe. Early on that day Bragg had written orders for an attack on the Federal left, which he supposed Crittenden held, for it was his plan to roll up the Union line from the northern end and sweep it back toward the mountains. Although Bragg would have preferred to open up on Crittenden, Thomas was to march all night and move into position to deliver the first assault on September 19. Bragg's attack, as it happened, had been delayed one day, and, except for cavalry skirmishes here and there, most of the Confederates were still on the other side of Chickamauga Creek.

Clearing the road for the wagons, Thomas's troops moved mostly in the open fields. Heavy flanking forces guarded the ammunition train and artillery which Crittenden began to hear creak past him at two o'clock on the morning of the nineteenth. Halts were frequent as the heavily loaded wagons broke down and were removed from the road or fresh mules were placed in the traces. The men warmed themselves by starting fires in the fences, which outlined the road in flame, the ammunition wagons riding perilously through. The air was thick with fog, dust, and smoke, the night "tedious and fatiguing." At eight o'clock, Brannan's column filed off the road near the Kelly house and stacked arms. The word was passed "twenty minutes for breakfast," and soon hundreds of little fires were kindled to heat the soldiers' coffee cans and broil the strips of bacon which one man cooked while another moistened and toasted the hardtack. But breakfast was hardly begun when it was unforgivably interrupted. "Here comes an aide at a furious gallop down the dusty road, a brief order delivered . . . and each regiment gets orders to take arms and march immediately," recounted Colonel Bishop of the Second Minnesota, to whom the scene was always vivid. "The bugle call to attention was drowned in a tempest of curses, but the order was promptly obeyed nevertheless, arms were taken and we filed out into the road . . . and briskly moved off northward in a cloud of choking dust. 'Dreadful! dreadful!' exclaimed our venerable chaplain as the air grew sulphurous with profanity. . . . 'Colonel,' " remarked a Chickamauga veteran a full quarter of a century later, " 'd'ye moind that breakfast we didn't ate at Chickamauga? Be jabers, oi can almost taste it yet.' "[32]

[32] Bishop, *Story of a Regiment*, 97.

X

Unbeaten on the Left

THE winding Chickamauga River coursed between the armies, trending a little eastward as it flowed north to join the Tennessee. The road which Thomas followed ran somewhat straighter north, and after reaching the Kelly farm, the divisions led by Baird and Brannan made their camp nearly three miles west of Reed's Bridge. The bridge provided a convenient route for Forrest's cavalry, which was covering Bragg's right flank, and in fact the Confederate mounted leader was already across. On the eighteenth Forrest had brushed with Colonel Robert Minty's troopers and with Colonel Dan Mc-Cook of the Federal Reserve Corps. Reinforced by General John Pegram's mounted brigade, Forrest rescued Reed's Bridge, which McCook had attempted to destroy, and slept on the west bank of the Chickamauga that night.

According to McCook, who talked with Thomas early on November 19, only a single enemy brigade had crossed over. He believed that the bridge had been burned behind it and that the brigade could be easily cut off. After leaving this information, McCook rode off to rejoin the Reserve Corps, which was guarding a road four miles to the north. On the basis of Mc-Cook's story, Thomas ordered Brannan, about eight o'clock, to attack the "isolated" enemy brigade. Brannan promptly swung eastward with Baird at his right and a little to the rear. Supported by Colonel Ferdinand Vanderveer on the left, General John T. Croxton of Kentucky led the first brigade to encounter Forrest. Croxton was a picturesque and rugged character with plenty of nerve, and after he had been roughly handled by superior numbers, the story goes that he sent an inquiry back to Thomas asking which particular brigade of the five or six over there he wanted captured. Another version has it that Croxton, overborne, returned and saluted Thomas: "General, I would have brought them in if I had known which ones you wanted!"[1]

This grim humor appealed to Thomas right in the middle of a large morning's work. Enough of the enemy was directly in front. Forrest's three brigades, fighting dismounted, were peppering the confused Federals from behind trees and underbrush. Pegram's and then another mounted brigade had joined Forrest, although infantry reinforcements were slow in arriving. Leaving the willing Pegram in charge, Forrest galloped off to urge on General W. H. T. Walker's infantry division, which had crossed the river some distance south. All of Brannan's men were warmly engaged, Thomas discovered. He hurried Baird into the fight, directing the brigade leaders to form their men in hollow squares and stand fast. Croxton was permitted to drop back to replenish his ammunition.

The crash of Federal artillery carried the sound of battle southward. Shortly before noon, all of Walker's division had arrived and a Union battery was taken. The blue-clads on the left were hotly pressed. "It seemed," said General Baird, "as if complete destruction was inevitable."[2] But Croxton returned to the line, Vandeveer held firm, and Thomas discovered new resources in three fresh divisions. Johnson of McCook's corps had been ordered on by Rosecrans, Crittenden had kept Palmer moving, and behind Palmer came Reynolds of the Fourteenth, who somehow had exchanged places with Johnson. McCook's men plunged into the fight to ease the pressure on Brannan and Baird, the Ninth Ohio Regiment fixed bayonets and rushed the enemy and recaptured the guns. There was a "great hurrah of victory."

Because of Dan McCook's simple error in information, the Battle of Chickamauga had been joined at a time and place which caught both Rosecrans and Bragg out of position. Thomas had only two divisions near him at the outset; Reynolds was

---

[1] H. M. Duffield, *Address at Dedication of Monuments*, September 18, 1895 (pamphlet), 3; James H. Wilson, *Under the Old Flag*, II, 169–70.

[2] *United Service Journal*, September, 1896, 221.

some miles in the rear, while Negley, in his advance, had run into Palmer's division, the latter moving ahead toward Thomas. Crittenden's corps, to which Palmer belonged, lay between Lee and Gordon's Mills and Crawfish Springs, which McCook had reached during the night. This left the entire army strung out over a space of six or seven miles. No time had been allowed o make ready and to form the divisions in line of battle following the night marches, and a wide gap existed between Thomas and Crittenden nearly all day. On the other hand, the opening of battle near Jay's Sawmill entirely upset Confederate plans. Bragg's purpose had been to "sweep up the Chickamauga toward Lee and Gordon's Mill" where Crittenden supposedly occupied the Federal left. But Thomas had by-passed Crittenden in the night. The Confederate leader, therefore, had to swing back to the north to meet the nocturnal extension of the Federal line.

As Thomas forced the fighting on the Confederate right, other divisions, both Union and Confederate, moved into the battle, each marching to the rescue of belabored forces as both sides clamored for help. Only gradually did the battle become general. The nature of the action is revealed in Rosecrans' report. The enemy, he wrote, was driving Baird's flank in disorder when Johnson struck it and chased it half a mile. Then Johnson's right flank became imperiled. Palmer came to the rescue, but his right was also overlapped. Then Van Cleve, said Rosecrans, arrived from Crittenden's corps in support of Palmer but was also thrown back. Reynolds' division came next "and was in turn overpowered." Davis's division of McCook's corps then dashed into the fight, driving the enemy, but was compelled to give ground by "a superior force." Thomas J. Wood's division (Crittenden's corps) next arrived "and turned the tide of battle the other way" but not for long, apparently. Sometime after three o'clock in the afternoon, Sheridan of McCook's corps "arrived opportunely to save Wood from disaster." At four-thirty o'clock, Negley tardily approached Rosecrans' headquarters at the Widow Glenn's house and was told to relieve Van Cleve. The enemy was driven back steadily "until night closed the combat."[3]

Thomas had his headquarters at the Snodgrass house, a mile in the rear of Kelly's, but he remained on his horse most of the day. Reinforced by Johnson and Palmer, his command grew steadily larger. His two aides, Captain Sanford C. Kellogg, his nephew, and Captain J. P. Willard, sweated in their saddles; other couriers were borrowed from division commanders. At a little after midday, when the guns were recaptured, Brannan and Baird were ordered to reorganize their commands, erect barricades, and hold the road to Reed's Bridge. The Confederate divisions were coming into the fight one by one. After Walker was overpowered, General B. Franklin Cheatham's division moved up on the double and "with indescribable fury" breached the lines of Johnson and Palmer.[4] General Alexander P. Stewart then fell on Reynolds, whom Thomas supported by moving Brannan far down to the right, Croxton's brigade reaching him just in time. General St. John Liddell flung two divisions into the conflict where Union artillery waxed hot; these forces lost heavily and had to withdraw. Bushrod R. Johnson, an Ohio officer gone South, came next; then John B. Hood with three brigades of Virginians, every rifle spitting fire. His arm in a sling, Hood arrived on the field about four o'clock with three of Longstreet's brigades and pushed the Federals back more than a mile. The struggle was a tonic for the Virginians, who had been sleeping on railroad trains. Above the crash of the guns the Rebel yell was heard, "savage, exulting." An officer with General Forrest described the nature of the action:

"Neighing horses, wild and frightened, were running in every direction; whistling, seething crackling bullets, the piercing screaming fragments of shells, the whirring sound of shrapnel and the savage shower of canister, mingled with the fierce answering yells of defiance, all united in one horrid sound. The ghastly, mangled dead and horribly wounded strewed the earth for over half a mile up and down the river banks. The dead were piled upon each other in ricks, like cordwood, to make passage for advancing columns. The sluggish stream of Chickamauga

3 *Official Records,* 1st Series, XXX, Part 1, 56–58.
4 *United Service Journal,* September, 1896, 223.

ran red with human blood. . . . I had been in 60 battles and skirmishes up to this time, but nothing like this had I ever seen. Men fought like demons."[5]

The day was long and sultry, the sun descending red in the sky. Men and animals were suffering from thirst, and the weary soldiers who had marched all night had only one meal until after sundown. As evening came on, Thomas sought out Johnson and Baird to move them back to higher ground for the encounter next day. After giving his orders, he located Palmer and Reynolds, whom he asked to move to a ridge five hundred yards east of the Lafayette road; but before Johnson and Baird could get in motion, the Confederate Pat Cleburne launched a terrific assault. "Confederate artillery filled the woods with their shells which in the twilight made the skies seem like a firmament of pestilential stars," narrated an officer with Johnson. "The 77th Pennsylvania of the first line was lapped up like a drop of oil under a flame."[6] One of Baird's brigades, advancing in support, nervously opened fire in the half-gloom on Johnson's troops, who returned it shot for shot, but fortunately the enemy failed to take advantage of the confusion and retired. The soldiers bivouacked for the night in their appointed positions. Nearly everyone shivered in the clear and cold autumn weather as most blankets had been tossed away during the battle. Stragglers and the disabled filled the hollows and woods.

Thomas and the other corps commanders were summoned to Rosecrans' headquarters at the Widow Glenn's house for the usual midnight council of war. Rosecrans asked first for particulars: What units had taken part in the battle and how had they fared? Thomas could report that every unit under his command had taken part in the action that day; in fact, only two brigades of the entire army had not taken part in the fighting. The Federal Army lacked reserves, while the enemy, Rosecrans emphasized, was being heavily reinforced. According to one of the early reports, 17,000 of Longstreet's men were coming

---

[5] Thomas Berry, *Four Years With Morgan and Forrest*, 243.
[6] *United Service Journal*, September, 1896, 223.

from Virginia, while the haul of Confederate prisoners that day included some of Hood's men, some from Johnston's Army of Mississippi, and a few of Buckner's troops from Knoxville. Taking into account all the possible and probable Rebel reinforcements, Rosecrans believed himself greatly outnumbered.

Although indications are that the opposing forces at Chickamauga were fairly evenly matched, with between 60,000 and 62,500 in action on each side, the fact that the Confederates were being reinforced carried a threat even though four of Longstreet's brigades and an artillery detachment failed to arrive in time. Only defensive measures, therefore, were discussed at the council. Thomas expressed his confidence that he could hold his position on the left but significantly urged Rosecrans to withdraw his right and center to the east slopes of Missionary Ridge and the transverse hills behind the Lafayette road. This would place the army in a more favorable position, since these heights commanded every route leading to Chattanooga except the Rossville road to the north, where Gordon Granger's Reserve Corps was posted. However, to abandon ground to the right, as Rosecrans pointed out, would mean the loss of Union field hospitals near Crawfish Springs. The army's present headquarters also would be given up. Thomas had little more to say and soon fell asleep. Whenever roused, he would rumble, "Strengthen the left," and again doze off.[7]

Although Rosecrans had few men to spare, he adopted Thomas's suggestion in part. Orders discussed and written down stipulated that the center and right would be withdrawn only a slight distance from their present positions, leaving Thomas commanding a salient east of the Lafayette road with the divisions of Baird, Johnson, Palmer, Reynolds, and Brannan. General Crittenden, to whom was left only the divisions of Wood and Van Cleve, was instructed to place the latter on the eastern slope of the Ridge in position to support either McCook or Thomas. McCook, who had Davis and Sheridan and Negley, was to close and cover the position at the Widow Glenn's. After Rosecrans was satisfied that everyone knew what was expected

[7] Charles A. Dana, *Recollections of the Civil War*, 113.

of him, hot coffee was served, General McCook sang "The Hebrew Maiden," and the council adjourned.[8]

Returning to his campfire in the woods, Thomas lay on the ground and studied a map which he held at an angle to the light. Near him slept his two aides and the other staff officers. Although no word was spoken, a sentinel walking his beat became aware of something unusual. In that glowing little amphitheater the fire dimly lit up the faces of hundreds of men peering intently out of the gloom. The sentinel saw them gazing upon the face of their commander "to divine if possible from the expression . . . what the chances of the morrow's fight would be.[9] They read their answer in his look and manner, entirely calm as usual; satisfied, they withdrew and slept again. The soldiers had a feeling of security under Thomas, a feeling so strong that it frequently aroused comment among them.

At two o'clock that morning, Sunday, September 20, Thomas received a message from General Baird reporting that his left did not quite extend to the road and that he could not reach it without weakening his line. Thomas then went back to sleep but aroused himself at six o'clock when he sent a note to Rosecrans asking that Negley take position on Baird's left and rear. Negley, who was in poor physical shape, had been consistently behind schedule during the movements of the last two days, and unfortunately for all concerned he was to prove late again.

The sun was rising in a red haze. General Rosecrans began the day with Catholic rites in his tent, then rode out to inspect the lines. Discovering McCook's right to be too far back and Crittenden too far to the left, he ordered the necessasry changes and asked at the same time that Negley should rejoin Thomas, directing McCook to fill the gap. Rosecrans then rode to the left of the line where he found Thomas strongly protected with log breastworks and his right and left flanks bent well back toward the road. All seemed to be in good order. Rosecrans paused to discuss in a good-humored vein one or two incidents of the

8 James H. Wilson, *Life of Charles A. Dana*, 260.

9 Military Order of the Loyal Legion of the U. S., District of Columbia Commandery, *War Papers*, II, 18.

previous day's battle and heard Thomas warmly praise a charge by his men. "Whenever I touched their flanks they broke, General, they broke," said Thomas, repeating himself "with unusual zest and evident satisfaction," according to war correspondent William Shanks who was making the rounds with Rosecrans. Shanks began to stare, upon witnessing this uncommon enthusiasm, and, as Thomas caught his eye, the blood mounted to his cheeks, "his eyes were bent immediately on the ground and the rest of his remarks were . . . brief."[10]

Rosecrans' good humor did not last long. Returning to Negley's position, which was near headquarters, he discovered that he was only then preparing to move and that no one had come to relieve him. Since Crittenden's corps was nearer at hand than McCook's, Rosecrans ordered that Wood be sent to replace Negley. Rosecrans then rode off to tell McCook what he had done, but upon returning, he found that Wood was moving too slowly. That unhappy officer received "peremptory orders," accompanied by a severe dressing-down. Meantime General Bragg had been shifting his forces. After Longstreet's arrival, he had reorganized his entire command. General Polk, as commander of the right wing, was to oppose Thomas with the corps of Daniel H. Hill, a former member of Bragg's Battery in the Mexican War. Under Hill were the divisions of Breckinridge and Cleburne, while Cheatham's division still remained on the right with Forrest's cavalry as the reserve. Under Longstreet, commanding the left wing, was Buckner's corps, comprising the divisions of Stewart and Preston, Hindman and Bushrod Johnson, and five Virginia brigades, which now had arrived, under Hood. Cavalry protection on the Rebel left flank was supplied by General Wheeler. Bragg's plan for the fight on September 20 was utterly simple. He again planned to turn the enemy left, where Thomas was firmly entrenched, and he expected to launch the attack at dawn.[11]

Fog and the tardiness of Bragg's generals prevented the assault from getting underway on time. General Polk had slept off the field, and the courier he sent to Hill with orders to at-

10 Shanks, *Personal Recollections*, 67.
11 Horn, *Army of Tennessee*, 259–60.

tack was unable to locate him. Hill was delayed, therefore, until well after breakfast. Just about the time that Rosecrans was rating General Wood, Hill was exchanging some sharp words with Bragg, pointing out that the commander had failed to reconnoiter the enemy. Bragg began to fume but was helpless. His generals all regarded him with hatred and contempt; nor was he ever cheered by the men of the line. He had only the status of his rank and the power of President Jefferson Davis behind him.

Time was allowed for the men on both sides to kindle their little fires and cook their coffee and bacon. General Polk, with Breckinridge in front, finally got started shortly after 8:30 o'clock. Supported by Forrest's division fighting as infantry, the Confederate line drove against Baird's breastworks; and the assault rolled southward all along the line as Bragg sent his divisions successively forward. Thomas, meantime, was still waiting for Negley to come up. The brigade of General John Beatty showed up and was immediately placed on the extreme left. After an hour's hard fighting, Beatty's line was shattered, and some of Forrest's men began working their way around to the rear. Most of these Confederates remained in their new positions throughout the day, but when another corps from Negley arrived, Thomas gathered up his reserves and regained the lost ground. "I am glad to see your troops in such good order," he remarked to Colonel Judson W. Bishop as the Second Minnesota Volunteers, veterans of Mill Springs, filed past him.[12] Thomas already had witnessed some disorder in the ranks under fire that morning.

The enemy continued to hammer at Baird, Johnson, and Palmer. As the din of musketry rolled southward, the assault engaged Reynolds and Brannan and seemed to threaten Rosecrans' headquarters. Charles A. Dana, assistant secretary of war, who was present as an observer, following two sleepless nights was catching forty winks under a tree when he was suddenly awakened by "the most infernal noise . . . never in any battle I had witnessed was there such a discharge of cannon and musketry. I sat on the grass and the first thing I saw was Gen-

[12] Bishop, *Story of a Regiment*, 108.

eral Rosecrans crossing himself. 'Hello!' I said to myself, 'if the General is crossing himself we are in a desperate situation.' I was on my horse in a moment. I had no sooner collected my thoughts . . . than I saw our lines break and melt away like leaves before the wind."[13]

Dana was witnessing a great Union tragedy at Chickamauga. It all began when one of Thomas's observers who was riding the lines informed the General that no troops were in sight on Reynolds' right and that a gap existed between Brannan and Wood. Actually Brannan had met a flank attack and had withdrawn a short distance into the woods. Unaware of the true circumstance, Thomas sent his aide, Captain Kellogg, to tell Rosecrans that Brannan was out of line and Reynolds' right was exposed. Rosecrans immediately dictated a hasty order that has been quoted in every detailed account of the battle:

"Headquarters, Department of the Cumberland
Sept. 20, 10:45 a.m.
"Brigadier-General Wood, Commanding Division.
"The general commanding directs that you close up on Reynolds as fast as possible and support him.
"Frank Bond, Major and Aide-de-Camp."[14]

The order was confusing. Was Wood to close up on the right or from the rear? Brigadier General James A. Garfield, chief aide to Rosecrans, had been writing all the orders from headquarters that day and so was presumably in a position to know the situation, but as he happened to be elsewhere just then, it was Bond who took down the message. Perhaps the order should have read: "Close to the left on Reynolds," for Rosecrans later contended that he ordered Wood to close up but that the latter decided to move "in support," or to Reynolds' rear. Since Wood was only a short distance from headquarters, he could have resolved his own doubts, but because he had found Rosecrans in a peremptory mood that morning, he at

13 Dana, *Recollections*, 115.

14 Van Horne, *Thomas*, 131–36; J. C. Ridpath, *Life of James A. Garfield*, 153.

once moved at a double-quick, facing his division to the rear and marching completely around Brannan to reach Reynolds. This ill-timed maneuver left a huge gap in the line.

Rosecrans now ordered Davis to close on Wood, supposing the latter to be still out in front, and in response to another appeal from Thomas for help, he asked Sheridan to go. Sheridan got there six and one-half hours later, via Rossville. The "most infernal noise" which had awakened Dana signaled the rush of Longstreet's corps into the opening left by Wood. Since the attack was merely coincidental with Wood's withdrawal, Longstreet was in luck.

Eight Confederate brigades arrayed in three solid lines swept wildly through the gap as the Rebels screamed exultantly. Two of Davis's brigades reached the opening and were instantly broken. "All became confusion," wrote Colonel Gates P. Thruston of McCook's staff. "No order could be heard above the tempest of battle. With a wild yell the Confederates swept on far to their left. They seemed everywhere victorious."[15] Davis was swept away in helpless disorder. Van Cleve, who was next in line, became confused and was soon thrown into disorder. Part of Sheridan's command seemed to disintegrate. "I have never," wrote Assistant Secretary Dana, "seen anything so crushing to the mind as that scene."[16]

Rosecrans gathered up his staff, and after endeavoring vainly to restore order, he galloped to safety along the Dry Valley road, the western route to Rossville. The entire right of his army was gone, with headquarters in the enemy's possession. The General made an effort to reach Thomas, but Longstreet had swung to the right, cutting him off. Thereupon he gave up the battle as lost. According to Garfield, Rosecrans "rode silently along, abstracted, as if he neither saw nor heard."[17] After a few miles had been covered, the aide volunteered to ride to Thomas and inform him of the disaster. The two officers then dismounted and with ears to the ground listened to the sound of the guns. The fire still came in regular volleys; Thomas, they

[15] *Battles and Leaders of the Civil War*, III, 664.
[16] Wilson, *Dana*, 264.
[17] Cox, *Reminiscences of the Civil War*, II, 10.

decided, still held his own. Rosecrans assented to Garfield's suggestion "listlessly and mechanically," telling him to inform Thomas that he could withdraw at his discretion.

For the commanding General, the road to Rossville and Chattanooga lay open. Rosecrans overtook a portion of his defeated army along the way. At four o'clock he reached the adjutant general's office in Chattanooga. His usually buoyant countenance was strangely shadowed. He seemed to be "faint and ill . . . stunned by sudden calamity," and had to be helped from his horse.[18] After him came two of his corps commanders, Crittenden and McCook, then two division commanders, Van Cleve and Negley. Sheridan and Davis were also in retreat.

The impetus of the rush through the center brought Longstreet around a right-angle turn to face Thomas's line to the north. Thomas's right, with flanks bent well back, now occupied two small hills facing south while Bushrod Johnson and Thomas C. Hindman of Longstreet's command gained a western slope. It was here, on "Horseshoe Ridge," that Thomas had urged Rosecrans to place the army for battle that day; now the line was here of necessity. Thomas's left wing, facing east, continued to hold its position across the Lafayette road but had not been engaged since late in the forenoon. Polk, Hill, and Breckinridge were taking time out on the enemy right.

Mystified by the nonarrival of Sheridan and hearing heavy firing coming from the direction of headquarters, Thomas had ridden along the Ridge shortly before noon to discover the cause. Along the way he met Captain Kellogg, who had been sent to hurry up Sheridan. Kellogg had been unable to get through. The enemy had gained Reynolds' rear, he said, cutting him off. An officer of Wood's division, which was not far away, had suggested that these troops might be Sheridan's coming up, although no one could be sure. Thomas rode over to the officer and told him to display flags, and if fired upon to resist the advance. Skirmishing soon commenced.[19]

Still there was no word from Rosecrans to explain what

18 *Ibid.*
19 Johnson, *Thomas*, 103.

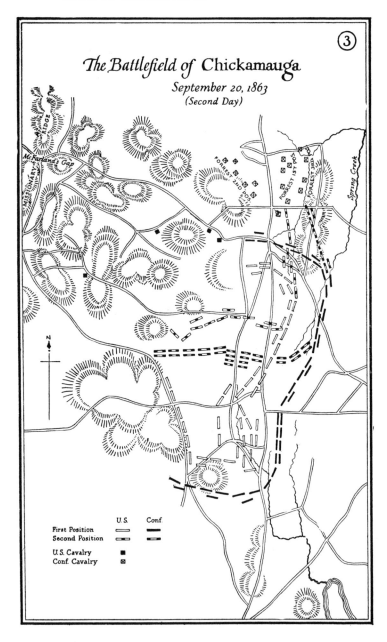

③

The Battlefield of Chickamauga
September 20, 1863
(Second Day)

	U.S.	Conf.
First Position		
Second Position		
U.S. Cavalry	■	
Conf. Cavalry	⊠	

might have happened to the center and right. About noontime, Thomas ordered Brannan and Wood to fall back on Horseshoe Ridge and erect barricades. He threw in Beatty of Negley's division and the fragments of two regiments which had survived the assault on Van Cleve. Negley finally arrived and was posted on the left. Against this improvised line, Longstreet now hurled his legions. While Hood, Stewart, and Kershaw attacked in front, Bushrod Johnson and Hindman swept Negley off the Ridge at the extreme right, gaining a foothold on the heights. Falling back half a mile or more, Negley managed to lose himself in the woods, and despairing of ever regaining Thomas's position, he resorted to a compass to make his way to Rossville. To make matters worse, he took Thomas's ammunition train in tow, and it was not long before cartridges became so scarce on the Ridge that the beleaguered fighters began searching the pockets of the dead and wounded for a handful of shells.

Thomas was still hopeful of relief from some source when his attention was directed to a dust cloud approaching his rear. He lifted his field glass and focused his eye on the banners raised above the earth-borne cloud. Did the dust conceal friend or Forrest? If the latter, the men on the Ridge surely faced disaster. Still trying to make out the up-raised colors, Thomas fidgeted and shifted his seat until his mount became uneasy and would not stand. The General later was to confess it the most anxious moment of his life. His nervousness was painfully apparent as he addressed no one in particular: "Here, take my glass, some of you whose horse stands steady—tell me what you see."

It was surely not Forrest's men, not cavalry, one of the officers argued, or the dust would be raised in spiral clouds instead of a mist. War correspondent Shanks, who had his own field glass, remarked that he was certain he could see the United States flag.

"Do you think so? Do you think so?" Thomas inquired nervously.[20] Captain G. M. L. Johnston of Negley's staff was asked to ride toward the approaching force and identify it.

General John Beatty voiced the fear and hope which agitated the defenders of Horseshoe Ridge as the dust cloud

[20] Shanks, *Personal Recollections*, 68–69.

drew nearer: "Are they friends or foes? The thunder of a thousand anvils still goes on in our front. Men fall around us like leaves in autumn. . . . The approaching troops are said to be ours and we feel a throb of exultation."[21] As the banners raised by General Gordon Granger's Reserve Corps grew plainer, Thomas visibly relaxed. It was a distinct relief, a bystander remarked, to see him recover his poise and exclaim, "Damn the enemy! Bragg is fighting without any system."[22]

Although Granger had been posted on the Rossville road to the north with orders from Rosecrans to stay there until further notice, the important General had watched the smoke and dust of battle as long as he could. "I'm going to Thomas, orders or no orders," he had exclaimed about eleven-thirty o'clock, after watching the progress of the fight from the top of a hayrick.[23] Thus, just before noon he began his march with 3,500 men under General James B. Steedman, who, then a colonel, had trained under Thomas at Camp Dick Robinson. The troops skirmished briefly with some of Forrest's men along the way and recaptured a Union field hospital. "I am very glad to see you, General," remarked Thomas to Granger about one o'clock. Steedman inquired where his men should take position. Thomas gestured in the direction of the enemy on the hill to the right and spoke briefly: "You see."[24]

The reserve had brought 10,000 rounds of ammunition. Valued far above gold and jewels, the fresh cartridges were placed in eagerly extended hands. Just before Steedman took leave of Thomas to advance his troops up the hill, he heard the General instruct an aide: "Go say to Colonel Harker to reinforce his right."

"Where will I find you, General, when I return?" the aide inquired mechanically.

Enough had been said of retreat that day. Thomas glared at the officer and thundered, "Here!"[25]

21 Beatty, *Memoirs of a Volunteer*, 251.
22 Shanks, *Personal Recollections*, 64.
23 *Battles and Leaders of the Civil War*, III, 666.
24 Society of the Army of the Cumberland, 1880 Reunion, *Report*, 35.
25 *Ibid.*, 30.

Steedman, grinning broadly, rode back to his force and timely took position between the slopes. Grasping a regimental flag he led the dust-covered troops up the hill occupied by Johnson and Hindman. The Confederate soldiers suddenly came to life and showered down a hail of lead, many bullets flying too high. Halfway up the slope the Federals halted for breath, then flung themselves upon the waiting gray-clads in a final lunge. There were a few minutes of savage fighting at close quarters with rifles, gun butts, bayonets, pistols, rocks, and stones, and the enemy was sent racing down the hill. Said General John Palmer, who watched the action through a field glass: "In all my experience I have never witnessed such desperate hand-to-hand fighting. The sound of musketry was so incessant and rapid that it was a continuous roar."[26] General Vanderveer, with his brigade of 1,200, now arrived from the Lafayette road and helped stem three bloody counterattacks. Directly after him came General William B. Hazen from Palmer's corps, but even with these reinforcements, Thomas's line had shrunk to half its original length, while a brief hour's fighting had accounted for full half of Steedman's men.

Taking his leave of General Rosecrans, Garfield started on his mission with two orderlies and Captain R. M. Gano, who had ridden to headquarters from Thomas earlier in the day and who believed he could find his way back. To circle some of Forrest's men who had penetrated far to the rear, Garfield made a wide detour through a wood, not turning back until he was close to Rossville. Two or three miles farther on he reached a cotton field where a fence suddenly glittered with rifles. Garfield shouted, "Scatter!" and wheeled to the left to gain the shelter of a ridge.[27] The rifles spat fire, dropping an orderly. Gano's leg was broken as his mount fell with a bullet through its lungs, but still he managed to crawl to the other side of the ridge. Garfield's horse, twice wounded, lasted the ten minutes more it now took to reach Thomas. The time, according to Garfield, was 3:35 P.M., and the news he brought, according to Thomas, was the "first reliable information that the right and

26 John M. Palmer, *Personal Recollections,* 84.
27 Ridpath, *Garfield,* 157.

173

center of our army had been driven."[28] In answer to the message brought from Rosecrans, Thomas informed Garfield that he had no intention of quitting the field before nightfall. Despite the heavy losses, spirits were still high. Garfield expressed the prevailing optimism in a note to Rosecrans: "Longstreet's Virginians have got their bellies full. . . . I believe we can now crown the whole battle with victory." General Granger rode with the message to the absent Commander-in-Chief.

East of the Lafayette road, division commanders Baird, Johnson, Palmer, and Reynolds faced an inactive Confederate line during the early part of the afternoon. They realized, however, that Polk would make another attack, but hearing nothing from Thomas for some little time, the four officers debated their best course. It was apparent that something had gone wrong with the right. All over the field, little knots of men discussed rumors that Rosecrans, Thomas, McCook, and Crittenden had been killed or captured. Some of the brigade leaders feared the worst. It was proposed that a general commander be named for the four divisions to march them to safety. However, Reynolds, the senior, declined to assume the command. When the proposal was laid before Palmer, an independent-minded civilian, he declared he would "rather be killed and be d——d than to be d——d by the country for leaving a battlefield under such circumstances."[29] Baird, it was said, also declined to retreat. This left only Johnson, who decided to stick it out. A short time later, Palmer witnessed Steedman's attack. Vanderveer and then Hazen were rushed over from the reserve.

Not until after four o'clock did Polk start another assault on the Union right, but the barricades could not be taken. Thomas, about this time, received an order from Rosecrans to take command of the army and withdraw to Rossville by nightfall. Granger, who brought the order back, later related that Rosecrans began to write in detail how the retreat should be conducted and how the troops should be placed, adding that campfires must be lit along the line to deceive the enemy, when

28 Johnson, *Thomas*, 104–105.
29 Palmer, *Personal Recollections*, 183–84; W. H. Hazen, *A Military Narrative*, 131.

Granger broke in with: "Oh, that's all nonsense, general. Send Thomas an order to retire. He knows what he's about as well as you do."[30] Rosecrans, speechless, at once obeyed. Thomas, receiving the brief order, rode off at once in search of Reynolds. Warned by some soldiers against capture by Confederates posted in the woods, he detoured to the left; but "just at this time," Thomas reported, "I saw the head of Reynolds's column approaching and calling to the general himself, directed him to form line perpendicular to the State [Lafayette] road, changing the head of his column to the left . . . and to charge the enemy who were then in his immediate front. This movement was made with the utmost promptitude."[31] A brigade led by the Russian General John B. Turchin drove into the enemy lines, rounded up 200 prisoners, became enveloped and cut its way out. General Willich, a German Republican of 1848, led the Ninth Ohio in a dash across the Kelly field. Three brigades were posted to hold the ground newly won as troops on the right and left retired under fire.

Both sides took prisoners; aided by two Confederate brigades firing into each other, the right wing in that sector got away without serious loss. General Charles Cruft's men, according to Palmer, left the field "as if on parade." Wood, Brannan, and Baird, protected by skirmishers, then withdrew on the left after sundown, and the yelling Rebels took over the field. All along the Ridge, Thomas's soldiers, their cartridge boxes empty, their bayonets stained ruddy, turned their backs on the enemy and marched proudly away. They left the Confederates beating out a grass fire which threatened the wounded on the ground.

Carts and ambulances cluttered the road to Rossville. The wounded and disabled lay alongside it, some calling out the names of their regiments, others too weak to utter a sound. The vividness and horror of the day's battle burned in the mind of General John Beatty as he rode along in the darkness. "We see again the soldier whose bowels were protruding and hear him cry, 'Jesus have mercy on my soul!' . . . A Confederate boy, who should have been at home with his mother and whose leg had

30 Shanks, *Personal Recollections*, 273.
31 Johnson, *Thomas*, 105.

been fearfully torn by a minie ball, hailed me as I was galloping by early in the day. He was bleeding to death and crying bitterly. I gave him my handkerchief and shouted back to him as I hurried on: 'Bind up the leg tight!' Sammy Snyder lay on the field wounded; as I handed him my canteen, he said: 'General, I did my duty.' "[32]

General Sheridan, returning to the army after going around by Rossville, met Thomas near the field and aided in covering his withdrawal. The two men rode back together as the moon rose. Reaching the outskirts of the village, Thomas halted, and both dismounted, sitting on a fence rail to watch the troops pass. Thomas seemed very exhausted, wrote Sheridan, "seemed to forget what he had stopped for and said little or nothing of the incidents of the day."[33] Finally Sheridan arose to bivouack his troops. Thomas then roused himself, remarking that he had a flask of brandy in his saddle and that he had stopped to offer Sheridan some, as he knew he must be tired. The flask was brought by a staff officer. Thomas took a sip and gave the rest to his companion. Refreshed, Sheridan mounted and rode off. Thomas later had coffee with Colonel B. F. Scribner of Baird's command, whose face was yet bloody from a wound, but still made no allusion to the fight or to any incident of the day. General Garfield could never forget an occurrence near the close of the action just after one of the divisions had fired its last cartridge and repelled a charge at bayonet point. Thomas, he said, took the hand of a soldier in one of his rare gestures of comradeship and thanked him for his valor and steady courage. The dazed private stood silent for a moment then cried out breathlessly, "George H. Thomas has taken this hand. I'll knock down any mean man that offers to take it hereafter!"[34]

[32] Beatty, *Memoirs of a Volunteer*, 253.
[33] Philip H. Sheridan, *Personal Memoirs*, 285.
[34] Van Horne, *Thomas*, 427.

XI

Chattanooga and Missionary Ridge

THOMAS well realized that the army was still in danger provided Bragg had the energy to pursue. He stationed his men in position to guard the three roads leading out of Rossville, but although some Confederate cavalry advanced close enough to capture some reconnoitering Federals the next morning, Bragg was strangely indifferent to Forrest's plea to smash the rest of the Union Army. Lapsing into one of his mental depressions, the Confederate leader was spiritually incapable of driving on to victory. However, since Bragg's quirks of mind were kept hidden while the energetic Forrest was still active and alive, Thomas advised Rosecrans early on September 21 to concentrate the army at Chattanooga. He went ahead with his preparations while awaiting a reply, and by seven o'clock the next morning the veterans of Horseshoe Ridge were safely lodged in the city. Rosecrans unfortunately decided to yield Lookout Mountain as well as Missionary Ridge, which caused some muttering among his officers since it meant abandonment of two Tennessee River ferries important to the supply line. After Bragg found it quite safe to approach, he posted his left flank on the mountain and his center and right along the wooded slopes of Missionary Ridge, which extended some miles east of the city. The Federal Army was now in a state of siege.

Chattanooga, in its beautiful natural setting, had been a queenly city of fine residences before being overrun by Confederate and Union forces, but a few weeks of war had turned it into a bleak and sad-looking place. Most of the better-class citizens had fled at the approach of the Yankees early in September, many women and children taking refuge in caves. The best houses had been ransacked for food and valuables; lawns and shrubbery were being eaten by mules. Chattanooga still had its dingy market, two or three hotels, a few churches, stores, and tenement houses with possibly a thousand dispirited whites and as many rejoicing Negroes still left. Shade trees were being felled and fences destroyed for firewood, while tents were pitched in gardens and fields. Just behind the city row upon row of crude army huts dotted the hills and the plain where swarms of soldiers labored with pickax and spade digging rifle-pits. Fort Wood and log breastworks were erected. Streets and camps were filled with arguments over the Battle of Chickamauga.

Most of the officers who had remained on the field were bitter against Rosecrans, Negley, Crittenden, and McCook, although Sheridan, Van Cleve, and Davis did not escape censure. It was argued that these generals could have joined Thomas on the Ridge and carried on the battle from there. "Old Pap" had not been exactly inaccessible. Dana had joined him by mid-afternoon after leaving Rosecrans, while Colonel Gates P. Thruston of McCook's staff had taken a message from the Ridge to Davis and Sheridan, whom Thomas asked to return to the front line. Davis had turned back and was approaching by the Dry Valley road when he learned that Thomas was withdrawing, but Sheridan had marched all the way around through Rossville, losing much valuable time. Van Cleve, who appeared too old for front-line duty, had become confused, while Negley had withdrawn without orders. Losses in the battle were too great for any temporizing with these "deserters." The Union estimate was 16,550 men killed, wounded, and missing, although the Confederates had lost about one thousand more. Since Rosecrans had been forced to retreat, the battle had decided nothing except that the Federals still held Chattanooga, which indeed had been theirs to retain two weeks before. And Braxton Bragg had escaped capture again.

The idol of the soldiers was "Pap" Thomas, the Rock of Chickamauga. "I confess I share their feeling," Dana notified Secretary Stanton. "I know of no other man whose composition and character are so much like those of Washington; he is at once an elegant gentleman and a heroic soldier."[1] So much praise of "Old Pap" was heard in camp that soldiers who had never seen him made efforts to do so. Supplying an answer to the question "How does he look?" a Chicago war correspondent told how the Rock of Chickamauga might be recognized in a crowd: "Well, if you will just think what manner of man he must be that should be hewn out of a large square block of the best-tempered material that men are made of, not scrimped anywhere, and square everywhere—square face, square shoulders, square step; blue eyes, with depths in them, withdrawn beneath a penthouse of a brow; features with legible writing on them and the whole giving the idea of massive solidity, of the right kind of man to tie to, you will have a little preparation for seeing him as he is."[2] The General's several nicknames—"Old Tom," "Old Reliable," "Old Slow Trot," "Old Pap," "Uncle George," and the "Rock," all meant about the same thing—the right kind of man to tie to.

Thomas himself had little to say as he busied himself with problems of supply and defense. His views of the campaign were not expressed until after the war. While he then blamed Rosecrans for leaving Chattanooga to pursue Bragg in McLemore's Cove, he characteristically held the War Department more at fault for ordering a pursuit. Thomas later maintained that Rosecrans should have stayed in Chattanooga to get "a good ready" no matter what Washington said, but it is also true that Rosecrans had found the official orders in line with his own mood. For the time being, however, no one in the army or in Washington knew what Thomas was thinking.

Ten days after the battle, the subject of promotions and demotions was discussed at a Cabinet meeting in Washington. Lincoln read aloud one of Dana's "confidential dispatches" which strongly criticized Rosecrans, Crittenden, and McCook. Navy Secretary Welles expressed the view that no one seemed as suitable for the command "or the equal of Thomas, if a change was to be made."[3] But while Crittenden, McCook, Negley, and Van Cleve were already on the skids, Rosecrans was

[1] Wilson, *Dana*, 265.
[2] Benjamin F. Taylor, *Mission Ridge and Lookout Mountain*, 192–93.
[3] Welles, Gideon, *Diary*, I, 447.

still being "tried," largely because northern politicians did not want to see Thomas promoted. The President delayed his decision for three weeks more.

Meanwhile the code messages of the articulate Dana, future editor of the New York *Sun,* continued to pour into Washington. While General Rosecrans, remarked Dana, abounded in friendliness, he was greatly lacking in firmness. "I have never seen a public man," read Dana's October 12 dispatch, "possessing talent with less administrative power, less clearness and steadiness in difficulty and greater practical incapacity than General Rosecrans. He has inventive fertility and knowledge, but he has no strength of will and no system in the use of his busy days and restless nights. . . . He is conscientious and honest, just as he is imperious and disputatious." Dana was not alone in his opinion of the commander's moral fiber. General Palmer, who believed Rosecrans drank and swore too much, although his tent and headquarters "was the resort of priests," wrote his wife that "self-indulgence and unmanly desire to escape personal damage and responsibility drove several officers of the highest rank into Chattanooga [where] they told horrible tales of route and disaster."[4]

When Thomas caught wind that his superior officer was under fire at Washington, he placed himself squarely on Rosecrans' side. Seeing that Dana had his nose deep in everything and learning the tenor of his dispatches through a clerk at the telegraph office, Thomas sent Garfield to warn his chief that "spies from Washington now in camp are working for your removal."[5] Thomas leaned over backward in avoiding any course which might make it appear that he was seeking the command. One evening Dana came to the one-story frame house he was using as headquarters and read him a laudatory telegram from Secretary Stanton, who was contending it was not his fault that Thomas had not been in chief command "months ago."[6] Thomas, said Dana, seemed "much too affected" to reply immediately. Possibly remembering Camp Dick Robinson, the

---

[4] George T. Palmer, *A Conscientious Turncoat,* 117.
[5] Society of the Army of the Cumberland, 1879 Reunion, *Report,* 176.
[6] Wilson, *Dana,* 275.

BRIGADIER GENERAL ROSECRANS

General ultimately remarked that he would have desired the independent command of an army organized and disciplined entirely by himself but added significantly that he did not wish to accept any command if exposed to the imputation of having intrigued to supplant his commander.[7] Evidently Thomas felt that even a private talk with Dana bordered on intrigue, but in any event his point was lost on the busy Assistant Secretary. When talk of his replacing Rosecrans still persisted in camp, Thomas asked Garfield to tell Dana bluntly that he never would consent to become Rosecrans' successor.

The issue, after all, would be decided not by Thomas but by Lincoln and the War Department. Conditions at Chattanooga in no way helped Rosecrans. After cutting the supply line to Bridgeport, Bragg hemmed the Federals in closer. Wagon trains coming from Nashville now had to make a seventy-mile detour over the steep and rocky roads of Walden's Ridge, a route doubly difficult after the fall rains set in. Short rations for men and animals created a vicious circle. The mules grew weaker from lack of forage and grain and soon could haul only the lightest loads. Many were dropping in their traces. Within a few weeks the mountain trail was lined by the bodies of thousands of draft animals which had perished from labor, hunger, and the desperate cruelty of their drivers. In the meantime, food was getting so scarce in camp that the surviving mules were guarded, while they fed, against foraging soldiers although the guards were privileged to share the meal. So, while hunger and discouragement hung over the city and stale hardtack sold for as much as twenty-five cents a piece, Rosecrans, according to Dana, was dawdling. On October 16 he telegraphed Stanton: "The incapacity of the commander is astonishing . . . his imbecility . . . contagious."[8] General James B. Steedman, a Western Democrat but a brave and honest soldier, arrived that day in Washington at Lincoln's request.

Lincoln greeted his visitor and shook hands with him; then asked abruptly, "General Steedman, what is your opinion of General Rosecrans?" Steedman demurred at first but was in-

[7] Dana, *Recollections*, 125.
[8] Wilson, *Dana*, 269 f.; Carl Sandburg, *Storm Over the Land*, 214.

duced to speak his mind when an opinion was "ordered." Rosecrans, he answered, was a splendid man to command a victorious army, but he believed that there were two or three men better able to command a defeated army.

"Who besides yourself, General Steedman, is there in that army who would make a better commander?" inquired the President, getting down to the point.

"General George H. Thomas."

"I am glad to hear you say so. That is my own opinion exactly," Lincoln responded.[9] However, only the day before, he told Steedman, a "powerful New York delegation" had come to him to protest against the man who had come from a Rebel state. Steedman gravely opined that Thomas, who had given up his home and family ties to be loyal, could be trusted in any position to which he might be assigned. That seemed to satisfy the President. Rosecrans, someone else had heard him remark, had been "confused and stunned like a duck hit on the head" ever since Chickamauga.[10]

His mind made up at last, Lincoln issued an order that day which covered considerably more ground than a new command for Thomas. At once straddling the political situation while placing the military reins in capable hands, the President united the departments and armies of the Ohio, Tennessee, and Cumberland in the Military Division of the Mississippi with General Grant at its head. While General Burnside continued as head of the Army of the Ohio, Grant would replace himself with Sherman as Army of the Tennessee commander; and with the appointment of Thomas as chief of the Cumberlanders left optional, although hinted at, Grant agreed to this change also. Meanwhile the army under Sherman was inching along over flooded country from Vicksburg to Bridgeport, while the Eleventh and Twelfth Corps of the Army of the Potomac, led by General Joseph Hooker, were being rushed west several weeks too late. Few new appointments had been made in the Army of the Cumberland. With McCook, Crittenden, Van Cleve, and Negley out, the Twentieth and Twenty-first Corps

9 Sandburg, *Abraham Lincoln: The War Years*, II, 434–35.
10 John Hay, *Letters and Diaries*, 106.

had been broken up and the regiments assigned to the various brigades, thus making some of them almost as large as divisions.

Hurrying east by rail, Grant wrote out several orders at Louisville for Rosecrans and Thomas. On the evening of October 19, upon returning to headquarters after examining the Tennessee River shore with a view to relief operations, General Rosecrans broke open the dispatches. He read them all carefully, then sent for Thomas and Granger and laid the papers before them. Rosecrans later detailed his own account of the headquarters meeting and the reaction from Thomas: "After he had read the papers over he drew a long breath and turned pale and was about to speak when I said: 'Thomas, don't say anything; there is no misunderstanding that can come between you and me. I know what you want to say, for Garfield has told me, but . . . what you have to do is to do it like a soldier.' . . . Upon that he said: 'Well, I suppose I must do so but I don't like it.' "[11] Rosecrans smiled and the tension subsided; chiefs of departments were summoned, and the generals got to work on the necessary orders and reports. As the welcome news filtered out of headquarters to the ragged and lean soldiers, "our hopes went up with a bound."[12]

Dana's dispatches had so alarmed Stanton that he journeyed west to meet Grant at Indianapolis, riding to Louisville with him. Stanton's anxiety became infectious, causing Grant to wire Thomas: "Hold Chattanooga at all hazards." This message, a poor introduction for Grant, was not well received. According to Rosecrans, who read it that evening, there was "astonishment and indignation at the outrageous implication it contained." Thomas replied with a oft-quoted dispatch: "We will hold the town until we starve."[13]

It would be a race between starvation and strategy, but Rosecrans had been waiting for Hooker to arrive at Bridgeport before entering upon his plan to relieve the city. While Thomas now approved it, he would have to wait for Grant. Preceding

11 Society of the Army of the Cumberland, 1869 Reunion, *Report*, 77–78; 1879 Reunion, *Report*, 176.

12 *Ibid.*, 1869 Reunion, *Report*, 78.

13 Van Horne, *Thomas*, 156.

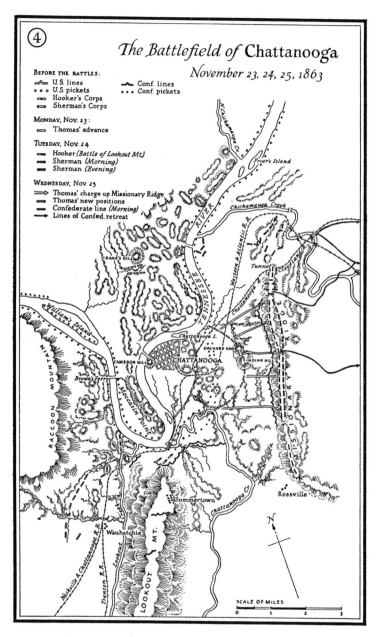

④ The Battlefield of Chattanooga
November 23, 24, 25, 1863

BEFORE THE BATTLES:
～ U.S. lines
o o o U.S. pickets
⊂⊃ Hooker's Corps
⊂⊃ Sherman's Corps

MONDAY, NOV. 23:
⊂⊃ Thomas' advance

TUESDAY, NOV. 24
▬ Hooker (Battle of Lookout Mt)
▬ Sherman (Morning)
▬ Sherman (Evening)

WEDNESDAY, NOV. 25
⟹ Thomas' charge up Missionary Ridge
⊂⊃ Thomas' new positions
▬ Confederate line (Morning)
⟶ Lines of Confed. retreat

～ Conf. lines
• • • Conf. pickets

SCALE OF MILES
0   1   2   3

the General to Chattanooga on October 23, Colonel James Harrison Wilson of Grant's staff was escorted to headquarters by Dana, who sang Thomas's praises along the way. Wilson later related that he was therefore "prepossessed in his favor and was ready to greet him as an able and reliable commander, but I am free to confess I was not prepared to see in him so many external evidences of greatness." Continuing, Wilson somewhat exaggerated Thomas's height and made the inevitable comparison with George Washington. (Somehow a man in the presence of Thomas always thought him two or three inches taller than he actually was.) "Six feet tall, of Jovelike figure, impressive countenance and lofty bearing, he struck me at once . . . as resembling the traditional Washington in appearance, manner and character more than any man I had ever met. I found him as calm and serene as the morning. . . . He expressed a modest confidence in being able to make good his hold on Chattanooga and at once inspired me with faith in his steadiness and courage." It was later made clear, the account adds, that the need of supervision from any source apparently "had never presented itself to his mind."[14]

Recalling the subject of his last interview with the Assistant Secretary, Thomas unbent himself enough to say, "Mr. Dana, you have got me this time but a man must obey orders." He inquired after Grant's health and asked when he might be expected. Although lamed by a fall from his horse, Grant was on the last leg of a fifty-five-mile horseback journey and was expected to arrive the next day. Observing military protocol, Thomas referred his visitors to General William F. ("Baldy") Smith, his chief engineer, and General Brannan, chief of artillery, for details concerning the army. Both Brannan of Chickamauga and Smith, veteran of Antietam and Gettysburg, were new appointments. Although Thomas had reorganized nearly every department in the army, promotions had been issued sparingly. Some of the volunteer officers who failed to qualify in energy, judgment, and sobriety had been disappointed. When Colonel Benjamin F. Scribner of Indiana complained that he had been treated badly, Thomas bared his own feeling

14 Wilson, *Under the Old Flag*, I, 272.

on the subject, saying, "Colonel, I have taken a great deal of pains to educate myself not to feel."[15] General Palmer, a good fighter at Stone's River and Chickamauga, now commanded the Fourteenth Corps, and General John J. Reynolds now served his commander as chief of staff.

Already conscious that affairs had taken a turn for the better, Wilson and Dana found Smith and Brannan in a businesslike mood and were assured that order and confidence already had been restored in the army. General Smith explained the plan originated by Rosecrans "for shortening the cracker line" to be put into effect as soon as Grant had approved it. Riding along the lines, Wilson and Dana found "short rations, little forage and many hungry soldiers and starving animals," yet spirits were buoyant. "Every vistage of discontent had disappeared," Wilson testified. "Everyone seemed cheerful and hopeful. Officers and men had regained resolution and courage."[16] Strength was at the helm.

Wet and hungry and covered with mud, General Grant and his party arrived betimes at nine o'clock that evening after their long horseback journey over rough and slippery mountain roads. Grant had pushed on relentlessly even after his horse had fallen again and bruised the leg which had been injured some days before in a similar accident. Two of Grant's aides carefully lifted him from his mount and placed him on Thomas's doorstep. The officers entered a large room in which a log fire was burning, but when Dana and Wilson arrived soon after, they discovered what seemed to them to be obvious neglect on the part of the host. Thomas was sitting on one side of the fire and Grant on the other over a puddle of water which still dripped from his clothes. General John A. Rawlins, Grant's chief aide, and other officers were sitting or standing about. Rawlins looked angry, Thomas preoccupied. Wilson nudged Thomas by speaking up: "General Grant is wet and in pain . . . " whereupon the Virginian sprang to action and gave his aides something to do. Dry clothes were produced and a hot supper laid. The embarrassment soon passed. Conversation

15 Shanks, *Personal Recollections*, 71–72.
16 Wilson, *Dana*, 280.

after the meal "became carefree if not hilarious," the West Pointers calling each other by their old nicknames.[17]

Still it was no welcome for Grant. Patrician and formalist, Thomas was not a man to appreciate Grant, nor did either officer ever like or wholly trust the other. Fortunately for the Northern cause, opposing temperaments never handicapped the Union Army one-tenth as much as the clashes which developed around Bragg impaired Confederate strategy. Hated by all his officers and men, Bragg was being maintained on the field by Jefferson Davis, who early in October had visited the Confederate Army entrenched on Missionary Ridge. Bragg was blaming the mud for his failure to attack the half-starved Federals in his front, and Davis weakly accepted the excuse. While Polk, Hindman, and Hill left in search of fairer fields following an open break with their commander, Davis still retained him, although "fully satisfied of his unpopularity and the decided opposition of the generals," according to a Confederate officer who was in a position to know. So Bragg continued his quarrels with Forrest and developed a psychological barrier between himself and his men.[18]

Military courtesy continued to be observed in the Federal camp. On October 27, Grant sent congratulations to Thomas on his promotion, effective that day, as brigadier general in the regular army. Although the promotion was tardy, Grant's message was not. From the evening of the General's arrival, however, members of Thomas's staff always imitated their commander in his attitude of reserve toward Grant.

Nature had broken up the great masses of land about Chattanooga into sharply defined mountains and hidden caves —the latter, hives of exploration for soldiers. Four miles to the southwest loomed craggy Lookout; to the south and east lay the indented summit of Missionary Ridge, separated from Lookout by the fortified plain. The circuitous Tennessee River dipped just west of the city to meet the mountain, carving out Moccasin Point on the north side, then took a wide bend to-

17 *Ibid.*, 281; *Under the Old Flag*, I, 272.
18 Horn, *Army of Tennessee*, 287–89.

ward unnavigable rapids known as the Suck. Military plans were governed by uncompromising topography which both sides sought to put to good use. Few secrets could be kept by the opposing camps. In the daytime, wrote Colonel Judson W. Bishop, "the enemy could look down upon us . . . from the surrounding and commanding heights of Mission Ridge, Orchard Knob and Lookout Mountain and doubtless amused themselves in watching our movements and speculating when they should close in upon us and capture us. We in turn could . . . trace their intrenched lines and note the location of their big guns and field batteries, and with field glasses could see their men whenever they appeared in or in front of their lines.

"But at night, when the grand semi-circle was lighted up with the enemy's little campfires whose light was continually intermitted by the squads of shivering, half-clothed rebels standing and moving around them, the spectacle was one we never tired of watching. Nearly every evening the signal torches on Lookout Mountain and on Mission Ridge were flashing messages to each other over our heads and across the valley. Our signal officers soon picked up their code so Bragg's messages were given to Thomas and Grant as promptly as to Hardee and Breckinridge. Occasionally a big gun on Lookout Mountain would open out in a flash like the full moon and then we suddenly became interested in locating the fall of the shell."[19]

Interesting as all this was, the soldiers could not dine or sup on scenery. A sample menu for one entire day at Chattanooga included "coffee" made from parched corn, wormy hardtack, green and yellow with mold, and a little beef from emaciated cattle, "dried on the hoof." Men quarreled over camp scraps and offal, searching the ground for grains of corn after the mules were fed. Help would come perhaps from General Joseph Hooker, bringing an army of Easterners from Virginia, who had arrived at Bridgeport. The time had come to open the cracker-line. Plans approved by Grant and Thomas called for the seizure of two ferries which provided access to points east and west of the long tongue of land cut off by the unnavigable

19 Bishop, *Story of a Regiment*, 117.

Suck. The operation had to be successful were the half-starved Federals to survive.

The first of a long series of movements began on October 24 when Thomas sent General Palmer and two brigades on a long march down the north bank of the river to co-operate with Hooker, who was to advance from Bridgeport and enter Lookout Valley while Palmer held the roads. A night expedition to Brown's Ferry, the first point to be taken, was assigned Baldy Smith, and during the night of the twenty-sixth simultaneous movements began. While General Turchin's brigade and three batteries moved overland toward the ferry, gliding along the north bank, General Hazen with two flatboats and pontoon boats manned with oars quietly drifted along the shelter of the bank as a slight mist veiled the full moon. Uniting opposite the ferry where Turchin had been hiding in the woods, all hands crossed over the pontoons to the south bank and rushed the enemy pickets in front. The Federals hastily entrenched on a hill and repelled a countercharge; after the artillery was ferried over, the position was made secure.[20] Meantime Hooker had seized Kelly's Ferry at the foot of the rapids and was marching along undisturbed in Lookout Valley. Although Bragg had been warned that a large Federal force had reached Bridgeport, he declined to credit the accurate reports of his signal corps. It was not until after Longstreet had ushered him to the top of Lookout Mountain on October 27 that he ceased to criticize what he had termed "sensational reports" and began to believe the evidence of his own eyes. There was Hooker, plainly visible below.[21]

This blond and rosy-faced Yankee general, a handsome soldier with a flair for the sensational, took position to guard the road to Brown's Ferry and encamped, stationing his rear guard some distance inland near the hamlet of Wauhatchie. Longstreet attacked at midnight but with only a single division which the economical Bragg had sent him after promising two. The Confederate force was virtually thrown away. One of

20 Horace Porter, *Campaigning With Grant*, 8; Walter E. Hebert, *Fighting Joe Hooker*, 256–57; Van Horne, *Thomas*, 158–59.

21 Horn, *Army of Tennessee*, 293.

Hooker's divisions under General John W. Geary met the assault coolly and held its ground while General Carl Schurz of the Eleventh Corps came up on the double and fell upon an enemy detachment posted to guard against just such a reinforcement. Discovering the Rebels on a steep hill to his rear, Corps Commander O. O. Howard ordered a brigade up the slope to scatter them at bayonet point. The fight grew hot; heavy guns flashed in the darkness, the echoes rolling back from the steep sides of Lookout. A timely diversion helped cut Union losses, for when the night firing scared the wagon-train teamsters away, the mules became very restive in their traces. Suddenly, "heads down and tails up," they rushed straight at the enemy "with trace-chains rattling and whiffle-trees snapping over the stumps of trees." Convinced that some Federal cavalry were upon them, the Confederates did not linger. Resistance collapsing, some 100 Rebel prisoners were taken and Geary buried 153 of the foe on his own front the next day. Union losses were 76 killed, 339 wounded, and 22 missing, considered a small price for the safety of the cracker-line. The mules received the extra rations due while General Howard's quartermaster, in his report, entered a request that they be awarded the "brevet rank of horses."[22]

All Chattanooga cheered the news that two pontoon bridges had been laid at Brown's Ferry with two steamboats running up and down the river between the ferry and the city. An immense wagon train was placed in motion over the eight-mile land route between the two ferries; 39,000 rations awaited to be taken overland from Kelly's. "We can easily subsist ourselves and will soon be in good condition," Thomas reported joyfully on October 31.[23] The needs of the men were taken care of first, however, and it was not for ten days that the horses and mules could be provided for. Some further assistance came to the besieged Federals when Bragg divided his forces at Jefferson Davis's suggestion, sending Longstreet and 18,000 men to attack Burnside at Knoxville. This news worried both Lincoln and Grant, and on November 7 Thomas received an order to

22 Porter, *Campaigning With Grant*, 9–10.
23 *Official Records*, 1st Series, XXX, Part 1, 41.

attack the enemy right on Missionary Ridge to create a diversion in the hope that Longstreet might be recalled.

Thomas read and re-read the order and laid it down. If he attempted to carry the Ridge, he remarked to Baldy Smith, his still hunger-weakened army would probably be beaten and Chattanooga uncovered. Food was still lacking for mules and horses, too few healthy animals were left to haul the artillery, and the men were short of rifles. Thomas mounted his horse and reconnoitered the Ridge from a hilltop, sizing up the number of enemy cannon and regimental flags. The movement was inadvisable, he reported back to Grant, until the arrival of the Army of the Tennessee under Sherman. Although Grant had the good sense to countermand the order, still it left a bad effect. It was asserted in the rival camp of Thomas that the order had been issued for political effect, while General Smith was to declare that Sherman with six well equipped divisions failed eighteen days later to carry the enemy right on the Ridge "at a time when Thomas with four divisions stood threatening Bragg's center and Hooker with nearly three divisions was driving in Bragg's left."[24] It was well that Grant was not blindly insistent. At least he could now tell Lincoln that he was unable to help Burnside.

Red-haired Cump Sherman with four divisions from the Army of the Tennessee had been riding the rails and marching along a difficult route from Vicksburg. Cumbersome wagon trains, compounding tardiness, followed in the rear of every division. Rain, deep mud, and swollen rivers piled up the days of delay. New bridges had to be built, trestles repaired, and miles of rails laid. When all else failed, steamboats were used as ferries. Leaving the vanguard of his force at Bridgeport, Sherman joined Grant and Thomas in besieged Chattanooga on November 14.

To introduce the newcomer to that rugged amphitheater of war, the bearded generals rode out of the city to have a look at the enemy lines. Sherman looked fit and alert, gesturing nervously as he talked. Grant rode with his coat unbuttoned

[24] *Battles and Leaders of the Civil War*, III, 715.

and unbelted, his white socks showing beneath his trousers legs untidily drawn up as he sat astride his horse. The commanding General smoked a large cigar energetically, his glance keen but impassive. Grave and silent as usual, Thomas was virtually ignored by his chief, who addressed himself almost wholly to Sherman, explaining that he was to bring his army past the city on foot by circling the hills on the opposite shore. He would then recross the river by night to surprise Cleburne and Hardee who occupied the enemy right. Cast in the stellar role, Sherman was to close the four-mile gap between himself and Thomas in the center by sweeping along the Ridge, while Thomas was to threaten from the plain and seize the first opportunity to attack. General Hooker, meanwhile, would continue to hold Lookout Valley. No further fighting was being planned for him. Sherman studied the terrain, telescoped his glass, and exclaimed confidently, "I can do it!"[25] It remained for him to get his army up by November 21, the date set by Grant.

As the officers and their aides returned to the city, Thomas gestured toward Bragg's headquarters on Missionary Ridge. Naturally curious concerning their old messmate at Fort Moultrie, Sherman inquired, "Tom, have you seen Bragg or had any communication with him?" Thomas's silver-blue eyes flashed. "Damn him, I'll be even with him yet," he flared.

"What's the matter now?"

Thomas answered by explaining that sometime ago an unsealed letter had come from the North addressed beyond the lines with a request to send it on by flag of truce. So he had put a slip of paper around it with a note asking his one-time friend Bragg to forward it to the given address. The letter, Thomas went on, came back with the endorsement: "Respectfully returned to Genl. Thomas. Genl. Bragg declines to have any intercourse with a man who has betrayed his state."[26] Nothing could wound Thomas more deeply than a slur upon his loyalty. As Sherman later recalled the incident, Thomas warmly uttered many threats of what he would do when the time came. "Few knew," another observed, "that he could flare up in that way."

Sherman returned to Bridgeport to bring up his four di-

25 Lewis, *Sherman*, 317.

visions and then the Heavens opened again and the pontoon bridges were broken by enemy rafts. Awaiting Sherman, Grant was forced to postpone his plans from day to day, issuing orders only to countermand them. Meanwhile the artillery posted on Lookout Mountain and Moccasin Point dueled fiercely, continuing a long feud. "These two batteries have a special spite at each other, and almost every day thunder away in the most terrible manner," observed General John Beatty, who took the rigors of war lightly. "Lookout throws his missiles too high and Moccasin too low, so that usually the only loss sustained by either is in ammunition. Moccasin, however, makes the biggest noise."[27] General Bragg was still making odd moves, sending Buckner to join Longstreet while only two brigades came from Johnston's army to reinforce the Ridge. Apparently the Confederate leader considered his position impregnable, taking as little heed of Grant and Thomas as of the Southern newspapers which had expressed great dissatisfaction at his failure to take Chattanooga. Thomas, whose secret service was still working well, discovered that Bragg probably had learned of Sherman's intended movement against his right and was preparing against surprise. On November 22, when Grant notified him of further delay, he went to his chief with a new plan.

Time could be saved and Bragg deceived, he suggested, by allowing Sherman to pick up Howard's Eleventh Corps in place of two divisions still far in the rear. Hooker's remaining troops and those of Sherman then in Lookout Valley could attack the enemy on Lookout Mountain "or at least divert his attention from Sherman's crossing above." Only one of Sherman's four divisions had reached its position across the river, but this had been reinforced by Jefferson C. Davis. With both Hooker and Sherman provided for, a simultaneous assault could be made on the Ridge and Lookout Mountain on the following day.

Grant permitted Howard to march into Chattanooga to join Thomas and agreed to let Hooker assault Lookout Mountain with the Twelfth Corps and one of Sherman's divisions

[26] Sherman to Garfield, July 28, 1870, Sherman Papers, Library of Congress; *North American Review*, April, 1887, 377.

[27] Beatty, *Memoirs of a Volunteer*, 259–60.

which remained in the rear, but he left it to Sherman to get most of his force in place by the night of the twenty-third. When it became apparent that he could not, Grant ordered a reconnaissance in force against Bragg's front to discover whether it was true, as a "deserter" had maintained, that the Rebels had fallen back, leaving only a strong picket line before Chattanooga. Locomotive whistles could be heard from the other side of the Ridge.

Orders to Thomas on November 23 asked merely that he drive in the enemy's pickets along the steep hill called Orchard Knob in front of the Ridge. Promptly following their noonday meal on the twenty-third, five divisions of the Cumberlanders and Howard's Eleventh Corps paraded before Fort Wood, a sizable work with emplacements for thirty-two-pound cannon. The soldiers were conscious that the eyes of two armies were upon them. Observed by all the ranking Union generals, and the Confederates on Missionary Ridge as well, the various corps assembled in style. "A grand and inspiring sight it was," according to one who marched that day. "Battle flags flapped and bayonets flashed in the sun as men with more strength in their legs than in days past moved smartly to the ringing commands. The sun shone brightly, the bands played stirring airs; tattered banners that had moved on battle fields from the Potomac to the Mississippi streamed out gaily as if proud of the battle scars they wore. Generals Grant and Hooker, and Sherman and Thomas and Logan and Reynolds and Sheridan and scores of others with their staffs galloped along the lines, and the scene that spread out around me like a vast panorama of war filled my heart with pride that I was a soldier and member of that great army. But what did it all mean?"[28]

Suddenly at two o'clock the gleaming bugles sounded their strident call. Thomas J. Wood's division rounded briskly into line and charged, Sheridan moving at the right. "Onward we moved in harmony with the grandeur of the scenery," related an officer with Hazen's brigade.[29] The inspired Federals raced

[28] Major James Austin Connolly Letters, Illinois State Historical Library *Publications*, XXXV, 298.

[29] C. G. Briant, *History of the Sixth Indiana*, 271.

past the first line of pickets, staining their bayonets with enemy blood, then continued straight on up the hill. Enemy riflemen sprang to action; the warning boom of cannon floated down from Missionary Ridge. Still the Yankees plunged ahead, flinging themselves into the "gopher holes" at the top of the Knob. Sheridan, after a struggle, carried Indian Hill on the right and planted his flag. Wood caught a signal from Thomas: "You have gained too much to withdraw. Hold your position and I will support you."[30] General Howard's troops were advanced to a position at Wood's left and Baird came abreast of Sheridan.

The men were ordered to fortify their positions, and the big guns began to roll up. Thomas mounted the hill on his powerful horse to shake hands with the officers and publicly thank the regiments standing at attention. They had done much more than had been asked. General Grant seemed entirely satisfied: "The troops moved under fire with all the precision of veterans on parade."

Superstitious soldiers encamped on mountain peak and hilltop in that rocky wilderness witnessed that night a demonstration of nature which caused some of them to cower. Over the face of a full moon the earth's shadow slowly crept. The more rational among the Federals argued that although it indicated an omen of defeat, it was not for them but Bragg "because he was perched on the mountain top, nearest the moon."[31] Convinced that this might be so, the men went to sleep. The darkness of the night helped cover the progress of Sherman's troops, who were laboriously rowing across the river in small boats and taking their positions east of the city. After one thousand had crossed over, a pontoon bridge was bumped into place to permit the rest to cross on foot. But two of Sherman's three divisions were hardly in condition to fight after their march of the previous day and the night crossing. Davis's troops were being held in reserve.

Sherman, who was to carry the day, ran into difficulty right from the start. His maps seemed to be wrong, for instead of climbing directly up the east slopes of Missionary Ridge, he

30 Van Horne, *Thomas*, 174.
31 Illinois State Historical Library *Publications*, XXXV, 299.

discovered himself faced by a series of fortified hills which masked the Ridge itself. He hustled his troops through a storm of canister to take the first two, which still left him some distance short of a railroad tunnel which he was supposed to occupy that day. Flattened out and disillusioned, Sherman entrenched behind a steep ravine and asked to be reinforced by the two divisions under General Howard.

The battle arena now shifted far to the right where Hooker was hurling two divisions and a brigade—nearly 10,000 availables—against the rocky sides of Lookout Mountain. Although the advancing Federals outnumbered the Confederates by four to one, the watchers on the plain grew anxious. "What, storm that mountain peak 2,400 feet high, so steep that a squirrel could scarcely climb it and bristling all over with rebels, bayonets and cannon?" So ran the pen of Major James A. Connolly of General Baird's division; but when spectators with field glasses saw the Confederates running and the Union colors emerging from a mist which encircled the lower part of the mountain, a great cheer went up in the valley, the bands played "Hail to the Chief," and fifty cannon thundered their salute. Bragg sent in reinforcements, prolonging the fight after dark as flashing guns played like lightning on the heights. As the Federals drew closer to the top, the gun muzzles no longer could be depressed enough to keep the range. Toward midnight the Confederate force under General Carter L. Stevenson was ordered to withdraw to Missionary Ridge, and Hooker's campfires began to sprinkle the mountainside with light. So far, every operation had gone well except Sherman's, which no longer bore any exact relation to Grant's original plan. Thomas had planned Hooker's fight and had carried his own to a point in advance of that which had been ordered while Sherman was still three miles from the plain.

General Howard moved his Eleventh Corps to the left to aid Sherman, who was ordered to renew his attack at dawn on the twenty-fifth while Thomas was to go forward "early in the day." But Grant had assumed in his orders that Sherman had gained more ground than he actually had. Throughout the forenoon, therefore, the Cumberlanders were held in their

GEORGE H. THOMAS

This rare portrait of Thomas in camp during the Georgia
campaign, 1864, was painted by the New York artist, Thomas
Nast "from a recent Photograph from life."

From a Johnson, Fry & Co. engraving
Courtesy Dr. Frederick M. Dearborn

places while Cump was given his chance. But the Ridge was still too broken to permit easy sailing. As soon as Sherman's men reached the valley in front, heavy boulders and shells with lighted fuses were bowled down upon them; once the next hill was gained, Hardee and Cleburne swept the heights with a hail of shells and canister. Noonday passed, and the Cumberlanders still waited. Thomas asked General Baird to march within supporting distance of Sherman, who was attempting to gain Tunnel Hill, through which the railroad passed. Although "difficulties of the ground" prevented Baird from getting into position until 2:30 P.M., the delay made little difference, as the Southerners charged downhill and drove Sherman from the tunnel, capturing a large number of prisoners and putting him out of action for the rest of the day.[32]

While he was still battering away at the hills and rocks, Sherman asked what Thomas might be doing. As yet he had seen or heard nothing of the promised forward movement "early in the day." The delay was Grant's; he still wished to give Sherman his chance to complete his assignment. The General considered Hooker's dash up Lookout "no action even worthy to be called a battle," and it was understood that Thomas would carry only the rifle-pits in his immediate front that day. So Grant continued to hold Thomas in reserve until urged to give the order by an impatient aide, General John A. Rawlins.[33]

Nor was Thomas disposed to hurry. For some little time after the word was given he continued to train his field-glass on the top of the Ridge. The officers and their aides were standing in a group near Fort Wood, where General Granger of the Reserve was sighting the siege guns at the Ridge, watching the effect of the fire and enjoying himself to the utmost. Rawlins, nervous and uneasy, spoke to Grant again. As Sherman's last assault failed, the Commander-in-Chief turned to Thomas and said firmly, "Now is your time."[34] The Virginian sent his aides

[32] Horn, *Army of Tennessee,* 299.

[33] James H. Wilson, *Life of John A. Rawlins,* 172; T. B. Van Horne, *History of the Army of the Cumberland,* I, 450.

[34] Hazen, *Narrative,* 173.

riding away to division commanders Baird, Wood, and Sheridan and signaled Granger to leave the guns. "Pay more attention to your corps sir," he said sharply. The signal to attack now came—six guns fired in quick succession from Fort Wood.

The three divisions of Cumberlanders facing the Ridge occupied a line two miles long. Although they outnumbered the Confederates in their immediate front by about five to four, forty-two big guns were counted pointing straight at them while across an open space of some 600 yards enemy riflemen fingered their weapons. This line only was supposed to be the target for the assault, although, according to Major Connolly, instructions were "to carry the Ridge if possible," even though Grant had not so ordered. As the final signal gun sounded from Fort Wood, the order "Charge" stiffened the men of the line. The waiting Federals threw themselves forward and scrambled up the steep slope toward the nearest Rebel pickets.

Shells and canister poured over their heads from guns in front and to the rear; "the very heavens above us seemed to be rent asunder."[35] A stream of iron was hurled at the summit by the thirty-two-pounders at Fort Wood, while Bragg's gunners worked their pieces desperately and hastily, most of the shells going high. Rifle fire was quite as inaccurate; for the Confederates to rise from their trenches and take deliberate aim was to invite suicide. Using bayonets and clubbed muskets, the Cumberlanders swept over the first line of rifle-pits with impetus and zeal unspent. The line just ahead invited them on, and the Ridge itself lay only 500 feet ahead. A corporal of the Ninth Kentucky Regiment rose from the ground and shouted, "By God, boys, let's go up," and away he went, the regiment, brigade, and all of Wood's division following hard after, swarming over the lower breastworks with bayonets still at their deadly work. They paused but a moment before chasing the Confederates up a steep and rocky ravine. About halfway up the men stopped to rest a few moments. They began to realize the problem they faced: What to do next?

"To our great surprise the enemy ceased firing . . . and the 32-pound guns also ceased as there was great danger they would

[35] Illinois State Historical Library *Publications,* XXXV, 303.

strike us," related a field officer. "I never felt so lonesome in my life."[36] But to the left, Baird's flag-bearers could be seen advancing the colors, the regiments crawling after them like ants while Sheridan's men on the right were smashing through some thickly felled trees and over the rapidly vacated rifle-pits, halting but a moment to re-form before starting on. A bugler from Turchin's brigade sounded the charge, and the blue-clads started their rush in the center. An officer with Sheridan's division described the din and clamor of victory:

"Those defending the heights became more and more desperate as our men approached the top. They shouted 'Chickamauga' as though the word itself were a weapon; they thrust cartridges into guns by handsfull, they lighted the fuses of shells and rolled them down, they seized huge stones and threw them, but nothing could stop the force of the desperate charge and one after another the regimental flags were borne over the parapet and the ridge was ours. The finest battery . . . in the Southern army was there, the ramrods half-way down the guns when captured. These were whirled around and fired in the direction of the flying foe. . . . What yells and cheers broke from the panting, weary but triumphant ranks. They threw their haversacks in the air until it was a cloud of black spots; officers and men mingled indiscriminately in their joy."[37]

General Wood, in gay mood, was heard to threaten his men with arrest for winning a battle without orders; Thomas, shrugging off Grant's sharp inquiry, "By whose orders is this?" as the Cumberlanders went tearing up the slope, was smiling imperturbably below. What had been planned as merely a covering movement for Sherman shone out as the great triumph of the day, "one of the greatest miracles in military history," according to Charles A. Dana, ". . . as awful as a visible interposition of God."[38]

36 Military Order of the Loyal Legion of the U. S., District of Columbia Commandery, *War Papers*, LIV, 11.

37 L. G. Bennett, *The 36th Illinois*, 529.

38 *Official Records*, 1st Series, XXXI, Part 2, 69.

Thomas rode up to the top of the hill. "I fell among some of my old soldiers, who always took liberties with me—who commenced talking and giving their views of the victory," he related. "When I attempted to compliment them for the gallant manner in which they made the assault, one man very coolly replied: 'Why, General, we know that you have been training us for this race for the last three weeks.' "[39] Grant held himself aloof from the general elation. According to Hooker, he was heard to remark, "Damn the battle! I had nothing to do with it."[40] The unaccountable Sherman would not allow himself to be left out: "We outwitted Bragg and took Missionary Ridge," he telegraphed General Stephen A. Hurlbut at Memphis.

[39] Van Horne, *Thomas,* 426.
[40] Lewis, *Sherman,* 423.

XII
Marching with Sherman

UNION soldiers who slept on bleak Missionary Ridge on the night of November 25 suffered from a cold bed until three o'clock in the morning when they were called up for an early breakfast before starting a chase after Bragg. Shivering men filed into columns. While Hooker's Eleventh Corps coursed to the left to flank the Confederate line of retreat through Ringgold, Thomas marched the Fourteenth at a lively pace through Rossville and Chickamauga Valley, where thousands of bushels of corn and several tons of corn meal were found ablaze. Chary Scotch-Irish General Bragg had been conserving his supplies for the invasion that never came off, and he was never known to allow his soldiers much to eat. For miles the road was white with meal, spilled as the Confederates fled. Delayed by a burning bridge, Hooker ran into surprisingly tough resistance when he reached Ringgold on the twenty-seventh, losing several hundred men in a fruitless drive against barricades. He waited for his artillery to come up and then shelled the enemy for an hour or two, until General Grant arrived and ordered the pursuit stopped. Hooker had to be content with the seizure of a few-score wagonloads of forage, plus large ammunition stores and some enemy caissons. Thomas had somewhat better luck, taking three pieces of artillery and several hundred prisoners on the first day after surprising the enemy rear guard. Early on the twenty-seventh he overtook a battery commanded by a son of General Beauregard and had manned it with infantry as the order came to halt. Although Bragg got away safely again, the Federals had gathered up a total of 6,100 prisoners, 7,000 muskets, 40 cannon, and "several miles of wagons" during the Chattanooga campaign. Some of the ragged and ill-fed Rebels were not averse to capture, confessing themselves "tired of running and being hunted like wild beasts."[1]

Grant halted the chase after receiving a wire from Lincoln: "Well done, Many thanks. Remember Burnside." Longstreet was still hovering about Knoxville. To relieve Burnside's little army of 12,000, which was believed in distress for lack of food, Grant pushed Sherman, Howard, and Granger toward the city at a rapid pace. The troops marched with scanty provisions and no wagons and never once took off their clothes while racing eighty-five miles or more on separate roads. Sherman, who had been reluctant to use up his troops, was a little disgusted to find the former Army of the Potomac leader safely entrenched behind impregnable barricades and very well fixed for supplies, his pens filled with cattle and warehouses with grain, while Longstreet had retired to the hills to bind up his wounds. The plight of East Tennessee was beginning to be overexaggerated. Responding to a suggestion from Grant that he pursue Longstreet into South Carolina, Sherman wired back: "A stern chase is a long one," and was permitted to give his Tennesseans a rest.[2] While Howard returned to Chattanooga and Granger went to Nashville, which Grant was making his center of operations, Sherman's army took up winter quarters at Bridgeport and Huntsville, Alabama. Only Thomas and Hooker of the high command now remained at Chattanooga. Since Sherman had gone to his Ohio home for the holidays, General Howard suggested to Thomas that he take a brief leave, but the General demurred: "Something is sure to get out of order if I go away. It was always so, even when I commanded a post."[3] With food and forage still short, the railroads needing repair, Longstreet to be watched, and dozens of letters to be answered, there was quite enough to do.

No further promotion fell Thomas's way after Missionary Ridge nor did he expect one, although General Garfield, writing from Washington, said that Secretary Stanton believed he should become the new leader of the Army of the Potomac,

1 Jenkin Lloyd Jones, *An Artilleryman's Diary*, 144.
2 Lewis, *Sherman*, 328.
3 Oliver Otis Howard, *Autobiography*, I, 495–96.

graveyard of many hopes. "I told him I hoped he would go no further than yourself in selecting a new commander," Garfield wrote Thomas, but it was Grant, promoted to lieutenant general, who ultimately received the command. General Bragg, it was learned, had a new position—Confederate chief of staff with headquarters at Richmond. His successor as commander of the Army of Tennessee, General Joseph E. Johnston, was feeding and clothing the defeated Confederates at Dalton, Georgia, a mountain-girt railroad junction about forty miles southeast of Chattanooga.

Thomas spent Christmas Day surrounded by his favorite officers of the elite Fourteenth Corps—General Palmer, commanding; Richard W. Johnson, an old Second Cavalry hand; and the dependable Absalom Baird. Absent was Jefferson C. Davis, slayer of General William Nelson at Louisville and perhaps too profane a man for Thomas's taste. Neatly written invitations inscribed "R.S.V.P." had been dispatched by Thomas's nephew and aide, Captain Kellogg. When Palmer, the only non West Pointer present, jocosely complained that he did not know what the inscription meant, Thomas assured him that it was all the Captain's work and that he had never dreamed of such refinement. At the dinner table, Palmer recalled, "all was etiquette, all seated and served according to rank and the utmost decorum prevailed."[4] The officers enjoyed a good meal topped off with brandy and gave thanks that they were men and not horses, which were again on quarter feed and in pitiful condition. "There is no suffering so intense as theirs," wrote General John Beatty at this Christmas season. "They are driven with whip and spur, on half and quarter food, until they drop from exhaustion and are abandoned to die in the mudhole where they fall. . . . A man can give vent to his sufferings, he can ask for assistance, he can find some relief either in crying, praying, or cursing; but for the poor exhausted and abandoned beast there is no help, no relief, no hope."[5]

Lack of strong horses was the greatest weakness of the Federal Army at Chattanooga. Grain was almost unobtainable in

4 Palmer, *A Conscientious Turncoat*, 126–27.
5 Beatty, *Memoirs of a Volunteer*, 267.

the devastated West and the wintry country was bare of subsistance. The army was weakened also by the absence of men. Thousands of volunteer officers and soldiers were either leaving for good or taking the thirty-day furlough which had been granted all who would "veteranize," that is re-enlist for the duration. The government also considered it necessary to pay $400 bounties to fresh volunteers, many of whom promptly deserted their companies to re-enlist in other states, some several times over or until they were caught.

Some of the gaps were being filled by Negro troops, which had been enlisted for the past several months, particularly in the East, on an experimental basis. Although Sherman and General Jefferson Davis disapproved their use, Thomas, when asked, expressed the opinion that the government had a perfect right to employ them. But the Virginian went a little farther than most Northern officers whose views inclined to the utilitarian. "The Confederates regard them as property," he advised the War Office. "Therefore the Government can with propriety seize them as property and use them to assist in putting down the Rebellion. But if we have the right to use the property of our enemies, we share also the right to use them as we would all the individuals of any other civilized nation who may choose to volunteer as soldiers in our Army. I moreover think," Thomas added, "that in the sudden transition from slavery to freedom it is perhaps better for the negro to become a soldier, and be gradually taught to depend on himself for support, than to be thrown upon the cold charities of the world without sympathy or assistance."[6] The more typical view had been expressed by Grant in a letter to Lincoln: "By arming the negro we have added a powerful ally. They will make good soldiers, and taking them from the enemy weakens him in the same proportion they strengthen us."[7] Thomas was the most patient of instructors—he had taught Negroes from childhood, and he took more than a Yankee's pride and satisfaction in witnessing the progress of colored recruits under his own eye at Chattanooga.

The continued menace of Longstreet in East Tennessee

[6] Thomas letter dated November 18, 1863, Historical Society of Pennsylvania Library.

still worried the authorities at Nashville and Washington. Grant's scouts believed that he was being reinforced by Johnston, although Thomas, who was in a position to know, had seen no signs of any such move. But since Grant was under pressure from Governor Andrew Johnson, he asked Thomas to send 10,000 infantry plus David S. Stanley's division as soon as the East Tennessee and Georgia Railroad had been repaired. Thomas continued to urge on the work throughout January and early February, but there was a lack of iron rails and the laborers seemed more interested in stealing chickens. To replace the divisions scheduled to go to Knoxville, Grant ordered up most of John A. Logan's Fifteenth Corps from Huntsville, where the soldiers had wintered comfortably in warm houses. The reinforcement arrived on February 13, 1864, the very day Thomas had satisfied himself that the railroad was in running condition, but just as he was ready to move, Grant suddenly countermanded the order. The peril to East Tennessee had been somewhat magnified, and Grant now believed it more important to protect a movement by Sherman, who was sweeping across Mississippi from Vicksburg to Meridian, a useful Confederate railroad center and arsenal.

Although belated, the order was welcomed by Thomas, who knew Johnston was the man to be beaten. On February 14, the day that Sherman rolled into Meridian, he was asked to descend on Dalton to prevent reinforcements being sent General Polk, commanding in Mississippi. Johnston already had sent on William J. Hardee's corps, although by the time it was well on the way, Sherman had destroyed $50,000,000 worth of Confederate property in Meridian, according to his own account, or $5,000,000 at least, according to the Confederates. But while Sherman had deceived General Polk, who had thought he might be headed for Mobile, he started back to Vicksburg on the twentieth with his mission only half accomplished. Seven thousand Federal cavalrymen from Memphis, which Sherman had counted on to help him find and defeat Polk, had been waylaid and defeated by 4,000 of Forrest's men.

7 Grant to Lincoln, August 23, 1863, Nicolay and Hay, *Lincoln*, VI, 466; James Ford Rhodes, *History of the United States*, IV, 334–36.

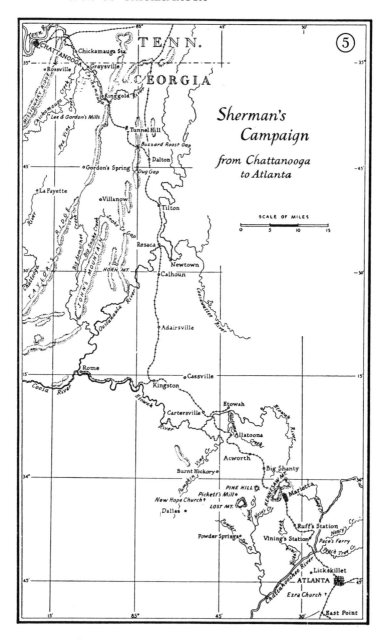

⑤

TENN.

GEORGIA

Sherman's
Campaign

from Chattanooga
to Atlanta

SCALE OF MILES
0   5   10   15

Chattanooga
Rossville
Chickamauga Sta.
Graysville
Ringgold
Lee & Gordon's Mills
Tunnel Hill
Buzzard Roost Gap
Gordon's Spring
Dalton
Dug Gap
La Fayette
Villanow
Tilton
Resaca
Newtown
Calhoun
HORN MT.
Adairsville
Rome
Cassville
Kingston
Cartersville
Etowah
Allatoona
Acworth
Burnt Hickory
Big Shanty
PINE HILL
New Hope Church
Pickett's Mill
Marietta
LOST MT.
Dallas
Ruff's Station
Powder Springs
Vining's Station
Pace's Ferry
Lickskillet
ATLANTA
Ezra Church
East Point

Despite the failure of Sherman's main plan, Grant considered that Thomas did not show up half so well in his stroke against Johnston. Handicapped by the lack of sound horses to haul the wagons and by his artillery limited to eighteen pieces, Thomas approached the fastness of Rocky Face Ridge and Buzzards Roost Gap on the twenty-fifth just in time to meet part of Hardee's corps returning from an interrupted march against Sherman. Thrown in with the divisions of Stewart, Walker, Cheatham, Stevenson, and Bate, plus Joe Wheeler's cavalry, this gave Johnston a preponderance of force against the four divisions which Thomas brought with him. A day of heavy skirmishing in the rocky vales and woods on both sides of the Gap convinced Thomas that it was impossible to carry precipitous Rocky Face Ridge by assault. Taking into account his limited transportation and artillery, the superiority of enemy cavalry, and the lack of subsistance in an area already stripped bare, Thomas decided independently to return to Chattanooga, which he reached late on the twenty-seventh, picking up two dispatches on the way. "It is of the utmost importance that the enemy should be held in full belief that an advance into the heart of the South is intended until the fate of General Sherman is fully known," warned the Commander-in-Chief. "The difficulties of supplies can be overcome by keeping your trains running between Chattanooga and your position. . . . Can't you draw teams from Bridgeport and Stevenson to send supplies to the front?"[8] But Thomas already had reconnoitered Johnston's force and drawn back the reinforcements being sent west against Sherman. Moreover, since the railroad to Knoxville had been repaired first, no trains were running south.

This was not precisely a meeting of minds. Although Thomas was correct in his strategy, his cool disposal of the situation did not set well with Grant. Apparently the Commander-in-Chief considered the Army of the Cumberland merely an auxiliary force to protect Sherman. Thomas, however, continued to shape his plans as the commander of an army which conceivably might be permitted to do something on its own account. Now that he had felt out Johnston's force and sur-

[8] *Official Records*, 1st Series, XXXII, Part 2, 480–81.

veyed the ground, he outlined plans for a march on Atlanta in the spring. "I believe if I can commence the campaign with the 14th and 4th corps in front, and with Howard's corps in reserve, that I can move along the line of the railroad and overcome all opposition as far, at least, as Atlanta," he notified Grant on February 28. "I should want a strong division of cavalry in advance."[9] However, since Sherman had the same idea and had been discussing it volubly all winter, Grant's choice of leaders could well be predicted. It was a time of great changes in the strategy of war. Summoned to Washington and appointed general-in-chief of all the armies in March, Grant returned west to mull over with Sherman the actual plans to be carried out. The two friends met at the Burnet House in Cincinnati. "We finally settled on a plan," Sherman related at the same place a quarter of a century later. "He was to go for Lee and I was to go for Joe Johnston. . . . It was the beginning of the end as Grant and I foresaw right here."[10]

The plan in rough detail was for Sherman to have top command of three armies—the Ohio, Tennessee, and Cumberland—the first two to form the wings, with the Cumberlanders in the center. The Ohio-born officers in their early thirties had been chosen to lead the flanking armies. James Birdseye McPherson, a handsome and gallant six-footer, number one in his class at West Point, took Sherman's place as commander of the Tennesseans. Burnside had been succeeded as Army of the Ohio leader first by General J. G. Foster, then by John M. Schofield, former commander of the Army of the Frontier in the Far West. Short and round-bodied, his beard long and sweeping, Schofield was an ambitious and restless character, just the man, it was thought, to command a fast-moving wing.

Naturally disappointed at being placed under Sherman, his junior in rank as major general of volunteers, Thomas uttered no word that was ever quoted by his officers, although they may have been partly responsible for a current rumor that he was dissatisfied. It was hardly likely that he relished being

9 Joint Committee on the Conduct of the War, *Supplemental Report,* I, 197.

10 Lewis, *Sherman,* 345.

placed under a volatile officer whom he had seen fail from lack of confidence in Kentucky and from overconfidence at Missionary Ridge. Guarding all roads north and south until Longstreet slipped off to rejoin General Lee in Virginia, Thomas continued to rebuild his cavalry and the railroad to Dalton, "Doorway of Georgia." He watched the daily progress of the colored troops in training and by April 5 reported six fully organized Negro regiments on duty, with three more organizing, plus a battery of light artillery. Another favorite project which he inspected nearly every day was a national cemetery for veterans laid out on the slopes of Orchard Knob. He had a prompt reply for an army chaplain who asked him if the soldiers' remains should be collected and buried in groups according to states: "No, no, no. Mix them up. Mix them up. I am tired of states-rights."[11]

The first of a campaign-long series of disagreements between Thomas and Sherman was threshed out early in April at Chattanooga. Knowing well the ground and the disposal of the enemy forces about Dalton, Thomas proposed to finish Johnston off in one stroke by a wide flanking movement through a gap which he knew to be unguarded below and to cut enemy communications between Dalton and Resaca, which lay fifteen miles beyond. "Let me take the Army of the Cumberland, move through Snake Creek Gap and get in the rear of Johnston," Thomas proposed. "He must come out and fight me, and I can whip him with the Army of the Cumberland alone. But . . . if he should get the better of me, you can come upon him with the Armies of the Tennessee and the Ohio and between us, we can rub him out. His men will take to the mountains, but he must abandon his artillery and trains, and there will be an end to the matter.

Sherman, however, was making his own plans. "No," he replied, "the Army of the Tennessee are better marchers than the Army of the Cumberland and I am going to send McPherson." Thomas said that on learning this, he put on his hat and

11 Van Horne, *Thomas*, 213.

returned to his quarters, "for I saw the game was up."[12] It was clear that if Johnston was to be caught, Sherman wanted McPherson to do it despite the common sense of Thomas's plan. Expertly trained and by far the most powerful of the three armies, the force under Thomas would number 61,000 men and 130 guns—two-thirds of the entire invading force—at the start of the campaign. Why not attack with the strongest force where the enemy was weakest and deliver a finishing blow? The proposed movement against Johnston, who would have only 53,-000 men when reinforced by Polk, would force him "either to retreat toward the east, through a difficult country, poorly supplied . . . or attack me, in which event I felt confident that my army was sufficiently strong to beat him," as Thomas later explained in his official report.[13] Nevertheless, although heeding Thomas's warning that neither Buzzards Roost Gap nor Dalton could be taken by direct assault, Sherman stuck to the original plan and selected McPherson's Tennesseans, who would number only 24,465 availables, for the vital flanking movement.

Grant and Sherman were concerting simultaneous movements against Lee and Johnston. While the Army of the Potomac was being patched up for Grant's Wilderness Campaign in Virginia, Sherman had more than a month to prepare. New rifles and guns came to Chattanooga, and fresh supplies and grain for animals whose ribs would have to be filled out before starting on the long campaign. Trains delivered hundreds more —horses, mules, hogs, and cattle. Late in April, General McPherson brought the long-haired and unshaven Tennesseans to Lee and Gordon's Mills by Chickamauga Creek; Thomas moved to Ringgold in the center with Schofield, marching from Knoxville, at his left. The armies stood in their positions and waited. Stores of food grew large; horses and mules were actually getting fat. Thomas had an experienced corps of engineers at hand to run the trains and repair damaged track.

Remembering how his wagon trains had bogged him down

12 John Watts De Peyster, "George H. Thomas," in Augustus C. Rogers, *Representative Men*, 569–70.

13 Joint Committee on the Conduct of the War, *Supplemental Report*, I, 201–202; Howard, *Autobiography*, I, 503.

on his march to Chattanooga during the previous fall, Sherman gave orders that no tents or baggage be carried en route—"only one change of clothing on our horses, or to be carried by the men and on pack animals by company officers; five days' bacon, 20 days' bread, ammunition, in quantity proportioned to our ability." The order was modified to some degree by most of the officers and was utterly ignored by Thomas and his staff, who would live in the style to which they were accustomed in a headquarters street with the General's big tent at the far end and five other tents in a row on each side. Most of the wagons, however, were filled with ammunition, officers being allowed space for only a tent fly, a small mess kit, and a few valises which might be tossed out en route. At the same time the men were burdened with extra ammunition—40 rounds in the cartridge box and 160 in the pocket—with all other equipment packed in haversacks or knapsacks and blanket rolls. From three to five days' supply of hard bread, pork, sugar, and coffee brought the burden to some thirty pounds per man to be carried in all kinds of weather and over all roads. Sherman estimated that his soldiers carried the equivalent of three hundred wagonloads of supplies on the march.[14]

Thomas consolidated the Eleventh and Twelfth Corps to form a new Twentieth with Hooker in command, and placed Howard over a newly organized Fourth Corps comprising the divisions of David S. Stanley, Thomas J. Wood, and John Newton, veteran of Gettysburg. On May 5 came the word "Ready" from Grant. A dozen aides raced about the camp with marching orders. "At daylight on the 6th the advance was sounded by the Army of the Cumberland like the explosion that blows up the dam," related Colonel J. S. Fullerton of Howard's corps.[15] Some 90,000 men and 254 cannon were rolling along. At Tunnel Hill, over which the wagon road twisted, the Cumberlanders fired the first gun early on the seventh. The entrenched pickets in front were quickly flanked and sent racing toward Buzzards Roost Gap with bullets whistling past their ears.

[14] Lewis, *Sherman*, 354; F. Y. Hedley, *Marching Through Georgia*, 79–80.

[15] Society of the Army of the Cumberland, 1893 Reunion, *Report*, 82.

The test of Sherman's strategy would come at Rocky Face Ridge, "a continuous craggy crest at least 500 feet high," split by Buzzards Roost. While McPherson slanted to the right to gain Snake Creek Gap, Thomas and Schofield were to hold Johnston in their front "at any cost." Thomas moved squarely up before the enemy's almost impregnable position; and on May 8, under cover of a morning fog, the Fourth and Fourteenth Corps threatened each side of Buzzards Roost, while Hooker's men mounted the steep sides of Chattogata Mountain and stormed the entrenchments of Dug Gap to the south. It was hard physical labor as well as bloody fighting. Howard's Fourth Corps drove up the side of Rocky Face, fighting with bayonets and clubbed muskets. A sweaty corporal transacted a bargain with some Confederates who were shoving boulders down from the heights—if they would only take a rest from their heavy work he would read to them the President's Amnesty Proclamation, which was agreed to and done.

Busily engaged on his front and flanks, Johnston gave no thought to Snake Creek Gap, which McPherson was approaching. Sherman, however, still seemed apprehensive. If Johnston spotted McPherson's move, the Ohioan would never get through. "Are you prepared to make an attack on Buzzards Roost Gap anyhow?" he asked Thomas that evening. Unwilling but dutiful, Thomas made his preparations to storm the heights. Soon after daylight he sent John Newton's division of the Fourth Corps, working with Schofield on the left, along the east side of the Ridge. A brigade under General Charles G. Harker drove up the eastern slope. "Harker fought up to and against stone walls, over the crest and down the east side of the mountain carrying the first line but with heavy loss," Fullerton related. "He got so near the enemy the men fought with clubbed muskets and hand-to-hand. Many were tumbled off the rocky palisades, falling . . . to the base of the perpendicular wall. On the east side impassable ravines stopped advancing troops. Other troops of the 4th Corps pressed up and southward along the mountain side toward Buzzards Roost Gap. In like manner, Hooker was fighting on Chattogata Mountain. Sherman, with anxious face and nervous actions, looked on."[16] A noonday dis-

Letter to the War Department from Thomas discussing the use of Negro soldiers

Courtesy The Historical Society of Pennsylvania

patch from McPherson arrived. News that he had passed through Snake Creek Gap with only a brigade of Confederate cavalry in his front caused Sherman to exclaim excitedly: "Mc-Pherson is through the Gap. Johnston's army is mine." Thomas was ordered to send one of Hooker's divisions to push through the Gap while the frontal attack was renewed in full fury to keep Johnston busy. Five more assaults were made and turned back as Confederate sharpshooters on the heights picked off their men. None of this would help McPherson. Once through the Gap, he had been stopped in his tracks by 4,000 Confederate cavalry; unable to reach the railroad, he retired at dusk to the protection of Snake Creek and started digging in.

Thousands of men had been sacrificed and Sherman's pride hurt. Thomas suggested next morning that Howard fortify his position in front of Buzzards Roost while he sent Hooker's corps to support McPherson, but Sherman, who disliked Hooker, was not disposed to accept this plan immediately. Johnston, meantime, had hurried three divisions under Hood to Resaca, which, indeed, was not yet threatened. After a long debate with Thomas over two alternative plans of action, one to cut loose from the railroad and move the whole army on the same objective point, Sherman belatedly decided to push his main force through Snake Creek Gap, leaving Howard, as Thomas had suggested, in his entrenchments in front of Buzzards Roost. Operations, however, had been delayed while Sherman was making up his mind. Early on the eleventh, the Twentieth Corps took up the march, followed by Schofield's troops and the rest of Thomas's army, while the Fourth Corps remained behind to watch Johnston. Placed on his guard, Johnston slipped away in the dark, moving rapidly back to Resaca, where he quickly fortified a strong position. Sherman realized that he had thrown away his chance. "Such an opportunity," he said after thinking it over, "does not occur twice in a single life."[17]

Johnston stood off the Federals for five days at Resaca, the Cumberlanders in front reporting 3,500 casualties; the Army of the Ohio, 840; and McPherson's Tennesseeans, less than 400.

16 *Ibid.*, 86.
17 Military Society of Massachusetts, *Papers*, VIII, 394; X, 188–89.

Although deploring the frontal assaults, Thomas was satisfied that his army, rated a good first in discipline and instruction, was fighting well. For the better part of a day, black and white signal flags waved between the headquarters of Division Commander Stanley, Corps Commander Howard, and the ranking General in a discussion of what should be done with a line captain, under arrest for some minor indiscretion, who refused to go to the rear. The answer, finally, came from Thomas: "Restore him to duty, and if he behaves well as a soldier in battle, I will take care of the charges." The discussion did not have to be renewed again.[18]

The contest of movement rolled southward, the armies skirmishing every day until dark. The Federals made faster progress after leaving Resaca. On May 17, Sherman approached Adairsville, halfway point to Atlanta. After skirmishing until twilight, the Cumberlanders prepared to rush the works early the next day, but McPherson and Schofield hung closely to the enemy flanks and forced a retreat before daybreak. Again, at Rome, Kingston, and Cassville, the rapidly moving columns of Schofield and McPherson touched Johnston's side and rear, while the powerful Thomas threatened in front, giving the Confederate leader no choice but to retreat across the Etowah River, burning his bridges behind him.

Sherman had now learned his lesson. Skirting two mountain ranges which blocked his path at Allatoona, he left the railroad and slid off to the right, aiming at the little town of Dallas, a road junction twenty miles west of Marietta, Johnston moving out and extending his entrenchments to keep his line opposed. The Cumberlanders bivouacked on the twenty-fourth at Burnt Hickory, "as desolate, rocky, dreary, and forbidding a resting place as ever sheltered an army," according to Captain Henry Stone, of Thomas's staff.[19] Next morning Thomas came up to Hooker, who was attacking a bridge fire at Pumpkin Vine Creek. No one as yet scented danger, but while the rest of the army was miles away on two other roads, Johnston's cavalry had spotted the movement and the Confederate

18 Isaac H. C. Royse, *History of the 115th Illinois,* 299.
19 Military Society of Massachusetts, *Papers,* VIII, 408.

line had been extended squarely in front. Hooker's leading division, commanded by J. W. Geary, ran into skirmishers and deployed in the woods. From the enemy side, Stewart's division of Hood's corps rushed upon the right. When prisoners were taken to be questioned by Thomas, they let it be known that Hardee's and Polk's corps were not far away.

The Confederate fire was growing hotter on that bright, cloudless day. Mindful of the mental attitudes of men under fire, Thomas believed it necessary to put on a bold front. He summoned Captain Stone and told him "almost in a whisper," as that officer related, "to ride back to Howard as fast as I could and hurry up the 4th Corps." Stone dashed off at a gallop only to be called back and cautioned to walk his horse until out of sight of the troops. As he started off more circumspectly, "there was a sudden outburst of musketry, kept up for some time, which filled me with dread." Reaching Howard on a narrow, dusty road six miles in the rear, Stone anxiously bade him hurry along, only to be told that a faster pace would use up the men. Stone then found General Alpheus S. Williams of Howard's corps in an open field and persuaded him to put some life into his column. Riding back to Thomas, he ran into Sherman, who was on his horse by the roadside, "showing great impatience." Sherman had a message for Thomas from McPherson, which he endorsed on the back, saying "somewhat testily and fretfully: 'Let Williams go in anywhere as soon as he gets up. I don't see what they are waiting for in front now. There haven't been twenty rebels there today?' "[20] But after Williams arrived to relieve the pressure on Hooker and Geary, the "twenty Rebels" plus a few more accounted for nearly 800 of his men in the first twenty minutes of fighting, while the stubborn Geary lost more than 500.

This slashing frontal engagement, the Battle of New Hope Church, ended for the day amidst a heavy thunderstorm which drenched the fighters and the suffering wounded, "greatly increasing the ghastly horror of the scene. It continued to pour till long after dark," as Stone related, "while tired soldiers . . . were doggedly making their way to the front through mud and

[20] *Ibid.*, 409.

water up to their knees or dropping exhausted by the roadside where they were often trampled on by the horses of bewildered staff officers. . . . Houses along the road were transformed into hospitals. Great bonfires were lighted in every yard to give light for the surgeons to carry on their work. . . . It was a weird, horrid picture, and the very heavens seemed to be in sympathy with the apparent confusion." Although Thomas was thankful for the shovels and axes which had saved Geary, Sherman still seemed nettled and dissatisfied because the army had stopped to entrench.

Thomas had entrenched because he felt that he had no alternative against a superior enemy force. Responsive to the feelings of his men, he had exerted himself to prevent uneasiness and panic. He taught himself something new, however, when a heavy cannonade dropped some balls around his headquarters street, causing him to shift his trains to a more protected spot. Seeing that the movement caused a flutter of nervousness among the men who were watching him, "he declared he would never do so again whatever the consequence might be to himself," according to one of his admirers. "As soon as he was settled down once more," continued Colonel John Watts DePeyster, "he began to speak on the art of castrametation, and said the world had never improved upon the camping arrangements of Moses."[21]

It took three more days of maneuvering and fighting to get a firm grip on Johnston. Early on May 27, Sherman ordered Howard's corps to seek out the enemy right flank and attack it. Pushing through thickets and across ridges and ravines, Howard was unable to find it, for Johnston was busily pushing his entrenchments all the way back to Pine Hill, bordering the railroad. The search for the end of the enemy line took nearly all day. About three-thirty in the afternoon, the Confederates on the other side of the line near Dallas opened an assault against the Army of the Tennessee supported by Davis of the Fourteenth Corps. Transmitting the order through Thomas, Sherman then gave the word for a frontal attack on the enemy

21 John Watts De Peyster, *Major General George H. Thomas* (pamphlet), 9.

right. Howard plowed through woods and brush for miles. Believing he had finally reached the end of Johnston's line, he
threw in Wood's division at five-thirty o'clock only to buckle
against strong entrenchments in his front. "A drawing back of
the trenches like a traverse had deceived us," Howard explained.
"Johnston had forestalled us and was on hand fully prepared."[22]
Against the alerted divisions of Hindman and Cleburne which
occupied that sector, General Wood lost "over 800 killed in a
few minutes" in this Battle of Pickett's Mill. Howard felt a shell
fragment slice its way through the sole of his boot and thought
for a moment that he had lost his left leg.[23]

Supported by Johnson's division, Wood made a fight of
it but had to retire shortly before ten o'clock to save his weakened flanks. Campfires revealed the woods full of wounded. The
Confederate assault near Dallas also failed against extended
Federal entrenchments. Enough ground had been gained at
Pickett's Mill for Sherman to continue moving his army toward
the railroad while McPherson occupied the ground previously
held by Hooker and Howard. It had been a difficult trap to
escape from. The battered Army of the Cumberland suffered
more than 3,000 casualties in and around New Hope Church;
summing up his losses as of May 31, Thomas reported 8,426
killed, wounded, and missing during the three weeks of campaigning, almost four times as many as among the other armies
combined.[24]

[22] Howard, *Autobiography*, I, 553.

[23] *Ibid.*, 535.

[24] Society of the Army of the Cumberland, 1893 Reunion, *Report*, 110;
Piatt, *Thomas*, 537.

XIII

Hood Escapes, Atlanta Falls

IT required 113 days for Sherman to get to Atlanta. After-
the start of the campaign on May 6, 1864, marches grew
shorter as heavy rains set in early in June, and for several
days the army waited. The enemy was constantly being reinforced by volunteers, many of them state guardsmen attended
by Negro servants and fighting in their best civilian clothes.
Johnston's force was gradually increased to 70,000 men. Hard-
working engineers kept one jump ahead of the Confederate
Army, laying down miles of entrenchments on each side of the
railroad and along designated lines of retreat. For the pursuing
Federals, the natural barriers presented no such problem as did
the man-made defenses, the piled-up dirt and slashings, the
sharpened branches of trees with points laid outward—Napo-
leon's abatis—the devilishly tangled chevaux-de-frise which had
to be flattened before cavalry could pass; the fascines, gabions,
and sandbags.

Thomas traced the course of the Army of the Cumberland
in a summary of operations from Dalton to Jonesboro, curtain-
raiser on the fall of Atlanta:

"Operations about Dalton, May 7–13; battle of Resaca,
May 14–15; action at Cassville, May 20; actions about New
Hope Church near Dallas, May 25–28; actions about Pine Hill,
June 15–16; at Mud and Nose's Creeks, June 17–19; at Culp's
Farm, June 22; battles of Kenesaw Mountain, June 27–29; at
Ruff's Station, July 4; crossing Chattahoochee River, July 12–
17; battle of Peach Tree Creek, July 19–21; siege of Atlanta,
July 22–September 2; battle of Jonesboro, September 1."[1]

[1] Society of the Army of the Cumberland, 1884 Reunion, *Report*, 38–47.

218

Three of the battles mentioned followed disagreements between Sherman and Thomas regarding tactics, and only the action at Peach Tree Creek was brought on by enemy assault. The Army of the Tennessee alone was concerned in two more battles. Although Sherman has been credited with skill as a flanker, nevertheless it was Thomas who annihilated the Confederate Army after receiving an independent command. On the march to Atlanta, Thomas was subject to orders from an officer generally regarded as not gifted at tactics, a commander-in-chief who later characterized himself as "scared as hell" for what the enemy might do out of his sight.[2] Thomas's admirers contended that for the distance covered and the forces opposed, two or three battles could have finished the Atlanta Campaign had Old Pap been the leader. The first opportunity to destroy the Confederate Army by flank attack had certainly been lost at Dalton and Resaca. Other favorable opportunities were to arise near Atlanta and were apparently thrown away.

About the first of June, two divisions of Federal cavalry occupied Allatoona Pass, now far in the Confederate rear. Johnston quit his position before New Hope Church and took up a prepared line around Pine Hill. McPherson dashed east to Acworth and followed the railroad down. Whittling away at distance, Thomas moved at his right with Schofield taking the right flank in place of McPherson. The Georgia mud was deep after the heavy rains, the water standing in pools. Thomas still clung to his eleven Sibley tents for the accommodation of himself and his staff on headquarters street. His adjutant general's wagon, the most complete in the military service, was fitted out with numerous pigeonholes and covered with an immense fly.

General Sherman would rein up his horse in front of the array of tents and ask, "Whose quarters are these?"

"General Thomas's, general."

"Oh yes, Thomastown—Thomasville, a very pretty place, appears to be growing rapidly."[3]

Observing that Sherman, with one old wall tent and a few flies, was living too Spartan a life for a commanding officer in

2 Lewis, *Sherman*, 424.
3 David P. Conyngham, *Sherman's March Through the South*, 40–41.

inclement weather, Thomas ordered a company of Ohio sharp-shooters to pitch new tents for general headquarters use, a service accepted for the duration of the campaign.[4]

After making the railroad safe, the Federals wormed through Big Shanty south of Acworth. Thomas inclined to the right and ran into Johnston's works on the east side of Pine Hill, breaking through and over after a two-day struggle. Railroad trains filled with supplies and bringing reinforcements for McPherson pushed through Allatoona. The sound of locomotive whistles signaled distance gained and that all was well behind. McPherson was joined by two divisions of the Seventeenth Corps of Tennesseans, 9,000 men under Frank P. Blair, Jr. of Missouri. Keeping west of the railroad, the Cumberlanders crossed Mud Creek Valley and Nose's Creek under artillery fire. Both sides were entrenching daily in the slow advance and retreat toward Kennesaw Mountain at a pace which sorely tried the impatient Sherman.

On June 18, from headquarters at Big Shanty, he sent a private letter to General Grant: ". . . My chief source of trouble is with the Army of the Cumberland which is dreadfully slow. A fresh furrow in a plowed field will stop the entire column and all begin to entrench. I have again and again tried to impress on Thomas that we must assail and not defend . . . and yet it seems that the whole Army of the Cumberland is so habituated to be on the defensive that . . . I cannot get it out of their heads."[5] Sherman also complained that Thomas had ignored his orders to leave his heavy baggage behind. Altogether, he made out a pretty good case against the commander of his largest force, and Grant would readily believe that Thomas was slow. Doubtless it was in this fixed belief that Grant published the letter for the world to read.

Sherman's restlessness and impatience came to a head as the Federals stood before the heights of Big and Little Kennesaw, which Johnston had fortified with every art at his command. There the Confederate leader waited at the top of his solid ramparts crowned with cannon, obviously ground to avoid.

4 Van Horne, *Thomas*, 230.
5 Piatt, *Thomas*, 534.

Elsewhere, however, the Confederate line had been thinned as it spread out toward Schofield on the right. Thomas could not help but suggest that McPherson could sweep past and attack Marietta, the next large town, from the north. Certainly Johnston could not place much of a force on McPherson's front without exposing his flank to Schofield. The situation was not dissimilar to that at Snake Creek Gap, save that McPherson now had 9,000 more men, but Sherman was in a mood for a frontal attack.

General John A. Logan of the Fifteenth Corps of Tennesseans, who happened to be at headquarters, thought he divined the reason. Sherman, he said, had been reading a newspaper which described Grant's head-on assaults against Lee's entrenched positions in Virginia. The newspapers naturally took notice inasmuch as the Wilderness Campaign, Spottsylvania Court House, North Anna, and Cold Harbor had cost the Federals 65,000 men. According to Logan, Sherman observed that the "whole attention of the country was fixed on the Army of the Potomac and that his army was entirely forgotten. Now it would fight. Tomorrow he would order the assault." When McPherson protested that Johnston could as well be flanked, Sherman replied that "it was necessary to show that his men could fight as well as Grant's."[6] The order went out on the twenty-fifth, two days before the time set.

As Thomas read it carefully, he observed to William D. Whipple, his adjutant general, "This is too bad."

"Why don't you send a written protest against the assault?" Whipple inquired.

"I have protested so often against such things that if I protest again Sherman will think I don't want to fight," rejoined Thomas. "But he knows my views."[7]

Nature had nothing to contribute to easing an impossible task. On June 26, the day before the battle, Thomas made a reconnaissance with Captain Stone to select a likely point of attack, riding almost within the enemy's picket line. "During that entire search of almost half a day I did not see one place

6 Lewis, Sherman, 375.
7 Society of the Army of the Cumberland, 1893 Reunion, Report, 118.

that seemed to me to afford the slightest prospect of success," Stone related. "The place finally selected was chosen more because the lines were nearer each other than because the enemy's line seemed vulnerable."[8] Thomas called upon Newton's division of the Fourth Corps and Davis's of the Fourteenth to make the assault, while the Fifteenth Corps of Logan was chosen by General McPherson. The soldiers wrote their letters home and slept fitfully in their tents during a warm and sticky night. Although Sherman was a talented leader of men, the Cumberlanders were still distrustful of a general who had yet to win a battle on his own responsibility. Thomas made two visits to headquarters that evening despite what he had said to Whipple.

Early on the twenty-seventh the sun rose in a murky blaze. The June days were hot, "awful hot," according to Major James A. Connolly of the Fourteenth Corps. "Why Ohio is an icehouse compared with Georgia in June."[9] The temperature that day reached 110 degrees. At 9:00 A.M., two hundred Federal cannon began to hurl iron at the Confederate works on Little Kennesaw. "Gun spoke to gun, Kennesaw smoked and blazed with fire, a volcano as grand as Etna," wrote Colonel Fullerton, Howard's adjutant general. "It seemed as though the whole earth was upheaving, that a grand explosion and then a downward crash would come. . . . Trees and houses fell before the cyclone."[10] The bombardment was all too brief, lasting only fifteen minutes. General Charles G. Harker of Newton's division took position in the woods, exhorting his troops. Colonel Dan McCook, former law partner of Sherman, recited Horatius' "Oration at the Bridge" to his men.

Resolution for the task ahead stiffened the ranks. As the cannon fire was silenced, the infantry columns raced toward the Confederate salient high above them. Thinned as they advanced, the brigades of McCook, Harker, John G. Mitchell, and George D. Wagner threaded the Confederate fire, threw aside the fallen trees, and broke down the palings before the first

8 Military Society of Massachusetts, *Papers*, VIII, 480.
9 Illinois State Historical Library *Publications*, XXXV, 342.
10 Society of the Army of the Cumberland, 1893 Reunion, *Report*, 119.

breastworks. Lethal rifle bullets and canister cascaded down thickly. Harker's men staggered and fell back, but the survivors were rallied and again led to the foot of the parapet. A few exhausted soldiers were left to plant their regimental colors on top of the Confederate works, where they were almost hopelessly outnumbered. A color sergeant shot a Confederate officer and received twenty-four balls in his body. General Harker lost an arm and soon died. When McCook was fatally wounded, his next in rank lived only a few minutes after taking over the command. Only Colonel Mitchell of Davis's corps succeeded in holding his sector of the Confederate line. The survivors among the other brigades withdrew in good order, however, seeking the protection of rocks and stumps on the mountainside while holding the Rebels closely to their works.

The troops in reserve below had been watching the assaulting column "with eager eyes, their bodies as well as their minds strained to the utmost tension," wrote Captain Stone, who stood at Thomas's side. "For an instant, as the wild cheering at the first encounter came to us it looked like success but almost as quickly the continuous cheering subsided into individual cries —and then a dread silence which told only of death and utter failure."[11] His field glass sharply focused on the smoke-wreathed mountain, Thomas was angrily muttering: "Too bad, too bad." "Do you think you can carry any part of the enemy's line today?" Sherman captiously inquired at 10:30 A.M. Thomas gravely reported his casualties among the officers. "The troops are all too much exhausted to advance but we hold all that we have gained."[12]

Nearly every colonel of McCook's brigade had been killed or wounded, and the Fourteenth Corps alone had suffered nearly 2,000 casualties. Attacking a slope less steep about a mile away, Logan found the going somewhat easier, losing only 500 men and gaining one hundred yards more ground, according to Sherman, who so reminded General Palmer of the Fourteenth the next day. A hundred more men were alive than there would

---

11 Military Society of Massachusetts, *Papers*, VIII, 480.
12 Van Horne, *Thomas*, 234.

have been had they gone as far as Logan, Palmer retorted, his temper flaring.[13]

As reserves rushed up with entrenching tools, the Cumberlanders dug in. "Davis's two brigades are now within sixty yards of the enemy's entrenchments," Thomas notified Sherman at 1:45 P.M. "Davis reports that he does not think he can carry the works by assault on account of the steepness of the hill, but he can hold his position, put in one or two batteries tonight, and probably drive them out tomorrow morning. General Howard reports the same. . . . From what the officers tell me, I do not think we can carry the works by assault from this point to-day, but they can be approached by saps and the enemy driven out."

Sherman's dispatches implied that the Cumberlanders had been found wanting in carrying out their assigned task. "The assault of the enemy's works was well arranged, and the officers and men went to their work with the greatest coolness and gallantry," Thomas replied firmly. "The failure . . . is due only to the strength of the works, and to the fact that they were well manned. . . . Both Generals Howard and Palmer think that they can find favorable positions on their lines for placing batteries for enfilading the enemy's works. We took between ninety and one hundred prisoners."[14]

If Sherman was determined on taking Kennesaw, he had only to adopt the recommended method of approaching from trench to trench with the aid of artillery. This the persistent Grant would have done. "I'm more nervous than he is," Sherman once said in comparing himself with his chief. "I am much more likely to change my orders or to countermarch my command than he is."[15] Sherman acted according to his character. Studying the casualty reports that evening, he decided to withdraw the troops on the mountain, issuing orders for a movement around the enemy left flank, which indeed could have been made at the outset. This satisfied Thomas, who promptly replied, "What force do you think of moving with? If with the greater part of the army, I think it decidedly better than butting

13 Palmer, *A Conscientious Turncoat,* 141–42.
14 Van Horne, *Thomas,* 235.
15 Lewis, *Sherman,* 375.

against breastworks twelve feet thick and strongly abatised."

Sherman would never admit his mistake. In a report of the campaign written two and one-half months later, he justified the assault on Little Kennesaw in this wise: "Failure as it was . . . I yet claim it produced good fruits as it demonstrated to General Johnston that I would assault, and that boldly."[16] Safely entrenched behind fortified breastworks, Johnston could wish for nothing better. "One or two more such assaults," Thomas had insisted on the day of the battle, "would use up this army." Still Sherman had come a long way since the early days of the conflict. While he was wont to magnify the strength of the enemy two or three times over as the war opened in Kentucky, on a front where his power was sure he could not accept the fact that a dangerous enemy yet lay in front of him.

Hacking at Johnston's flank while swinging around Kennesaw, the Federals were eager to cross the Chattahoochee River, a rain-swollen stream only a few miles outside the fortress of Atlanta. At Ruff's Station, halfway between Marietta and the river, a line of Confederate barricades awaited the invaders, and even more elaborate entrenchments were in place above the north bank where Johnston was collecting his wagon trains. Sherman issued vehement orders to catch Johnston before he reached the river or "in the act of crossing." On July 2, after waiting for supply trains to come up, the Cumberlanders dashed ahead and overtook the enemy rear guard below Marietta. The Confederate line proved stubborn. Heavy skirmishing occupied Thomas all the way to Ruff's Station, where early on the Fourth of July he ordered Howard's corps to strengthen skirmish lines and rush a three-ply row of rifle-pits in front. Sherman rode up impatiently as the army prepared for action. "Johnston is crossing the Chattahoochee," he informed Howard. "There is nothing in front of you but skirmishers."[17] Howard opined that a "bad accident" might occur if he rushed out ahead but promised, "We will hurry." After the artillery came up, the lines of skirmishers moved along followed by Sherman, who left his

[16] *Official Records,* 1st Series, XXXVIII, Part 4, 60.
[17] Society of the Army of the Cumberland, 1898 Reunion, *Report,* 123.

horse behind and walked on foot down the main road. Howard's men crossed a field and came to a wood where, as Colonel Fullerton related, "a rattling fusillade of musketry and artillery fire opened on our lines. I looked back at the road not a quarter of a mile distant and saw the commander-in-chief making more than double-quick time down the road . . . in search of his horse."[18]

The artillery hammered briskly at the rifle-pits, and the troops swarmed over. Confederate uniforms stuffed with straw were discovered guarding a rail fence; a soldier dived in a tackle and started a boisterous game of football.[19] Only one more line of entrenchments—Johnston's ninth since Dalton—stood between the Federals and the Chattahoochee River. All three columns were now west of the railroad. Temporarily posted on Thomas's right, McPherson encamped on Nickajack Creek while Schofield was placed in reserve several miles back at Smyrna. Johnston's line above the Chattahoochee accordingly extended far to the Federal right; but since little ground was fortified east of the railroad, Sherman had only to side-step in that direction. He therefore adopted the wise course of sending McPherson around on a long punitive expedition to the factory town of Roswell, which lay about twenty miles northeast of the railroad as the river coursed; Thomas likewise slanted eastward, throwing up breastworks in his front. Despite Sherman's dislike for protective fortifications, the Cumberlanders were not going to be caught by surprise.

The army of the center made a great noise on July 5 after crossing a wide, wooded valley and gaining a high bluff near Vining's Station. Only eight miles distant across the Chattahoochee the spires of Atlanta were in sight. Major Connolly was thrilled to his bones, hurrying word home: "Mine eyes have beheld the promised land! . . . There lay the beautiful 'Gate City' in full view. . . . In a very few moments Generals Sherman and Thomas were with us . . . and the two veterans, for a moment, gazed at the glittering prize in silence. I watched the two noble soldiers—Sherman stepping nervously about, his eyes

[18] *Ibid.*, 124; Howard, *Autobiography*, 596–97.
[19] Henry F. Perry, *History of the 38th Indiana*, 143.

sparkling and his face aglow. . . . Thomas stood there like a noble old Roman, calm, soldierly, dignified; no trace of excitement about that grand old soldier who had ruled the storm at Chickamauga. Turning quietly to my General [Palmer] he said: 'Send up a couple of guns and we'll throw some shells over there,' pointing to some heavy timber across the river."[20]

Two miles across, on the south bank, Johnston's untiring engineers had constructed another line of fortified works, but these extended eastward in the direction of McPherson. The line just over the north side of the river was still intact. Mulling over the situation next day, Sherman got word that a detachment of Thomas's cavalry, escorting McPherson, had entered Roswell and burned the largest woolen factory in the South. It seemed the proper course to continue moving in this direction. Schofield therefore was ordered to make a sweep from Smyrna to the mouth of Soap Creek, halfway between Thomas's position and Roswell, where a crossing could be made. Keeping connection with Schofield, Wood's division of the Fourth Corps moved in that direction and located a ford near Pace's Ferry. While Wood and Schofield made their crossings, Thomas occupied Johnston with frontal attacks until, on July 9, the Confederate leader discovered that his flank was again threatened. The Confederates picked up their property and abandoned the elaborate works that night, burning their bridges behind them. Trains from Chattanooga brought Thomas new-type pontoons for bridges—tight canvas boats to supplant the easily punctured India-rubber pontoons.[21] Taking all precautions against surprise, Thomas saw that Wood got over safely on the left and followed him with most of the main army on July 17.

Only two more lines of fortifications now lay between Sherman and Atlanta. If Johnston was to hold the Federals in check, he would have to fight, although doubt existed among the Confederate high command that he so intended. The strain of the campaign was proving too great for Jefferson Davis and the general staff at Richmond. There had been endless newspaper criticism, Cabinet pressure, visits from citizen delegations, and

20 Illinois State Historical Library *Publications* XXXV, 346.
21 Henry Hitchcock, *Marching With Sherman*, 118.

letters from army officers, notably Lieutenant General John B. Hood, who had campaigned with Johnston all the way from Dalton and who now complained that his commander had "lost 20,000 men without having fought a decisive battle."

Although the Confederate Army had been capably handled and was still confident of its ability to trap Sherman before he reached Atlanta, a written exchange of views between Davis and Johnston failed to satisfy the President. Sounding out General Lee about Hood's merits, Davis was advised that General Hardee, second in command, possessed more experience in handling an army. Chief of Staff Bragg, however, was already on the ground. Bragg advised Davis on July 15 that Hood "would give unlimited satisfaction," which was all too true if the Federal view were taken into account. Headlines blazed on July 18: "Hood Supplants Johnston."

After reading the news in an Atlanta paper, Sherman tossed a few questions at Schofield, who had known Hood at West Point. The new Confederate commander, Sherman learned, "was bold even to rashness and courageous in the extreme," an estimation shared also by Thomas, who had known Hood as a Second Cavalry lieutenant.[22] There existed no doubt that Hood was courageous and martial. A wound at Gettysburg had deprived him of the use of his left arm, and a leg had been amputated after Chickamauga. Every morning he had to be strapped into his saddle, but he was still fiery and aggressive at thirty-three. Sherman passed along word that the change meant fight. At last the Rebels would come out from behind their bristling fortifications.

But the change was not welcomed in the Confederate camp. According to a Mississippi lieutenant who wrote a letter home that day, "Hood is the most unpopular Gen¹ in the army & some of the troops are swearing they will not fight under him. Brig Gen¹s Cols and company officers have been called together to forestall anything like an outbreak . . . & all regret that Johnston is gone."[23]

Losing little time, the belligerent Confederate leader plan-

[22] Sherman, *Personal Memoirs*, II, 72.
[23] Wiley, *Life of Johnny Reb*, 241.

GENERAL JOHN B. HOOD

ned to attack the Cumberlanders first. With McPherson and Schofield both far to the left, the former headed toward Decatur, Hood decided to take advantage of a gap existing between Schofield and Thomas. After annihilating Thomas's command, he could envelop the other two armies in turn. The scheme was well devised. McPherson and Schofield were engaged in railroad-destroying expeditions, and Sherman expected that Hood would attack them first to protect his line of communication with South Carolina. Sherman called upon Howard to take two of his divisions to the left and partially fill the gap. This would leave Thomas, Sherman advised Old Slow Trot on the nineteenth, free "to walk into Atlanta." Howard went to Thomas early next morning to make sure his assigned position was correct. It was according to orders, Thomas reminded him. "We must act independently," he said with a smile.[24]

Thomas said good-bye to Howard and swung two miles to the left, leaving only Newton of the Fourth Corps on the direct road to Atlanta. Crossing Peach Tree Creek that day, Thomas advised Sherman about noontime that Davis was skirmishing with the enemy on the right flank, while the corps of Palmer and Hooker and Newton's division were advancing one mile beyond the south bank. Newton encountered skirmishers and at once began to entrench on a ridge, raising a rail barricade. With Hood on the loose somewhere in front, the situation, he remarked to Thomas, had an "ugly look." But no one seemed to know what Hood might be doing or what his plans were. To deceive Sherman, Hood had detailed Joe Wheeler with 2,500 cavalrymen to hold Schofield and McPherson in check, throwing in Cheatham's corps to widen the gap between the Federal left and right. Delayed while Cheatham tardily got into position, the Confederate commander launched his assault on Thomas's depleted force at 4:00 P.M.

"Yelling like furies . . . like wild beasts let loose," racing masses of gray-clads poured out of the woods and covered the open ground in front.[25] The Cumberlanders faced greater peril now than at any other time in the campaign. Newton, scenting

24 Howard, *Autobiography*, I, 607.
25 Society of the Army of the Cumberland, 1893 Reunion, *Report*, 130.

danger, had stopped to entrench, a move in which Thomas concurred, but since the army had been given the all-clear signal by Sherman, most of Palmer's and Hooker's corps were breezing along. The onset of the attack fell mostly on Newton, fortunately, spreading to Hooker who was next in line, but the Confederates had concentrated 30,000 troops against some 20,000 on Thomas's left flank. It was for the artillery, which had been trained for such moments, to save the army. Hastily assembling all available guns along Newton's line, Thomas urged on the horses, as they raced past, with blows of the hand. He directed the fire in person, pouring shells, canister, and solid shot into the Confederate ranks; but the impetus of the attack could not be halted. Colonel Benjamin Harrison's brigade was flanked right and left on the ridge, and although he received permission to withdraw if he wished, the grandson of "Old Tippecanoe" declared, "Here we shall stay."[26] Racing past Newton, William B. Bate's division of gray-clads wheeled around in the rear with seemingly nothing to oppose them.

Hurrying to Hooker, Thomas gathered up the batteries of the Twentieth Corps and double-shotted them with canister. Sweating Federal gunners decimated Bate's men at short range. The Rebels retreated, re-formed, and were again driven back. For a third time the attack was renewed while Hardee and Stewart drove into Hooker's line in front. Messages from Sherman began to arrive, the first reiterating orders of the nineteenth for a forward movement, since there were "none of the enemy's troops between Peach Tree Creek and Atlanta."[27] The battle was still hot when a more subdued note arrived from the Commander-in-Chief: "I have been with Howard and Schofield all day and one of my staff is just back from McPherson. All report the enemy in their front so strong that I was in hopes none was left for you."[28] Nothing was said about any reinforcements, and Thomas continued his battle without relief.

Artillery raced farther to the right, and Hood plumbed for weak spots in the Federal line. The darting flame of cannon

26 *Ibid.*
27 Van Horne, *Thomas*, 245.
28 *Official Records*, 1st Series, XXXVIII, Part 4, 196.

fire was cleaving the dusk as Hardee, Stewart, and Bate sought the shelter of the entrenchments Johnston had built, leaving a frightful slaughter behind them. Hood's loss as estimated by Confederate sources was 5,000 killed, wounded, and missing, but no report was ever made. The Army of the Cumberland, according to Colonel Fullerton, lost 1,699 killed and wounded, which is perhaps a conservative figure since Hooker's corps and a part of Palmer's had fought in the open. But the army had never doubted its victory. Two soldiers recalled glimpses of Thomas at Peach Tree Creek. Observing Thomas's expression as a clue to how the battle might be going, General Newton saw him "calm and resolute" as he directed the artillery fire and rescued his flank.[29]

To an officer of the Sixtieth Indiana, Thomas was not so imperturbable. General Thomas, John L. Ketcham related, "is always working at his short, thick whiskers. When satisfied he smooths them down, when troubled he works them all out of shape. The rebels were advancing on us and we on them; we met in a hollow between the cedar knoll and the hill we afterwards occupied. The general could see neither party, and it was at that moment, when our right and left, fighting in the woods, seemed ready to give way, he had his whiskers all out of shape. He gave orders to his bodyguard to hold the bridge across Peach Tree Creek and cut down any armed soldier who attempted to cross. But when he saw the rebels running, with us after them, he took off his hat and slung it on the ground and shouted, 'Hurrah! Look at the Third Division. They're driving them!' His whiskers were soon in good shape again."[30]

Failing against Thomas, although he had dealt him a solid blow, Hood gave McPherson his chance two days later, sending General Hardee and nearly the same attacking force against the Tennesseans. The action was as desperate as that at Peach Tree Creek, and Hood was very nearly successful. According to General Blair of the Seventeenth Corps, the Confederates lost out only because Sixteenth Corps troops happened to be temporarily out of place. While tenacious resistance can hardly be

29 Van Horne, *Thomas*, 244.
30 Merrill, *The 70th Indiana*, 149.

231

discounted, Blair relates that he was posted at McPherson's extreme left, which Hardee endeavored to turn after driving Logan from his entrenchments on the right; but as the Southerners swung around Blair in their surprise assault, they ran straight into the Sixteenth Corps of Grenville M. Dodge, who had halted in Blair's rear while awaiting orders.

"The position taken up accidentally by the Sixteenth Corps prevented the full force of the flow from falling where it was intended to fall," Blair related. "If my command had been driven from its position at the time that the Fifteenth Corps [Logan] was forced back . . . there must have been a general rout . . . of the army commanded by General McPherson."[31] But the Tennesseans had as bitter a taste of Hood as Thomas's army. Early in the day McPherson was lost—shot from his horse on a lonely road before the fighting fairly started. Fighting to revenge his loss, the Tennesseans with Logan in command beat off seven Confederate assaults that afternoon. Attacked from the rear, Blair's corps of 9,000 leaped to the other side of their works and fought in reverse, scattering the enemy just in time to scurry back and fight off another frontal attack. Logan's men flung themselves at the enemy with the cry "McPherson and revenge!"[32] The death of McPherson, a beloved associate, kept Sherman from feeling any elation over the victory, even though his favorite Tennesseans had won.

Although the Cumberlanders had been fairly busy that day, they were disappointed in not being asked to do more. Thomas advanced his skirmishers early, entering the first line of enemy works south of the Chattahoochee. After the movement had got underway, orders from Sherman came by courier, whose arrival was described by Captain Stone: "The sun had already risen . . . when Colonel [Charles] Ewing, Sherman's brother-in-law and aide, dashed up to Thomas's tranquil headquarters frantic with excitement, swinging his cap wildly about his head and without saluting or dismounting shouted at the top of his voice: 'The rebels have gone. March right through Atlanta and go into camp on the other side,' then fiercely gal-

31 John B. Hood, *Advance and Retreat*, 189.
32 Lewis, *Sherman*, 385–86.

loped away without a word of detail or explanation or giving a chance to ask a question. The excitement was all his own, but the order was General Sherman's."[33]

Thomas placed Palmer on the Atlanta road, joining him at the head of the column and moving cautiously forward. Shortly before noon he received a note from Sherman marked 11:00 A.M.: "We find the enemy in force inside Atlanta. . . . I have sent word to Howard that we were mistaken in finding the enemy gone. . . . I wish you to press down from the north and use artillery freely, converging in the town. I will then throw McPherson again on your right to break the Macon road."[34] Obviously Hood had marched through Atlanta on his way to attack McPherson on the east side of town, the maneuver leading Sherman to believe that he had taken position behind the fortifications. Hood's surprise attack prevented the Tennesseans from co-operating that day, although Thomas received no further word from Sherman. Playing his guns on the northwest fortifications, Thomas discovered the enemy "in masses in front . . . his positions covered by two intrenched lines of skirmishers," according to a dispatch to Sherman marked 5:00 P.M.[35] Confederate guns were replying "with much spirit."

There Thomas remained within hearing of the duel between Logan and Hood but was ordered neither to storm the town nor to assist the hard-pressed Tennesseans. Sherman explained the riddle in his *Memoirs.* It was his "inference," he wrote on second thought, for Thomas "to take advantage of the opportunity to make a lodgement in Atlanta if possible." He had kept Schofield and Thomas from having any share in the battle, he said, on the ground that "if any assistance were rendered by either of the other armies the Army of the Tennessee would be jealous."[36] The implication in this surprising remark is that the armies of the Ohio and the Cumberland were subordinate to the Tennesseans, an army which Sherman fondly called his "whiplash." Hood retreated into his defenses around

---

[33] Military Society of Massachusetts, *Papers,* VIII, 444.
[34] *Official Records,* 1st Series, XXXVIII, Part 3, 223.
[35] *Ibid.*
[36] Sherman, *Personal Memoirs,* II, 77, 82.

the city that night, and the opportunity for "lodgement" slipped away.

Thomas met Sherman next morning at General Thomas J. Wood's headquarters, when the only subject of discussion seems to have been a new leader for the Army of the Tennessee. Logan, a civilian soldier who had succeeded McPherson as senior officer among the three corps, was distrusted by Thomas as theatrical. In talking with Sherman, Thomas explained that Logan "is brave enough and a good officer but if he had an army I am afraid he would edge over on both sides and annoy Schofield and me. Even as a corps commander he is given to edging out beyond his jurisdiction."[37] Then General Howard was suggested for the place. The officer from Maine was known to be dependable, willing, and devoid of temperament, and after a prolonged discussion he was accepted. Sherman had no cause to regret his decision. "Howard is a Christian, elegant gentleman," he reported to General Halleck some weeks later. "In him I made no mistake." Thomas received credit in the letter for being "slow but true as steel."[38]

Howard's appointment was the first of several replacements made as the army settled down to siege before Atlanta. When General Hooker, commanding the Twentieth Corps, felt aggrieved because a junior in rank had been favored, he offered his resignation on the ground that his "rank and service had been ignored." Thomas did not hesitate to let him go, forwarding the application to Sherman "approved and heartily recommended."[39] Hooker had given some trouble by exaggerating enemy numbers in his front and requiring support when he might have done as well without it, and he had been reluctant on occasion to throw his support to the other corps. Therefore, Hooker departed to take over Northern Department headquarters at Cincinnati. Oddly or not, Hooker had only praise for Thomas thereafter, while Sherman, he always contended, was "crazy."[40] Howard was replaced as Fourth Corps leader by

[37] G. Dawson, *Life of John A. Logan*, 516–18; M. F. Force, *General Sherman*, 331–32.
[38] *Official Records*, 1st Series, XXXVIII, Part 3, 793.
[39] Sherman, *Personal Memoirs*, II, 86.
[40] Hebert, *Fighting Joe Hooker*, 294.

David S. Stanley of Ohio and West Point; but in filling Hooker's place, Sherman unhesitatingly nominated Henry W. Slocum of New York, who had nourished a long-standing hatred for the former commander of the Twentieth Corps. The third replacement came a few days later when General Palmer of the Fourteenth Corps declined to support Schofield in a movement before Atlanta because he was Schofield's senior and so would not take orders from him. Ill, homesick, and generally out of sorts, Palmer considered himself the object of persecution. Although Thomas had favored him over every other civilian general in giving him the command of the elite Fourteenth Corps, there was no place in the army for injured pride. Recommending that Sherman let him go, Thomas replaced him with Jeff Davis of Indiana, an officer with more staying power. General Palmer, a future Illinois senator and presidential candidate, was another to swear by Thomas after the war, and with such effect that the Virginian's name was given a grandson.[41]

Hood made one more attempt at battle, sending General Stephen D. Lee to seize the roads at Ezra Church, due west of Atlanta, where Howard took position on the twenty-seventh. The Tennesseans worked busily next day entrenching behind parapets, and Lee smashed into the position as they were still digging in. Savage fighting lasted from midafternoon until nearly nightfall; after five attacks had been beaten off, dead Rebels lay "in windrows" and Lee sullenly withdrew. Confederate morale, which had been dwindling ever since Hood's appointment, sank even more rapidly after this third defeat. According to General Hardee, "No action of the campaign probably did so much to demoralize and dishearten the troops engaged in it."[42] President Jefferson Davis was so shocked that he sent word to Hood to avoid any further frontal attacks. New siege guns for the Federal army arrived by rail, and Sherman began to shell the city in earnest while the cavalry dashed about on railroad-destroying missions. Great fires burned within the city; Rebel nerves weakened, and desertions increased. "There

41 John M. Palmer, *Autobiography*, 214; G. T. Palmer, *A Conscientious Turncoat*, 147–48.
42 Southern Historical Society, *Papers*, VIII, 340.

is no peace," Sherman advised the War Department, "inside or outside of Atlanta."

The month of August was for siege guns and cavalry raids, the latter productive of exaggerated reports concerning work accomplished and opposing enemy strength. Since Sherman's line was spread too thin around Atlanta for a direct assault at any one point, a contemplated flank movement was postponed from day to day while cavalry detachments under Hugh J. Kilpatrick and Kenner Garrard haphazardly raided the country. Shells poured into the city at regular intervals throughout the day, many flying far above Hood's fieldworks. While the Federals stood and waited behind extensive redoubts, Captain Henry Stone of Thomas's staff set down a few notes concerning his favorite commander, later converting them into an extended criticism of the Atlanta campaign. Wrote [Colonel] Stone in a paper read before the Military Society of Massachusetts:

"One secret not only of Thomas's unvarying success but of his wonderful hold upon the confidence and affections of his army is the fact that everyone in it was to him a man and a soldier. . . . He was unremitting in his effort that they should be well supplied, well looked after, and always brought to the right place at the right time. . . . When every day brought at least a skirmish he invariably made his way to the head of the column . . . where he often dismounted and walked to the outer skirmish line to reconnoiter. . . . His woodcraft was almost unerring. He could make his way through the thickest forest and come out at the spot he aimed for. When under fire, his movements . . . were as deliberate as at any time. . . . He was never seen riding up and down his lines waving his sword, shouting, or going through ceremonies. . . . Whenever and wherever his soldiers saw him they knew that all was right and they read in his fixed countenance the . . . harbinger of victory. On the march nobody ever saw him, with an escort trailing, dashing past a moving column of troops, throwing up dust or mud and compelling them to leave the road. If any had the right of way, it was they. He would break through the woods or flounder across a swamp rather than force his men from the road and wear them out by needless fatigue.

"He sometimes had terrific outbursts of temper. It was usually under complete control but when it did break out it was volcanic. He once so alarmed a teamster who, when his mules were stalled, was beating them over the head with the butt of his whip, that the poor fellow took to the woods to escape he knew not what fate. Again when the servants and orderlies about his headquarters were chasing a stray goose and making a great shouting and disturbance he flamed out so that everybody ran and hid from his wrath while the poor goose, after a short circling flight, lighted at his feet as if for protection and safety. To all dumb animals he was a friend and protector. . . . It was exhibitions of meanness and cruelty to those who could not defend themselves, rather than any great faults or crimes, which chiefly stirred his passion. He . . . liked as he sat by the campfire to hear the droll anecdotes and adventures of his soldiers. . . . He liked to occupy himself with some mechanical work for which he had great fondness and aptitude, or with the study of science, history or philosophy. . . . He was well versed in constitutional law, or rather, perhaps, in the Constitution itself."[43]

Reflecting occasionally upon tactics, Thomas made two proposals to Sherman, when the army finally moved out—suggestions which, if they had been adopted, might have trapped Hood's army. On August 26, the besieging forces began to withdraw from their positions around the city preparatory to cutting two railroad lines south and southeast of Atlanta where the cavalry had done no effective work. Howard's Tennesseans made a wide swing which took them on the outside perimeter of three flank movements converging on Jonesboro and Flint River, about twenty miles south. Thomas took the middle course as usual, with Schofield on his left. At the same time, Slocum's Twentieth Corps was moved back to the old Confederate entrenchments near the Chattahoochee River to keep contact with the railroad line running from Chattanooga and to counter a possible attack by Hood. On the twenty-eighth Thomas and

43 Military Society of Massachusetts, *Papers*, X, 195–97.

Howard reached the first railroad, the Atlanta and West Point, and spent the next day breaking it up. Rails were heated in bonfires kindled from the ties and wrapped around trees or telephone poles, a favorite trick of Sherman's. General Hood, meantime, had been trying to guess what was actually happening; then finally comprehending the Federal objective, he flung out the corps of Stephen D. Lee and Hardee, with the latter in command. Only one corps—Stewart's—now remained in Atlanta. On the morning of August 31 Hardee's course took him not two miles distant from Renfrew, where the Cumberlanders were drawn up in order of battle. Spotting the dust cloud thrown up by enemy infantry, Thomas urged Sherman to permit him to attack in flank but the Commander-in-Chief declined to allow the move. Colonel Fullerton, who was present at the parley, later maintained that Sherman was very much concerned over the Army of the Tennessee, which was entrenched behind breastworks at Jonesboro, "and would not allow Thomas to move out of position from which he could quickly go to its support."[44] Thomas rushed up a division to assist Howard, who managed to hold firm along most of his line and at the same time deal out severe punishment. Late in the afternoon the assaulting line withdrew behind its own breastworks east of the town.

In the belief that Hardee would move back to Atlanta, Sherman continued to make the railroad his main object of attack, sending Stanley of the Fourth Corps and Schofield to destroy the Macon and Western tracks as they advanced from Rough and Ready, north of Jonesboro, to Lovejoy's Station, seven miles below. Thomas's mind still revolved around the Confederate Army as the principal target. He suggested taking his army down to Lovejoy's Station to cut off the line of retreat to Macon while Howard and Schofield held the Rebels at Jonesboro. But Sherman did not wish to countermand his emphatic orders to Stanley and Schofield. "I don't believe anybody recognizes how important it is to tear up this railroad," he notified Thomas. " . . . As soon as it is demonstrated on what road it [the enemy] retreats we can arrange to head it off."[45]

[44] Society of the Army of the Cumberland, 1893 Reunion, *Report*, 139.

Hood withdrew Lee's corps part way toward Atlanta, leaving Hardee to face the enemy at Jonesboro the next day. Then, on September 1, as Stanley and Schofield moved south along the railroad line, Thomas confronted Hardee's entrenchments within the town and watched his old Fourteenth Corps storm the works and take two hundred prisoners. Holding the Army of the Tennessee motionless, Sherman called for Stanley to hurry forward and cut off Hardee, but the harassed Fourth Corps had to fight its way through some dense wooded growth on its way down and arrived too late. The railroad-wrecking job had been poorly timed. Hardee made good his escape to Lovejoy's, where Thomas had sought to be, and threw up strong fieldworks. Here the entire Confederate Army was to find sanctuary.

Aside from the minor victory at Jonesboro, it had been a day of frustration and short temper. Thomas sent two of his aides to hurry the unhappy General Stanley along, finally riding off himself at an unusually fast pace. "His old stout horse that hated to trot when laden with 200 pounds actually roused himself to a gallop and his master was almost furious," General Howard related.[46] Sherman said that it was the only time during the campaign that he saw Thomas urge his mount into a gallop, but the fact was that Old Slow Trot seldom could hurry his horse without reviving sharp twinges of his old spinal injury. Sherman was quick to blame Stanley for the failure to intercept Hardee, but according to the Fourth Corps commander, the fault lay in Sherman's "want of generalship in using a large force to destroy a useless railroad—useless to Hood's army—when that force should have been hastened to hunt up the enemy and to attack him at once."[47] During that night the wind brought faint sounds of explosions from the direction of Atlanta. Federal chagrin was mollified when news arrived early on September 2 that Slocum had crept cautiously forward and entered the city.

45 *Ibid.,* 140–41. *Official Records,* 1st Series, XXXVIII, Part 5, 718.
46 Military Order of the Loyal Legion of the U. S., New York Commandery, *Personal Recollections,* Series I, 300.
47 D. S. Stanley, *Personal Memoirs,* 182–83.

The operation had not been a difficult one since General Hood was no longer there. After burning his warehouses and a number of railroad trains laden with ordnance and ammunition, Hood had marched south to join Lee near Atlanta and rendezvous with the rest of his force at Lovejoy's. Sherman, meantime, had started in pursuit of Hardee, but Hood managed to get around him unscathed. Two or three assaults on the fieldworks at Lovejoy's left the Federal commander with a great curiosity concerning what Atlanta looked like, and so the campaign against Hood's army was abandoned as the blueclads moved north. Long a symbol of Confederate hope and defiance, Atlanta seemed a prize worth taking in hand. Occupation of the fallen city, rather than operations against an elusive enemy, now constituted the greater objective for the commander who had held a loose net.

XIV
Victory at Nashville

UNABLE to whip each other soundly, Hood and Sherman went looking for something else to do. It was Sherman's tactic to depopulate the city of Atlanta, evicting the citizens from houses to be used for storage and occupation. Homes on the outskirts of town were to be burned and the lines of defense closed in. Sherman was preparing for more war in and around Atlanta, although it never came. After Mayor James M. Calhoun and two aldermen had made the protests, receiving a volley of words in reply, the townspeople packed their belongings in wagons and rode or trudged south past the army of Hood, who helped them on their way. Another backwash of the war occupied the Confederate General for a week or two while he removed some 20,000 Union prisoners from the notorious Andersonville prison camp in his rear, transferring them to Florida where they would be safe from Federal liberators. Jammed into a narrow area and fed with meager scraps, the prisoners were skeletonlike and ragged specimens, their uncut locks full of lice. A few men escaped by night to tell their pitiful stories to Sherman.[1] One out of every four lodged at Andersonville had died there, but as Sherman reminded Mayor Calhoun in his reply to the latter's protest against eviction: "War is cruelty and you cannot refine it."[2]

Although Sherman's belligerency for waging war in the field plainly had evaporated, Hood could not be idle long. It was his plan to raid the single-track railroad which supplied Sherman from Chattanooga and Nashville. The road was an obvious target, but somehow the Rebels had delayed concentrating

1 Sherman, *Personal Memoirs*, II, 112.
2 Lewis, *Sherman*, 415.

upon it even though General Robert E. Lee, early in July, had recommended that all Confederate cavalry in Mississippi and Tennessee be sent against the vulnerable communication line. Had this been done promptly and effectively, the march through Georgia would have taken another turn. Sherman had worried constantly over the safety of his railroad, which was protected only here and there by blockhouses. Whenever it had been damaged by guerrilla raids, expert construction gangs had moved in and speedily repaired it so that trains bringing fresh troops and supplies never were long delayed. Still no powerful Confederate force such as the army of General Forrest had been ordered to attack it. The responsibility of stopping Sherman had been placed entirely upon Johnston, and, when it was too late, upon the daredevil Hood.

In a spirit of desperation just before the fall of Atlanta, Hood made an attempt to disrupt Sherman's communications by sending Wheeler's cavalry on a wide swing into East Tennessee then across the Cumberland Mountains and on to Sherman's railroad, but very little had been accomplished against the Federal forces left at Chattanooga and Murfreesboro. Hood now sent out a call for Forrest, who had been occupied during the summer in western Tennessee and Mississippi. Toward the latter part of September, Forrest marched from Meridian to Tullahoma, capturing two Federal garrisons on the way and destroying a part of the Nashville and Decatur Railroad. The Nashville and Chattanooga main line was to be threatened by foraying parties sent on ahead.

These raids—or possibly Forrest himself—aroused grave concern in Atlanta and in Washington. On September 26, Sherman received a message from Grant ordering that Forrest be driven out of Middle Tennessee, and it was for this express purpose that Thomas was detached from the army three days later and sent to Chattanooga. Preceded by Newton's division of the Fourth Corps, Thomas was accompanied by a Fourteenth Corps division under James D. Morgan of Boston, who had succeeded Davis. Meantime General Hood was girding himself and his rested army for nothing less than an invasion of Middle Tennessee, operating on the railroad in Sherman's rear.

Putting up at the Crutchfield House in Chattanooga, Thomas found the city overcrowded with officers on leave and furloughed troops. "No more should be allowed to leave Atlanta until the road is clear to Nashville," he wired Sherman on September 30. "From what I can learn about Forrest I think I will have to send General Morgan's division to Tullahoma."[3] Although Forrest had sent two small parties to damage the railroad leading to Nashville, it had been repaired and was in good order by the time Thomas and Morgan reached Tullahoma on October 2. Thomas continued to Nashville to direct operations against Forrest's raiders and reorganize the Federal forces in Tennessee. General Rousseau, who had been in command of the district, was started south with two divisions to threaten the invaders, while General Steedman entrained from Chattanooga to reinforce the garrisons at Bridgeport and Stevenson.

Still farther west of the Nashville-Chattanooga line, Forrest marched as far north as Columbia, where he tore up more track in that sector and then escaped into northwestern Alabama while Morgan was seeking him out. It was a race between Morgan and Forrest to Pride's Ferry near Florence, where the Confederates hoped to cross the Tennessee River and fight another day. While the Confederate Fourth Alabama marched to Shoal Creek to delay Morgan, Forrest ferried his artillery across the swollen, mile-wide river on the fifth. He continued working busily all night and for the next two days passing troops and equipment to a large island about seventy yards offshore. From there they were ferried across the main stream in safety as boats became available. While Morgan was driving the Fourth Alabama through the town, Forrest's rear guard mounted horses and swam to the island.[4] A single company of Rousseau's cavalry reached Morgan on the evening of October 6 to find the enemy gone. "Forrest has escaped us," Thomas was notified—disappointing news.[5] Still, the Nashville and Chattanooga railroad had been saved, and it was unlikely that Forrest could damage it further now.

3 *Official Records*, 1st Series, XXXIX, Part 2, 465.
4 Robert Selph Henry, *"First With the Most" Forrest*, 362.
5 *Ibid.*, 361; *Official Records*, 1st Series, XXXIX, Part 3, 140.

Taking up the reins at Nashville, Thomas found himself busier than at any time since the dismal siege of Chattanooga one year ago. Military affairs in the capital city, he reported, were in considerable confusion. To the southward, Hood was on the loose again, hurling his troops against Sherman's communications stretching north of Atlanta. Sherman had no choice but to take most of his army and follow along, retracing the very ground he had won by hard fighting that summer. Reaching Kennesaw Mountain on October 4, he was warned that his chief supply depot at Allatoona was threatened, but the garrison managed to hold out after some hard fighting, saving one million rations. Hood now swung west, crossing Coosa River and by-passing Rome on the tenth. Thomas wired the news to Stanton that very day: "Am making such disposition of my force as will, I hope, prevent his crossing the Tennessee River . . . and while I hold him in the front, Sherman will attack him in the rear."[6] Sherman, however, had his mind on greater things and was leaving Hood entirely to Thomas. "Let him [Hood] go north, my business is down South,"[7] he was heard to say as the Rebel chief again turned against the railroad, tearing up the tracks from Resaca to Tunnel Hill and seizing the Federal garrison at Dalton. Dispatches to Grant carried the idea of marching seaward, destroying "roads, houses and people," as Sherman wired on October 9; "I can make the march and make Georgia howl."[8] Grant interposed a few objections. Thomas, he thought, might be defeated if left alone to face Hood. Sherman declined to believe that Hood would enter Tennessee. Even if he did, Thomas would have sufficient force, declared Sherman, to beat him.

Two days later, after convincing Lincoln that Sherman's idea was politically feasible, Grant wired that he could make his march. Sherman, in other words, could turn his back on Hood, with whom, indeed, he had not sought battle. Hesitating and dallying at Hood's heels, Sherman had shown little disposition to fight. What troops would he leave for Thomas? His

6 *Ibid.*, 175.
7 Lewis, *Sherman*, 430.
8 *Ibid.*, 429.

WILLIAM TECUMSEH SHERMAN

natural choice was to retain the subordinate officers he liked best and the most efficient troops for his foray against "roads, houses and people." He believed he could get along without Stanley of the Fourth Corps, Army of the Cumberland, but would keep the Twentieth Corps and Thomas's prized Fourteenth. General Dodge of the Sixteenth Corps, Army of the Tennessee, had been wounded and his command broken up, and most of these troops were now slated for Thomas. But Thomas was to return Morgan and Newton together with 5,000 fresh volunteers as replacements. Sherman also planned to retain the Fifteenth and Seventeenth Corps of the Army of the Tennessee, General Schofield's command, and a division of the best cavalry.

With these several units, the pick of the lot, Sherman proposed to organize an army of 60,000 to 65,000 men with which to destroy Atlanta, Macon, Augusta, and Savannah and teach the South a moral lesson. He outlined his plans to Thomas under date of October 20: "I propose to demonstrate the vulnerability of the South and make its inhabitants feel that war and individual ruin are synonimous [sic] terms," he wired Thomas from Summerville, Georgia. "To pursue Hood is folly, for he can twist and turn like a fox and wear out an army in pursuit. . . . I know I am right in this. . . . I propose to take Howard and his army, Schofield and his, and two of your corps, viz Davis [Fourteenth] and Slocum [Twentieth]. I propose to remain along the Coosa watching Hood till all my preparations are made, viz till I have repaired the railroad, sent back all surplus men and material and stript for the work. Then I will send Stanley with the 4th Corps. . . . I want you to retain command in Tennessee and . . . will give you delegated authority over Kentucky and Mississippi, Alabama etc. whereby there will be unity of action behind me. I will want you to hold Chattanooga and Decatur [Alabama] in force and on the occasion of my departure . . . you shall have ample notice to watch Hood close. I think he will follow me at least with his cavalry in which event I want you to push south. . . . We must pursue a *large* amount of secrecy."[9]

9 Sherman to Thomas, October 20, 1864, Dearborn Collection.

The unit which Thomas desired most of all was not to be his, apparently. This was the elite Fourteenth Corps, the first brigade of which he had organized at Camp Dick Robinson, nucleus of the division which had won the Battle of Mill Springs. Sherman could not bear to see the Fourteenth go, refusing Thomas's request with a tribute to its fine efficiency: "It is too compact and reliable a corps for me to leave behind. I can spare you the Fourth Corps and about five thousand men not fit for my purpose, but which will be well enough for garrison duty at Chattanooga, Murfreesboro' and Nashville. What you need is a few points fortified and stocked with provisions and a good movable column of twenty-five thousand men that can strike in any direction."[10] Sherman was still assuming that Hood did not intend to invade Tennessee, although before many weeks had passed he would be advising Thomas to concentrate all his troops at one point and attack the invader.

Ten thousand more men were designated for Thomas when General Schofield showed little inclination to accompany Sherman. Shrunken through losses and expirations of terms of service, the Army of the Ohio was contracted into the Twenty-third Corps, which made up for the loss of Newton and Morgan. Thomas also received about 5,000 cavalry troops minus horses and all the damaged artillery from Sherman's "surplus." To bring his army up to the point of opposing Confederate strength, he called on William Starke Rosecrans, now commanding in Missouri, to lend him General A. J. Smith and two divisions of the Sixteenth Corps, Army of the Tennessee, which had remained behind to fight General Forrest that summer. Since Smith recently had been engaged in driving the Rebel Sterling Price from western Missouri, his troops were not very accessible; but after Grant had given his consent to the transfer, General John A. Rawlins entrained for St. Louis to obtain river passage for Smith and at the same time to rustle up some additional men. Since Smith had to march all the way across the state of Missouri, he would not reach St. Louis until November 24. Meantime the various additions to Thomas's command would comprise a net somewhat less than the forces of Forrest and

10 Van Horne, *Thomas*, 261.

Hood, while there were a dozen cities and towns to garrison against a possible Confederate strike.

Thomas's present army of 31,000 was spread so thin, in fact, that early in November, Forrest made one of his great sweeps of the war. First he began blockading the winding Tennessee River at Johnsonville, ninety miles due west of Nashville, a main army depot with acres of Federal supplies. Confederate land batteries laboriously hauled into position waylaid and captured several small Union craft, and a lubber river navy was organized. On November 4, Forrest attacked Johnsonville and some Federal gunboats from both land and water, throwing shells from all directions. Before the tireless Rebel raider had finished, he had destroyed or captured "three gunboats, eleven steamers and fifteen barges, a portion of the latter laden with quartermaster and commissary stores." Flaming vessels set fire to docks, warehouses, and sheds along the shore; several hundred barrels of liquor exploded, mingling blue flame with red, a scene described by a dazed Federal eyewitness as "awfully sublime." Schofield happened to arrive at Nashville the very next day and immediately was put on the cars going west for a glimpse of Forrest's heels as Thomas conservatively estimated the property loss at one and one-half million dollars.[11]

Sherman had followed Hood at a safe distance as far as Gaylesville, Alabama, where he tarried a week while shaping his plans. His troops were in fine health and spirits; not a man had been lost in a fight since the Confederate attack on Allatoona. Hood, during the last week in October, was marching from Gadsden to Guntersville, then to Decatur and Tuscumbia, seeking the most suitable crossing of the Tennessee River and quarreling along the way with General Beauregard, newly appointed chief of the Military Division of the West. Sherman was not sorry to see Hood out of the way. "If he'll go to the Ohio River," he remarked, "I'll give him rations."[12] General Grant, however, had misgivings. He still felt that Sherman's chief assignment was Hood. "If you see a chance of destroying Hood's

11 Henry, *Forrest*, 371–79; *Official Records*, 1st Series, XXVII, Part I, 589–90.
12 Lewis, *Sherman*, 430.

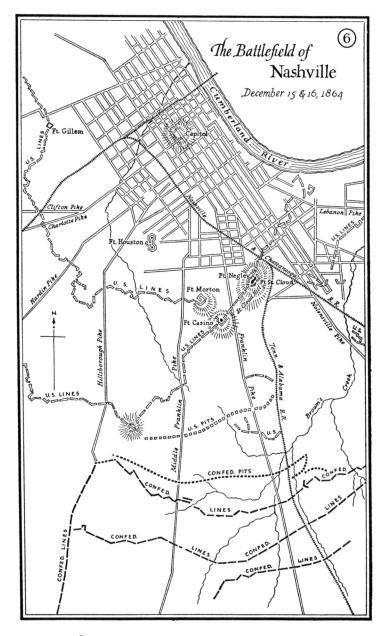

The Battlefield of
Nashville
December 15 & 16, 1864

army, attend to that first and make your other move secondary," he wired on November 1.[13] Sherman, who had informed Thomas that he would be "script for the work," now argued that he was encumbered by heavy wagon trains while Hood was traveling light and so could never hope to overtake him. Grant gave in again and telegraphed, "Go as you propose." So Sherman started on his long march. Following some rapid exchanges of telegraph dispatches with Nashville, wire connections were severed on November 12. "I am now convinced that the greater part of Beauregard's army is near Florence and Tuscumbia, and that you will have at least a clear road before you for several days, and that your success will fully equal your expectations," read the final message from Thomas.[14]

The dirt was flying in and around Nashville as work was speeded on a long line of entrenchments starting at the river bank and encircling the city. Thomas still needed time to collect arms, horses, mules, and men. Anxious uncertainty whether Hood would cross the Tennessee or follow Sherman hung over the Federal camp. Thomas stationed the major part of his force at Pulaski, near the Alabama line, ordering Schofield to join Stanley there and take command of both the Fourth and the Twenty-third Army Corps. Most of the available cavalry was watching Hood's movements from the north side of the river at Florence. Another question was how soon could General Smith arrive.

Hood presented Thomas with two precious weeks in November while the Confederate Army waited at Tuscumbia for supplies to come by rail from Corinth, Mississippi, and for Forrest to appear. With ten miles of track out of operation, repairs proceeded at a snail's pace as heavy fall rains set in. General Stephen D. Lee's corps got safely across to the north side of the river, but then a precious pontoon bridge was swept away by high water. Remiss in checking the crossing, four brigades of Federal cavalry under General Edward Hatch hovered cautiously on Lee's front. General Forrest reported for duty on the

13 Van Horne, *Thomas*, 259.
14 *Ibid.*, 269.

fourteenth, receiving the command of all the cavalry operating with Hood, a depleted force numbering only 6,000 men. Hood crossed the river to place himself out of Beauregard's way. He had never been willing to accept orders from the French Creole. Without waiting for any further railroad repairs, the divisions of Cheatham and Stewart with some newly arrived infantry troops began to pass over a new pontoon bridge, and on November 21, Hood began a forward movement with the intention of cutting off or destroying the 23,000 Federals under General Schofield at Pulaski.

The march was taken up under the worst conditions the Army of Tennessee had faced since the days of General Bragg. Winter was coming early and the late November weather felt harsh and raw. Chilling rain and snow fell on the shoeless and ragged invaders who were using rawhide, hats, and even coat sleeves to protect their feet from the frozen ground. Blankets and food were very scarce. "There were times when in some of the commands rations of corn, 3 ears to a man, were issued and occasionally nothing but cornmeal was to be had," commented Captain R. W. Banks of the Thirty-seventh Mississippi. "It was a time that tried the strength and spirit of soldiers to the limit."[15] A gaunt and fanatical figure strapped to his saddle, Hood was pushing blindly forward toward bitter tragedy for the Army of Tennessee. Had he been able to cut off Schofield, then retreating by day and night marches to Columbia, there would have been little to stop him short of the Ohio River, the goal of which he dreamed. But as the two armies milled around Columbia, a Federal infantry division under General Jacob D. Cox rescued Hatch's cavalry from a severe drubbing, seizing a vital crossing of Duck River just in time. Schofield threw up fortifications on the south side of the river where Thomas had ordered a stand to be made. After sparring against dismounted cavalry for two days and infantry columns for two more, Schofield crossed the river on November 28 only to find that Forrest already had gained the north bank by distant fords to his left.

Thomas's new chief of cavalry, twenty-seven-year-old James H. Wilson, had brought reinforcements, but Forrest dashed be-

[15] R. W. Banks, *Battle of Franklin*, 24–25.

tween him and Schofield to sever practically every means of communication between them. Had Schofield lingered longer, he would have been caught in the trap, but Thomas, doing his thinking for him, ordered him to march swiftly twenty-four miles to Franklin and fortify a new position to be held if possible until A. J. Smith should arrive. Warned that the Confederates had started a turning movement, Schofield hurried Stanley forward as far as Spring Hill, junction of several country roads, to cover the wagon trains. Hood feinted with two of Lee's divisions to delay Schofield and dashed ahead with Cheatham and Stewart to Spring Hill. The jaws of the trap were poised wide open as Schofield filled the road with crawling wagons and crept along with the Twenty-third Corps in the rear.

Riding at the head of Pat Cleburne's division, Hood had fair hopes for the success of his ruse, but there followed one of the most costly Confederate failures of the war. Through some misunderstanding or physical exhaustion or too much whiskey going the rounds, a courier failed to deliver an order to Cheatham who had been stationed in the path of the advancing Federals.[16] With the order to attack resting in someone's pouch or pocket, there was no attack. The dilatory Schofield scurried past Hood's sleeping army toward midnight along a road where the lines were so close that straggling Union soldiers began to wander into the enemy camp. "It was like treading upon thin ice covering a smouldering volcano," related General Stanley. "At any moment the line of soldiers might spring to their feet, advance a few hundred yards and pour destruction into the flank of our retreating columns. . . . The 4th Corps was left to confront the enemy and to save the material of the army if possible. From one o'clock on that star-lit night until five we put across one bridge, only wide enough for one wagon at a time, nearly 11,000 teams—army wagons, caissons and ambulances."[17] The army safely reached Franklin, twelve miles away, and threw up strong hillside works on the night of November 29.

Instead of cleanly flanking his way around, the mortified Confederate leader attacked the entrenchments in successive

16 Horn, *Army of Tennessee*, 386–92.
17 Stanley, *Personal Memoirs*, 204.

waves, exposing Cheatham and Stewart to a "holocaust, a whole-sale massacre," in the words of a Confederate officer who fought. "The loss inflicted on the assailants was almost equal to the entire force within the works. Eleven of the best officers were killed or wounded, including Pat Cleburne, the Stonewall of the West." With Lee's corps far in the rear and Forrest's cavalry running errands and uselessly divided, 6,000 Confederates were sent to their deaths or to improvised field hospitals in "a concentrated roar of musketry."[18] Where the assault was most desperate, trenches were glutted with bodies piled in heaps six or seven deep or wedged in upright on their feet. Two Federal batteries were captured just before dark and were turned right and left to enfilade the lines, but Colonel Emerson Opdyke of Stanley's corps ordered a bayonet charge by his Second Division brigade which ended the fight. Schofield, who left the battle almost entirely to Stanley, was properly excoriated by that officer for having stationed himself with a reserve division two miles away on the north bank of the Harpeth River. It was common knowledge in the army that the cautious Schofield would never expose his skin.[19]

Thomas decided to take no more chances with Schofield, ordering him to race for Nashville, eighteen miles away. Schofield needed no urging with Hood and Forrest still at his heels. As the Confederates marched over the bloody field next morning, Captain Banks of the Thirty-seventh Mississippi had a moody valedictory for the charnal-house scene: "Of all the gruesome sights of war, nothing better calculated to affright and demoralize an army could have been devised than that exhibition of the dead. . . . Why any considerable portion of the army which had encountered so many dangers and undergone so many discouraging, heartbreaking experiences in the recent past should have been permitted to witness that sickening, blood-curdling, fear-kindling sight is difficult to understand when it might so easily have been avoided by a slight detour in

[18] Green, *Recollections and Reflections*, 81.

[19] Stanley, *Personal Memoirs*, 214; newspaper clippings, MSS. Division, Library of Congress, accession 4642; *Tennessee Historical Magazine*, VII, 88–91.

the line of march. . . . The hell of war was depicted cruelly in the ghastly upturned faces of the dead."[20]

Worrying over Schofield and the delayed arrival of Smith, Thomas was having an anxious time of it in the besieged city. On November 24, fifty-nine river transports loaded down to their guards had started leaving St. Louis. As the steamer *Imperial,* carrying quartermasters' stores, was shoving off, General Dodge called to the captain from the shore: "Make all haste to Nashville, Thomas needs you!"[21] The water in the Mississippi River was low, and one overloaded boat was snagged and wrecked on a sand bar. Soldiers and stores had to be taken off and packed into already overcrowded transports. The Ohio and Cumberland rivers, fortunately, were in an improved stage. A fleet of gunboats patrolled back and forth as the transports entered the Cumberland on the last lap of their journey. Although Thomas had sent a fast steamer down the river to hurry the Westerners forward, no word had come since Smith's arrival at Paducah on the twenty-seventh.

Except for 3,500 men under General Rousseau at Murfreesboro and necessary garrisons at Chattanooga, Bridgeport, and Stevenson, all troops from outlying posts had been called in—odds and ends from scattered depots. Steedman marched from Chattanooga with two brigades of Negro troops and the miscellaneous troops discarded by Sherman. Food and fuel were scarce in Nashville—hardly any part of the western country had been foraged upon as much as Middle Tennessee. In sore need of draft animals as well as horses for Wilson's cavalry, Thomas had sent Quartermaster James L. Donaldson into Kentucky to buy mules. During the careworn weeks of November, the General was seen wearing his military hat pulled down over his grave eyes. "Habitually during all that period he . . . was reticent and gloomy," testified General James T. Rustling, assistant quartermaster. With the arrival of good news from Franklin, the turning point came on the evening of the thirtieth. "Now his hat lifted, his broad brow cleared up and his strong

20 Banks, *Battle of Franklin,* 85.
21 John Scott, *The 32nd Iowa Volunteers,* 309.

and massive face began to shine with the fierce light of impending battle," continued Rustling. "I dropped into his headquarters about 9 P.M. to inquire more about Franklin. His hat up and face all aglow, Thomas handed me a telegram from Schofield, announcing that he had defeated Hood."[22]

Thomas asked Rustling for news of Smith, but there was none to report. Buoyed up by the change in his commander's demeanor, Rustling hurried off to a party at the home of Judge John A. Campbell, returning to the St. Cloud Hotel about midnight. There he found Thomas talking busily with Schofield and Thomas J. Wood, just arrived from Franklin. Wood had succeeded Stanley, wounded in the fight.

Rustling had news. "Smith is all right," he announced. "Just as I came in I heard his steamers tooting along the levee." He had no sooner finished speaking than in strode Smith, a big Westerner, grizzled and rugged. Thomas "literally took Smith in his arms and hugged him, for he now felt absolutely sure of coping with Hood." Maps were spread over the floor, and as Rustling left the group at 1:00 A.M. all four generals were down on their knees examining the positions to be taken that day. Rustling ran into a rough-looking set of men bivouacked along the levee. "We're A. J. Smith's guerrillas," a bearded veteran announced. "We've been to Vicksburg, Red River, Missouri and about everywhere else . . . and now we're going to Hades if old A. J. orders us."[23]

When Schofield's fagged-out soldiers reached the city a few hours later, they flopped down on the cold ground and slept nearly twenty-four hours. Thomas wired General Halleck at Washington that he was only waiting for Wilson to remount his cavalry for the protection of the flanks. Thousands of horses had been worn out by hard work and many of the men had yet to receive saddles and suitable mounts. "If Hood attacks me here, he will be more seriously damaged than he was yesterday," Thomas maintained. "If he remains until Wilson gets equipped, I can whip him, and will move against him at once."[24] He

22 James F. Rustling, *Men and Things I Saw in Civil War Days*, 86.
23 *Ibid.*, 87–88.
24 Van Horne, *Thomas*, 300.

counted on the presence of two Federal ironclads and several gunboats in the river to prevent Hood from crossing or blockading it, but the Cumberland was blockaded nevertheless. To get Wilson ready, Thomas ordered the seizure of every mount to be found anywhere in Kentucky, Tennessee, or northern Alabama. The horses of the local streetcar company were corralled, the trained animals of a wandering circus, and Governor Johnson's fine stable, but it would still take a full week to accumulate enough mounts for Wilson.

Thomas's wire to Halleck was intended as reassurance that Hood's army might well be defeated and destroyed once the cavalry was remounted. However, the word had been freely passed around in Washington that Thomas was "slow." Halleck turned the telegram over to Secretary Stanton, who talked with Lincoln that same day. At 10:30 A.M. on December 2, Stanton sent a wire to Grant, then confronting Lee at City Point, Virginia: "The President feels solicitous about the disposition of Thomas to lay in fortifications for an indefinite period 'until Wilson gets replacements.' This looks like the McClellan and Rosecrans strategy of do nothing and let the enemy raid the country. The President wishes you to consider the matter."[25]

Grant attacked the problem with vigor, sparing no means at his disposal to get Thomas in hand. Two telegrams went out from City Point that same day, advising an attack "before Hood fortifies," and supplying details. "Arm and put in the trenches your quartermasters employes, citizens, etc." Saturday, December 3, was a day of great preparation in Nashville. Now numbering nearly 50,000 men properly equipped, the Federals were posted along two lines of unfinished entrenchments about the city. Heavy skirmishing to the southward marked the arrival of the Confederate Army. The Confederates were clearly visible from high points in the suburbs, and the flashes of enemy guns could be seen plainly enough from fortified Capitol Hill. Thomas marshaled 5,000 quartermaster's employees and other hands, his officers waylaying citizens on their Sunday promenade next day.[26] Besides the long outer line of works, occupied by

25 *Ibid.*, 301.
26 John Wooldridge, *History of Nashville*, 199.

soldiers, a seven-mile-long inner line enclosed the hospitals and stores. Here the auxiliary workers were placed. Smith's command moved one and one-half miles southwest of the city and began additional field entrenchments with an abatis of timber and sharp-pointed stakes firmly planted along the entire line. Running across hills, knobs, and ravines, the work was completed by Monday, December 5. However, Thomas was not yet willing to launch his attack. He further explained his position to Grant: "I have infantry enough to assume the offensive if I had more cavalry, and will take the field anyhow as soon as the remainder of General [E. M.] McCook's cavalry reaches here, which I hope it will in two or three days. . . . It must be remembered that my command was made up of two of the weakest corps of General Sherman's army, and all the dismounted cavalry except one brigade."

Some scattered actions occupied the land and water forces as heavy cannonading shook the town. One of Forrest's busy regiments set up a blockade of the Cumberland eighteen river-miles below the city and captured two transports carrying 197 horses and mules only to lose them in a midnight battle to Federal gunboats. On Monday a cavalry engagement on Hillsboro pike south of the city ended in a Confederate defeat. General Forrest happened to be absent on a foray against the garrison at Murfreesboro but was repulsed on the seventh in fine style. More mules and horses were on the way. When Quartermaster Donaldson showed up in a dither one evening for fear his agents had bought twice too many, Thomas dissolved his anxiety in an instant: "25,000 did you say? Is it possible that you have this number? Donaldson, accept my heartfelt thanks."[27] After a fall of rain and sleet, six-mule teams would be required to haul each ammunition wagon through the deep clay mud and up the hills surrounding the city.

Telegrams continued to fly between Washington, City Point, and Nashville. Everyone from the President down expressed concern lest Thomas fail to attack before Hood entrenched, before he wrecked the railroads, before he moved into the rich cattle-grazing lands of Kentucky and to the Ohio

[27] *Century Magazine*, August, 1887, 617.

River. A cavalry raid into southern Kentucky which McCook took care of aroused the further anxiety of Grant. "Attack Hood at once and wait no longer for a remount of your cavalry," he wired on the sixth. And to Halleck on the eighth: "If Thomas has not struck yet, he ought to be ordered to hand over his command to Schofield. There is no better man to repel an attack than Thomas, but I fear he is too cautious to take the initiative."[28] Orders were passed along the lines at Nashville that same afternoon: "Be ready in two hours."

Then fog swept in, chilly and cold. Rain descended, freezing as it fell. As the ground became one vast sheet of ice, the order was recalled. Next day sleet and snow fell upon the shivering picket lines. Movement even along level ground was hazardous and was impossible up the slopes. Thomas's aides saw the careworn expression return to his face. "While the rain was falling and the fields and roads were ice-bound he would sometimes sit by the window for an hour or more not speaking a word, gazing steadily out upon the forbidding prospect as if he were trying to will the storm away," related Captain Stone. "It was curious and interesting to see how in this gloomy interval his time was occupied by matters not strictly military." Now a delegation of city fathers would drop in to discuss some military regulation, now a citizens' committee seeking wood to keep poor families from freezing—another task for Quartermaster Donaldson. "Of evenings, Governor Johnson, the new vice president elect, would unfold to him, with much iteration, his fierce views concerning secession, rebels and reconstruction," Stone continued. "To all he gave a kindly and patient hearing."[29]

Less patience was demonstrated at the headquarters of Grant. At 11:00 A.M. on December 9, the Commander-in-Chief flipped an ace on the table, demanding that the War Department replace Thomas with Schofield. After Secretary Stanton made out the necessary orders, Halleck entered a protest and left the way open for a change of mind. "If you still wish these orders telegraphed to Nashville, they will be forwarded," he

28 Van Horne, *Thomas,* 303.
29 *Century Magazine,* August, 1887, 609.

257

wired Grant at four that afternoon. Informed by Thomas of the freezing rain, Grant saw fit to suspend the order "until it is seen whether he will do anything." Thomas telegraphed resignedly that same day: "General Halleck informs me you are very much dissatisfied with my delay in attacking. I can only say that I have done all in my power to prepare, and if you should deem it necessary to relieve me, I shall submit without a murmur."[30]

For several days, Thomas kept the contents of the daily telegrams to himself, but after the storm had spent its full force, the corps commanders were invited to St. Cloud Hotel headquarters on the evening of December 10. Thomas now laid down Grant's orders and his own replies, explaining that he had acted entirely upon his own judgment and was prepared to take the consequences but still wanted his generals to know the full situation.

Wilson, the junior officer present, spoke first. He had been Grant's chief topographical engineer during the operations around Vicksburg and an aide at Chattanooga, and he knew the Commander-in-Chief well. His comment was: "Nowhere and never, perhaps, in Grant's life can be found an episode which better illustrates that trait in his character which Mrs. Grant had in mind when she said: "My husband is a very obstinate man.' "[31] Thomas, Schofield, Wood, Smith, and Steedman now heard Wilson espouse everything that had been done at Nashville so far as well as commend Thomas's delay. No hostile operation of any kind, avowed Wilson, should be attempted until a thaw had set in, permitting his cavalry to move. The attack should be made only when the ground had become passable for both horse and foot. Wood, commanding the Fourth Corps, was pleased to concur. Smith and Steedman "were equally outspoken," Wilson related, "and as none present denied or criticised my proposition or the conclusion drawn from it, the meeting was shortly dissolved." Only Schofield had sat silent, nursing his thoughts.

Thomas asked Wilson to stand by as the council broke up.

[30] Van Horne, *Thomas*, 304–305; Piatt, *Thomas*, 570–71.
[31] Wilson, *Under the Old Flag*, II, 93.

The commander opened his heart. "Wilson," he said, "the Washington authorities treat me as if I were a boy. They seem to think me incapable of planning a campaign or of fighting a battle. If they will just let me alone till thawing weather begins . . . I will show them what we can do. I am sure my plan of operations is correct and that we shall lick the enemy if he only stays to receive our attack."[32]

Freezing weather still hung on. Fuel was consumed at a great rate, but although Thomas had woodcutters out every day, there were no big fires for the soldiers to warm themselves. Only fires for cooking were allowed. No day was complete without a nagging telegram from Grant. "If you delay attacking longer, the mortifying spectacle will be witnessed of a rebel army moving for the Ohio, and you will be forced to act, accepting such weather as you find," the General-in-Chief wired on the eleventh. "Delay no longer for weather and re-enforcements."[33] But it was hardly possible for Hood to move if Thomas could not. "I will obey the order as promptly as possible, however much I may regret it, as the attack will have to be made under every disadvantage," replied Thomas in a stubborn frame of mind. "The whole country is covered with a perfect sheet of ice and sleet, and it is with difficulty that the troops are able to move about on level ground."[34] General Whipple, Thomas's chief of staff, began to declare that someone was using the wires to undermine his commander at Washington. Thomas sent for Steedman, able veteran of Chickamauga. Could it be Governor Johnson? he asked. Steedman did not think so. He had talked with Johnson and knew him to be aboveboard at least. Thomas suggested that he look into the matter.

Steedman returned to his headquarters and assigned some detective work to an aide. This officer, Captain Marshall Davis, went to the telegraph office and picked up a message from Schofield to Grant: "Many officers here are of the opinion that General Thomas is certainly too slow in his movements." Steedman hastened with the message to Thomas, who examined it care-

32 *Ibid.*, II, 101–102.
33 Van Horne, *Thomas,* 306.
34 *Ibid.*

fully and inquired, "Steedman, can it be possible that Schofield would send such a telegram?" Steedman remarked that Thomas should be familiar with the handwriting of his own general. Thomas put on his glasses and held up the message before the light. "Yes, it is General Schofield's handwriting. . . . Why does he send such telegrams?" Several years later Steedman recalled that he "smiled at the noble old soldier's simplicity and said: 'General Thomas, who is next in command to you, and would succeed you in case of removal?' 'Oh, I see,' he said as he mournfully shook his head."[35]

Apparently even Grant distrusted Schofield by this time. On December 13 he ordered John A. Logan, who happened to be on a visit to City Point, to hurry to Nashville and assume the command provided that Thomas had not advanced by the time of his arrival. Ice still covered the ground that morning. Moody and beset, Thomas was heard to remark that Sherman had taken the pick of his army for operations against an inferior force, while Grant with 100,000 troops had been confronting Lee for nearly seven months. He was heard to declare that he felt like telegraphing, "If you want me to go out at Hood with inferior forces, why don't you go in at Lee with superior forces?"[36] Newspapers received in camp denounced Thomas for "idle stupidity" while Hood hemmed him in, but despite the mass of expert opinion developing elsewhere, Captain John Scott of the Thirty-second Iowa knew better: "How grandly some of our friends at home, seated in a nice, well-furnished room or office by a warm fire, could fight our battles for us! They understood the moves that should be made on the warring chessboard to perfection, just when and how to make them. And they had a better place in which to make the moves than the men in the trenches in that pitiless storm of sleet and snow, or in that dense fog and mud; but the men of the line, in their simplicity, had all confidence in 'Old Pap Thomas.' "[37]

During the afternoon of the thirteenth, all hands were

[35] Newspaper clippings, MSS. Division, Library of Congress, accession 4642 (from Cincinnati *Enquirer*).

[36] De Peyster, "Thomas," in *Representative Men,* 571.

[37] Scott, *The 32nd Iowa Volunteers,* 312.

relieved to see the ice gradually disappear before a warm southern wind. At 8:00 P.M. on the fourteenth, Thomas explained his orders for battle to the various corps commanders and telegraphed General Halleck: "The ice having melted away the enemy will be attacked tomorrow morning." At that, related Captain Stone, "he drew a deep sigh of relief and for the first time in a week showed something of his natural buoyance and cheerfulness. He moved a little more briskly; he put in order all the little last things that remained to be done; he signed his name where it was needed in the letter book and then, giving orders to his staff officers to be ready at 5 A.M., went gladly to bed."[38] General Logan, that evening, was well on his way to Cincinnati. Apparently more concerned over a distant enemy than one near at hand, General Grant was preparing to start for Nashville the very next day.

With no lack of men for either attack or defense, Thomas planned to feint with Steedman at the enemy left, drawing reinforcements from Hood's outer line. Wood and Schofield were to carry the fighting in the center while Wilson and Smith pounded Hood's right flank. Including Quartermaster Donaldson's forces and the regular Nashville garrison under General John F. Miller, Thomas had nearly 55,000 men in the field. Enemy forces around Nashville, following the losses at Franklin, could not have numbered more than 25,000, and Hood would have to fight without Forrest, who was still sniping away at Murfreesboro and at railroad blockhouses. Although Thomas had erred in overestimating enemy numbers, which he believed to be about 40,000, he had no means of knowing in advance that Forrest would be out of the fight. As matters now stood, Wilson had approximately 12,000 mounted troops ready to descend like an avalanche on three scant brigades of horse commanded by General James R. Chalmers. Here on the enemy left, where only two brigades of infantry remained, the Confederate line was spread far too thin. Occupying strong works along Hood's center and right were the corps of Stewart, Lee, and Cheatham, which blocked four turnpikes and two railroads radiating out from the city. Hood had been so concerned over guarding this

[38] *Century Magazine*, August, 1887, 609.

cluster of communication lines which happened to run south and southeast that the result was an unbalanced arrangement of forces.

Thomas methodically checked out of the hotel at 5:00 A.M. on December 15 and handed his packed valise to an orderly. A damp fog shrouded the countryside as he rode with his staff to field headquarters. Although the troops had begun to move up to their new positions, the fog delayed Steedman's attack until eight o'clock and there were waits of an hour or two longer elsewhere. The mixed white and colored troops under Steedman, a reconciled Democrat, handled their task well. Bold skirmish lines thrust aside enemy pickets and charged a battery planted in a rocky ravine. Although the position could not be carried, the violence of the attack caused Hood to withdraw troops from the center to strengthen his right, and Steedman managed to keep Cheatham pretty well occupied all day. At ten o'clock Wilson swung around on the rim of the wheel to envelop Chalmers, holding him in place with only a part of his force, and fighting infantry with the rest. Wherever resistance was encountered, Wilson's corps dismounted and rushed the breastworks, capturing cannon, taking flags, and gathering in prisoners. Smith got into action as the fog lifted. From Thomas's hilltop position the lines of infantry blue, dotted with regimental flags and the national colors, could be seen threading knolls and ravines, passing over fences and around scattered farm buildings.[39] Smith took a breather at midday in front of a steep hill. After his artillery had been drawn up in position, a strong skirmish line scrambled up the slope as the Federal batteries flicked branches and dirt from the hilltop. Enemy guns replied only distractedly. The blue-clads worked their way through the abatis and stormed the entrenchments.

A halt was ordered for the breathless men to re-form. Wild cheering swept across the valley as the Federal colors waved from the parapets. So many prisoners were taken that observers at field headquarters, watching them file into the Federal line, thought for a moment that the enemy had rallied in a counterattack.[40] When Schofield proved a little slow, Thomas rushed

[39] Scott, *The 32nd Iowa Volunteers*, 314.

over to lend impetus to his advance. Wood's Fourth Corps slithered through a pasture, across a ravine, and up Montgomery Hill, crowned by a substantial brick house where enemy sharpshooters were taking their toll. A well-aimed shot from the Sixth Ohio Battery exploded at the instant it struck the building; charging with a fierce yell, the Fifty-first Indiana took the hill at one o'clock.

Dense smoke rose from the valley, mingling with shreds of fog. Hood smashed through two enemy redoubts along Hillsboro pike and began to roll up Stewart's line against Granny White pike, occupied by Lee on the enemy right. Stewart held on stubbornly, his troops pouring down artillery fire from another hilltop. Thomas sent an aide with orders to storm it, and although one of Wood's brigade commanders called it "suicide sir, perfect suicide," the salient was carried without great difficulty.[41] Nevertheless, the movement took some time; and Wood was unable to reach still another assigned position, bivouacking for the night along the east side of Granny White pike. The fast-moving Wilson found himself two miles beyond the infantry line at nightfall, while Smith and Schofield had cleaned up the sector adjoining Wood. Although the Federals had made a late start, some 1,200 prisoners and sixteen guns had been taken and the entire enemy line shoved several miles over toward Cheatham on the right. Gathering up troops already in retreat, Hood fell back two miles to another fortified series of hills.

Thomas readjusted his position for the battle next day. Continuing his first-day plan of attack, he called upon Wilson to make his move along the right flank first, while the center was to demonstrate strongly until the enemy's left was turned. Wilson was instructed to press the enemy's left flank and rear "as soon as I could see to move, with all the force I could bring to bear," according to the cavalry leader's version of the verbal order.[42] Smith and Wood now occupied the center while Steedman continued to hold the left, where his provisional detach-

40 *Century Magazine*, August, 1887, 613.
41 *Ibid.*
42 Wilson, *Under the Old Flag*, II, 113.

ment had more than accomplished its first day's task. Hood made several important changes in his line, moving Cheatham from the right to the extreme left, opposite Schofield; Stewart became the center and Lee the right, facing Steedman. Some six miles long on the first day, the Confederate line was now contracted to about three miles.

"So far I think we have done pretty well," Thomas remarked as he started back to Nashville to wire Grant of the day's success. "Unless Hood decamps tonight, tomorrow Steedman will double up his right, Wood will hold his center, Smith and Schofield will again strike his left while the cavalry work away at his rear."[43] Thomas was hailed by some rebellious Confederate prisoners from South Carolina who complained of the presence of their colored guard. They would rather die, they maintained, than enter Nashville in charge of "nigger soldiers." The General's natural sympathy for human suffering failed him. "Well, you may say your prayers and get ready to die, for these are the only soldiers I can spare," he said coldly.[44] His wire to Grant: "Attacked enemy's left this morning; drove it . . . about eight miles," caused the Commander-in-Chief to retrace his journey from City Point to Washington where he was about to entrain for the West.[45]

Friday, December 16, dawned chilly and slightly foggy. Riding to the front with his aides, Thomas heard a window slammed down and was greeted by a look from a young Rebel lady "the reverse of angelic." The General rode on "with an amused smile," related Captain Stone. "The young lady in process of time became the affectionate wife of an officer then serving in Thomas's army."[46] The party encountered a group of Confederate wounded lying neglected and forgotten. An orderly was sent back to the city to bring up an ambulance and a surgeon, stimulants were provided from the flasks of the party, and another orderly was left on watch until assistance arrived.[47] Thomas rode along the lines on an inspection tour and received

43 Rustling, *Men and Things*, 96.
44 Johnson, *Thomas*, 196–97.
45 Coppée, *Thomas*, 269; Porter, *Campaigning With Grant*, 348.
46 *Century Magazine*, August, 1887, 614.
47 De Peyster, *Thomas* (pamphlet), 13.

informal greetings from the ranks. An earlier start was made that morning, the three infantry corps and the cavalry getting underway at 6:00 A.M.

Advanced enemy batteries opened on Steedman as he ascended the first hill on his front. Steedman halted for orders as he had been directed. Wood was energetically shelling Overton Knob, the northernmost summit, but was also waiting in place. While Wilson hacked away at the enemy left flank, Thomas permitted Smith's first division to charge one of the hills, but the enemy artillery proved too strong. Confident that the right moment would come for a general assault, Thomas waited for Wilson to get around Hood's left. Wilson made progress slowly although gathering in several hundred prisoners by noon. It was becoming a cat-and-mouse game; not until midafternoon did Thomas permit Wood to attack a salient hill. The blue-clads squeezed through long lines of sharpened stakes firmly planted in the ground and crept steadily along. Keeping the battered Union line well in range, four fieldpieces and six lines of infantrymen poured down canister, solid shot, and rifle fire. It was down on stomachs until relief came. Troops of the Eighty-ninth Illinois saw a cannon ball tear through the left side of Lieutenant Peter G. Tait. As the officer fell, his heart and left lung dropped out on his right arm, crossed over his body. The dangling heart, a comrade related, continued to throb for twenty minutes.[48] Federal artillery opened rapid fire; under this friendly cover the line fell back about three hundred yards where it re-formed and charged again. Gaining the parapet, the breathless Federals clubbed the gunners from their pieces and turned them about on the scurrying foe.

Wilson hastened over with news. A dispatch from Hood to Chalmers had been captured: "For God's sake, drive the Yankee cavalry from our left and rear or all is lost."[49] The cavalry commander found Thomas and Schofield standing together on a small hill from which the enemy line could be seen less than a mile away. "My dismounted men, their guidons fluttering in

48 W. R. Hartpence, *The 51st Indiana*, 265.
49 *Tennessee Historical Magazine*, VI, 258; Wilson, *Under the Old Flag*, II, 115.

their air, flanked and covered by two batteries of horse artillery, were in plain sight moving against the left and rear of the enemy line," Wilson recounted. "Pointing at the favorable condition of affairs, I urged Thomas with ill-concealed impatience, to order the infantry forward without further delay. Still the stately chieftain was unmoved. . . . He lifted his field glasses and coolly scanned what I clearly showed him. It was a stirring sight, and gazing at it, as I thought, with unnecessary deliberation, he finally satisfied himself. Pausing only to ask me if I was sure that the men entering the left of the enemy works above us were mine . . . he turned to Schofield and as calmly as if on parade directed him to move to the attack with his entire corps."[50] Thomas rode over to Smith and pointed to the hills beyond: "Order the charge." Aides were racing to Steedman and Wood.

About four o'clock a blast of artillery fire opened all along the line. From ammunition teams stuck fast in the mud, groups of soldiers carried shells and solid shot to the batteries. Hatch's division of infantry dismounted and hauled two artillery pieces up a hill. Inspired soldiers raced up the slopes, broke down tangled barricades, and entered the Confederate works as the hills quaked and roared. Every rifle and artillery piece not disabled was engaged in the grand duel against a background of dark hills and lowering clouds. General Rustling recalled how "grape and canister shrieked and whizzed; bullets in a perfect hailstorm. . . . The whole battlefield at times was like the grisly mouth of hell, agape and aflame with fire and smoke, alive with thunder and death-dealing shots. The hills and slopes were strewn with the dead; ravines and gorges crowded with wounded. I saw men with their heads or limbs shot off; others blown to pieces. I rode by a tree behind which a Confederate had dodged for safety, and a Union shell had gone clear through both tree and soldier and exploded among his comrades."[51] Loud cheering echoed back to headquarters—"the voice of the American people," said Thomas.

It took an hour or more to convince Hood of the futility of his task. A steady drizzle of rain had set in as the decimated

50 *Ibid.,* II, 116.
51 Rustling, *Men and Things,* 100–101.

Rebels slammed down their arms or raced from the field in a confused mob. If an estimated Confederate loss of 13,189, including 4,462 prisoners, is correct, more than half the enemy force had been put out of the fight. Hood's soldiers would never fight again as an army. Fifty-three guns and twenty-five flags had been taken in the two-day battle. Although badly mauled in their thrust against Lee, Steedman's colored troops brought in their share of the spoils. Union casualties, out of 50,000 men actually engaged in the fight, were reported as only 3,057, less than one-fourth the enemy loss.

Thomas lingered a few moments to commend his elated soldiers and to get Wood started in pursuit. Leaving his aides busy on the field, he rode off alone. Wilson, who was still pursuing Confederates down Granny White pike, heard a heavy gallop on the macadam behind him. Could it be Thomas—galloping? "As it came nearer and clearer the intuition flashed through my mind that it might be Thomas. . . . It was too dark to see or to recognize anyone, but reining up my horse and pulling him toward the side of the road a heavy figure loomed abreast of me, calling out: 'Is that you, Wilson?' Recognizing the voice, I halted and answered, 'Yes, General Thomas.' By the time these words were out, the dignified commander shouted so that he might have been heard a quarter of a mile off: 'Dang it to hell, Wilson, didn't I tell you we could lick 'em, didn't I tell you we could lick 'em?' With scarcely a pause for my reply, the General wheeled about and galloped for Nashville with a word of praise for the cavalry. He disappeared in the darkness shouting: 'Continue the pursuit as far as you can tonight and resume it as early as you can tomorrow morning.' "[52]

[52] Wilson, *Under the Old Flag*, II, 125.

XV

An Army Dispersed

SOME important men in Washington dictated telegrams to Thomas at the close of the first day's battle. "I rejoice in tendering to you and the gallant officers and soldiers of your command the thanks of this department for the brilliant achievement of this day. . . . E. M. Stanton, Secretary of War."[1] From General Grant: "I congratulate you and the army."[2] "Please accept for yourself, officers and men the nation's thanks for the good work of yesterday," President Lincoln telegraphed during the forenoon of December 16. "You have made a magnificent beginning; a grand consummation is within your easy reach. Do not let it slip."[3] Before leaving the field of battle, Thomas published these telegrams to the army in general orders which closed the day: "The major-general commanding with pride and pleasure . . . adds thereto his own thanks to the troops for the unsurpassed gallantry and good conduct displayed by them in the battle of yesterday and today."[4] A final message responding to telegrams received went out to Lincoln, Grant, Stanton, and Governor Johnson, the vice president–elect who now sat secure in Nashville's high-pillared capitol: "The army thanks you for your approbation of its conduct yesterday and [wishes] to assure you that it is not misplaced. . . . I have ordered the pursuit continued."[5]

The usual high commotion after a great victory reverberated over the land. Amid the playing of bands and much cheer-

1 Johnson, *Thomas,* 198.
2 *Ibid.*
3 *Ibid.,* 197–98; original letter in Dearborn Collection.
4 *Official Records,* 1st Series, XLV, Part 1, 50.
5 *Ibid.,* Part 2, 210.

ing, one hundred guns awoke Washington City the next morning. Grant ordered another hundred fired at City Point, and General Meade, commanding the Army of the Potomac, did likewise. Phil Sheridan's Army of the Shenandoah touched off a similar salute near Winchester, and when General John D. Stevenson followed suit at Harper's Ferry, artillery thunder rolling over the spruce-clad hills caused a Union brigadier at Martinsburg to inquire, "Any news from the front? Heavy firing has been heard here this afternoon."[6] Warm congratulations from Meade and Sheridan to their old associate were taken down in the busy telegraph office at Nashville. But of all the memorabilia of praise Thomas appreciated most the sentiments of Secretary of State Chase: "We all feel profoundly gratified to you and your gallant Army for the great success over Hood. I rejoice that you were in command."

General Sherman received the news on December 23 and wrote Thomas on Christmas Day. He had reached the sea in the meantime, entering Savannah on December 22 after the Fifteenth Corps had stormed lightly held Fort McAlister, fifteen miles inland, on the thirteenth. His letter to Thomas reflected a sense of relief rather than warm praise: "I have heard of all your operations up to about the 17th and I do not believe your own wife was more happy at the result than I was. Had any misfortune befallen you I should have reproached myself for taking away so large a proportion of the army and leaving you too weak to cope with Hood. But as events have turned out my judgment has been sustained," wrote Sherman, self-preoccupied, "but I am none the less thankful to you. . . . Here I am now in a magnificent house. . . . The old live oaks are beautiful as ever, and whilst you are freezing to death in Tennessee we are basking in a warm sun."[7] Thomas showed the letter to Colonel Rustling, who viewed it in the same light as the General, then cast it aside.

Cavalry leader Wilson clattered down Granny White pike on the heels of Chalmers' mounted men. Intense darkness and

---

[6] *Ibid.,* 1st Series, XLIII, Part 2, 796.

[7] Sherman to Thomas, December 25, 1864, Henry E. Huntington Library; Rustling, *Men and Things,* 104.

a dismal fall of rain marked the night of December 16; men and animals were almost spent. General Wood followed along with some straggling infantry but was soon outdistanced. About ten o'clock, four miles north of the Harpeth River, Hatch's mounted division discovered the enemy formed behind a fence-rail barrier laid across the road. Part of the division dismounted, deployed, and scattered the Confederate line. Some of the commands got badly mixed up in the running fight. Colonel George Spalding seized the bridle and then the sword of General E. W. Rucker of the Confederate cavalry. Both large and powerful men, the two officers grappled with each other in the darkness, each wresting away the other's saber to slash out with the exchanged weapons.[8] A stray shot which broke Rucker's sword finally decided the issue between the two.

Three fieldpieces were captured as the Rebels raced for Franklin. Taken to Wilson, Rucker stoutly declared, "Forrest has just arrived . . . and will give you hell tonight."[9] Forrest, in fact, was then on the run, but the bluff worked and Wilson desisted as the Confederate cavalry and infantry under General Lee patched up a strong line at Hollow Tree Gap. Most of Hood's worn-out foot soldiers and his wagons were crowding down Franklin pike, a parallel road to the east. Thomas never forgave himself for not having detached a mobile force to cut off the enemy rear. This failure, he later maintained in the presence of friends, was a "grave error of judgment"; Hood's army "ought all to have been captured."[10]

The Federals would not be able to do it through tail-end pursuit. Although Wilson managed to break through Hollow Tree Gap on the seventeenth, the fight was stubborn, and precious time was lost. The Confederate rear guard fell back through Franklin, destroying a Harpeth River bridge. After crossing the river by fords above and below the town, Wilson discovered the Rebels in an open field raked by artillery fire. Wilson thrust furiously at both flanks and then at the center, taking some two hundred prisoners and three more guns. "Had

8 Piatt, *Thomas*, 589.
9 Henry, *Forrest*, 410.
10 Van Horne, *Thomas*, 344.

not night settled we would have captured almost the entire rear guard of the enemy ... which ran like a flock of sheep," declared Thomas.[11] Meanwhile, Forrest had slanted cross-country with his cavalry and droves of cattle and hogs, joining the main army at Columbia the next day. While Wilson's hungry men and horses waited for supplies to come up, the Confederates escaped over Duck River.

More rain and the heavy roads detained Thomas and the infantry at Spring Hill. Renewing the chase on the nineteenth, Wilson's corps began to straggle. "With five brigades well in hand, [I] lost not an hour night or day that could possibly be avoided," the cavalry commander recounted. "But with rain and frost to chill and distress both horses and men, and the country getting wilder and more desolate as we pushed into it, we could not get forward fast enough on the flanks of the enemy's rear guard. ... The country ... was the worst we had yet seen ... entirely stripped of forage and supplies."[12]

When not engaged in hurrying the supply trains forward, Thomas applied himself to admonitory telegrams received from Grant and Halleck. "Great precaution should be taken to prevent [Forrest] crossing the Cumberland or Tennessee River below Eastport," wired Grant. "Permit me, General, to urge the vast importance of a hot pursuit," Halleck ventured politely. "Every possible sacrifice should be made."[13]

Thomas felt his ready indignation return. "General Hood's army is being pursued as rapidly and as vigorously as it is possible for one army to pursue another," he reminded Halleck on the twenty-first. "We cannot control the elements. ... I am doing all in my power to crush Hood's army and, if it be possible, will destroy it. But pursuing an enemy through an exhausted country, over mud roads completely sogged with heavy rains, is no child's play. ... I hope, in urging me to push the enemy, the department remembers that General Sherman took with him the complete organization of the Military Division of the Mississippi, well equipped in every respect, leaving me only two corps

11 *Official Records*, 1st Series, XLV, Part 2, 249.
12 Wilson, *Under the Old Flag*, II, 139–41.
13 Johnson, *Thomas*, 200–201.

partially stripped of their transportation. . . . This army is willing to submit to any sacrifice to crush Hood's army or to strike
any other blow which may contribute to the destruction of the
rebellion."[14]

Most of all Thomas missed his Fifty-eighth Indiana Regiment of trained pontoniers and bridge-builders which Sherman
had taken. Hardly a single bridge was left anywhere in the rear
of the fleeing Confederates. The situation was made worse by
the error of a staff officer who wrote "Murfreesboro" instead of
"Nolensville" on an order which was to have outlined an open
route for a pontoon train; and although the train was recalled
after it had gone two miles, a full day's time had been lost before
the infantry could cross Duck River on the twenty-second.[15]
Secretary Stanton and General Grant made some attempt to
soothe Thomas's ruffled feelings, the one assuring him of "un-
bounded confidence in your skill, vigor and determination . . .
to pursue and destroy the enemy"; the other compounding
"congratulations" with further unwanted advice.[16] Thomas
anticipated one of Grant's commands by sending General Steedman by rail to Decatur, Alabama, to block the river there while
Admiral Samuel P. Lee's gunboat flotilla coursed up the Tennessee to prevent a crossing above Florence. But after Forrest
led two savage rear-guard actions below Pulaski, the Confederate infantry made "double distance on half rations," reaching their river haven near Florence on Christmas Day.[17]

The ten-day pursuit was mostly a fight against exhaustion.
Wilson wore out 5,000 horses before his pressure began to
diminish against last-ditch defense by Forrest and the dauntless
rear guard of cavalry and infantry, many of the latter fighting
barefooted. While guns behind light field entrenchments held
off Wilson and Hatch north of the river, Hood and Forrest got
most of the army over the floating bridge between December 25
and 28, snatching up their pontoons behind them. On the
twenty-seventh, Lee's gunboats gingerly pushed through Muscle

14 *Ibid.*, 201–202.
15 Van Horne, *Thomas*, 354.
16 *Ibid.*, 358–59.
17 Henry, *Forrest*, 415.

Shoals but shied at engaging the enemy closely and failed to destroy the bridge. The omission was ascribed by Wilson to "the independence of the navy and the natural timidity of a deep-water sailor in a shoal-water river,"[18] but it was Thomas who would be blamed at Washington. The long pursuit came to an end at the river bank. Thomas had forced his men over 120 miles of soggy roads and a dozen swollen streams in an implacable chase through rain, snow, darkness, and frozen mud. He would punish men and horses no longer.

Despite all these difficulties, Grant could see only sunny skies and a wide-open road for Thomas. To General Sherman he gloomily remarked: "His pursuit of Hood indicated a sluggishness that satisfied me he would never do to conduct one of your campaigns."[19] This criticism served to veto Sherman's suggestion that Thomas should follow Hood as far as Selma, Alabama, if necessary. Concerning General Sherman, Grant had wired Halleck: "It is refreshing to see a commander, after a campaign of seven months' duration, ready for still further operations and without wanting any outfit or rest."[20] Thereupon Sherman lingered untroubled at Savannah a full month while receiving reinforcements from Thomas.

A message from Stanton to Thomas dated December 24 plunged the General deep in thought. There was nothing wanting in the wording of the telegram: "With great pleasure I inform you, that for your skill, courage and conduct in the recent brilliant military operation under your command, the President has directed your nomination . . . as a major general in the United States Army, to fill the only vacancy in that grade. No official duty has been performed by me with more satisfaction, and no commander has more justly earned promotion by devoted, disinterested and valuable services to his country."[21]

Thomas's mood, however, could not be changed by praise. Chief Surgeon George E. Cooper, who was standing by at Pulaski field headquarters, saw the General sit motionless and

18 *Ibid.*, 416.
19 Van Horne, *Thomas*, 361.
20 *Official Records*, 1st Series, XLV, Part 2, 264.
21 Van Horne, *Thomas*, 371.

silent with the telegram in his hand. The sensitive commander could reflect that he had been passed over not once but several times, as after Mill Springs, Chickamauga, and Chattanooga. As the higher commissions had been granted, one by one, they had gone to Sherman—August 12, 1864—to Meade on August 18, and to Sheridan, Thomas's junior in the service by thirteen years, on November 8. Sherman had been promoted to regular major general during the siege of Atlanta, Meade had received his commission in due course of events rather than for any single engagement, and Sheridan had been given his for the Battle of Cedar Creek which had caught him napping twenty miles away at Winchester. It had been fourteen months since Thomas had received his previous promotion—a commission to brigadier which had followed the dismissal of Rosecrans as commander of the Army of the Cumberland. Now there seemed to be no one else available to fill the vacancy created by the resignation of General McClellan, a presidential loser in November. Another very sore point with Thomas were rumors that he was to have been relieved while getting the army ready at Nashville.

Thomas turned to the surgeon and handed him the dispatch, saying: "What do you think of that?"

Cooper read the message and responded, "It is better late than never."

"I suppose it is better late than never but it is too late to be appreciated," Thomas replied moodily. "I earned this at Chattanooga."[22]

Thomas debated overnight what he would say to Stanton in reply, revealing the tenor of his thoughts in a message dated December 25: "I am profoundly sensible of the kind expressions in your telegram . . . instructing me that the President had directed my name to be sent to the Senate . . . and I beg to assure the President and yourself that your approbation of my services is of more value to me than the commission itself."[23] The incident did not pass without further expression of feeling, this time Quartermaster Donaldson, whom Thomas had known since the siege of Fort Brown in the Mexican War. As Donald-

---

[22] *Ibid.;* Rustling, *Men and Things,* 104.
[23] Piatt, *Thomas,* 377.

son later reported the conversation to Quartermaster-General Montgomery C. Meigs, "He [Thomas] feels very sore at the rumored intentions to relieve him and the major generalcy does not cicatrize the wound. You know Thomas is morbidly sensitive and it cut him to the heart to think that it was contemplated to remove him. He does not blame the Secretary, for he said Mr. Stanton was a fair and just man."[24]

This left, particularly, Grant. Alexander K. McClure, the Pennsylvania politician and antislavery publisher, had a theory: "I fear that Grant . . . never fully forgave Thomas for that wrong that Grant had done him in regard to the battle of Nashville."[25] The remark was clever but an oversimplification of the difficulty. Grant could only be greatly relieved by Thomas's victory since it justified Sherman's march to the sea and left that officer in the clear. The relationship between Grant and Sherman had been very close: they had been as brothers ever since Shiloh. Cast aside and humiliated during the march on Corinth, Grant had been buoyed up and encouraged by Sherman's faith and kind words. He naturally would respond in kind. While Thomas had been placed over Sherman during the campaign, Grant thereafter saw to it as well as he could that Sherman, another temporary underdog, came out on top. Although Sherman had been defeated at Missionary Ridge while Thomas won the great battle of the day, that was not the plan, and the fundamental character of the situation remained unchanged. Sherman was Grant's confidant, his loyal admirer, his dependent younger brother; Thomas, it appears, a man to receive orders from both. A few months after Chattanooga, Sherman was writing Grant, now a lieutenant general, in courtier-like terms:

"I believe you are as brave, patriotic and just as the great prototype Washington; as unselfish, kind-hearted and honest as a man should be; but the chief characteristic is the simple faith in success you have always manifested, which I can liken to nothing else than the faith a Christian has in a Savior.

"This faith gave you victory at Shiloh and Vicksburg. Also

24 *Official Records*, 1st Series, XLV, Part 2, 461.
25 McClure, *Lincoln and Men of War Times*, 341.

when you have completed your last preparations, you go into battle without hesitation, as at Chattanooga—no doubts, no reserves; and I tell you it was this that made us act with confidence. I knew wherever I was that you thought of me, and if I got in a tight place you could come if alive. . . . You are now Washington's legitimate successor."[26]

Even without this sweeping salute, Sherman would have received the principal command in the Atlanta Campaign. Now after Nashville, when Sherman was prompt in reminding Grant that he could use some of Thomas's men, his wishes would still come first. Thomas wanted to give his men a rest, such as Sherman's had enjoyed after their Tennessee campaign and were having now in the pleasant warmth of Savannah. The services of Thomas himself had been almost unbroken in the field since the beginning of the war. Only during the month of October had he permitted Mrs. Thomas to join him at Nashville, their first meeting since August, 1861.[27]

Announcing the end of the campaign against Hood on December 29, Thomas ordered Smith's corps to go into winter quarters at Eastport near Corinth, Mississippi; Wood's Fourth Corps, at Huntsville and Athens, Alabama; Wilson near Huntsville with a single cavalry division left at Eastport; and Schofield, at Dalton, Georgia. At the same time, Thomas drew in the limits of his military rule by suggesting that Governor Johnson reorganize Tennessee rule along civil lines: "All should certainly now feel that the establishment of rebel authority in the State of Tennessee is hopeless," he reminded the Governor.[28] Although the suggestion to Johnson was accepted, Thomas was brought up short by a wire from Halleck dated December 31: "Lieutenant-General Grant does not intend that your army should go into winter quarters. It must be ready for active operations in the field."[29] Thomas later discovered that this did not mean that he was to conduct any further campaign. Al-

26 Lewis, *Sherman*, 343.
27 Coppée, *Thomas*, 309.
28 Van Horne, *Thomas*, 369–70.
29 *Ibid.*, 376.

MAJOR GENERAL GEORGE H. THOMAS

A disillusioned officer, tardily promoted to major general, United States Army, following the Battle of Nashville

From an engraving by J. C. Buttre of a photograph by George N. Barnard
Courtesy Dr. Frederick M. Dearborn

though Sherman had suggested that the western army should penetrate middle and southern Alabama, a country rich in supplies, and Thomas was agreeable to a campaign in the spring, Grant demurred. Thomas, he theorized to Sherman by telegraph, "is too ponderous in his preparations and equipments to move through a country rapidly enough to live off it."[30] As a matter of fact, Grant seemed unwilling to give Thomas any opportunity to prove himself otherwise. Rather than try him in middle Alabama, which was still unforaged, he would retain him in a territory which already had been ransacked by marching armies a dozen times.

Grant responded to Sherman's request for more men by ordering Thomas to send him Schofield's Twenty-third Corps, raising the total for the Carolina campaign to 89,000 men. Thomas was being held at the end of a string; the Army of the Cumberland was not to be allowed to fight again under its own leader or as a single unit. Meanwhile, Grant remained motionless before the Confederate forces at Petersburg, replying to a delegation of Philadelphians who came to protest his inaction: "Just as soon as I hear that Sherman is at some one of the points designated on the seacoast, I will take Richmond. Were I to move now without advices from Sherman, Lee would evacuate Richmond, taking his army somewhere South, and I would have to follow him."[31] Whether or not this surmise was correct, Grant continued to linger at City Point for three months after Sherman had taken Savannah. Not until Goldsboro had fallen, in the interior of North Carolina, did he make his move. As long as all went well with Sherman, who could go where he wished, the war would be prolonged.

The dispersal of Thomas's army continued throughout the winter and early spring. After Schofield marched to aid Sherman and Wilson's headquarters were transferred to Waterloo and Gravelly Springs, Alabama, Thomas was ordered to supply the needs of General Edward R. S. Canby, who was operating along the Gulf. First the army of A. J. Smith was sent, then a division of Wilson's cavalry. Another mounted de-

[30] Piatt, *Thomas*, 578.
[31] Lewis, *Sherman*, 458.

tachment led by General George Stoneman was ordered to prepare for a campaign into East Tennessee and the Carolinas,
destroying railroads and raiding towns which lay west of Sherman's path and protecting his left flank. The situation was
puzzling to Wilson. "Just what they counted upon or expected
from Thomas, whom they had promoted to major general of
the regular army . . . was never made clear," he attested. "They
sent Schofield with one army corps to the east, Smith with another to Alabama, and Wood to Huntsville. In other words,
they scattered their infantry around as well as the splendid body
of cavalry I had got together with so much trouble."[32] Wilson's
special complaint was based upon the fact that after James F.
Knipe's division had been ordered to join Canby, he was asked
to send a similar mounted force to occupy Forrest by demonstrating against Tuscaloosa and Selma in the heart of the Alabama coal and iron region.

Finding himself immobilized, Thomas already had directed
Wilson to prepare for this very campaign. He recognized the
West Pointer, former aide to McClellan and Grant, as a good
disciplinarian and trustworthy and so gave him a free hand "to
drill, instruct and discipline both officers and men as well as
to build up, train and break in the horses for the spring campaign." The entire cavalry corps was being collected and remounted between Waterloo and Gravelly Springs, where can-
tonments of newly built log cabins and lean-to stables dotted
the countryside for miles. By the first of March, reinforcements
from Thomas had raised the corps to more than 27,000 men,
of whom 20,000 were mounted, with 15,000 armed with the
coveted Spencer magazine rifle. Wilson accurately described
his force as "the largest body of cavalry ever collected on the
American continent."[33]

But the mounted leader demurred at having his strength
frittered away; therefore, Thomas went up the river by steamboat to review the splendid corps and discuss what should be
done. Boarding the steamer at Waterloo, Wilson argued that a
"demonstration" in any direction would be but a useless waste

32 Wilson, *Under the Old Flag*, II, 180.
33 *Ibid.*, 165.

of strength. If permitted to take his entire available force, he promised not only the defeat of Forrest but the capture of Tuscaloosa; Selma—busiest arsenal center in the South; Montgomery—the first Confederate capital; and Columbus, Georgia —seat of gun, sword, and pistol factories. After the cavalry had passed in review with arms stiffly poised, bands playing, and guidons a-flap, Thomas assured Wilson that he could make his march. The suggestion was relayed to Grant, who also agreed but with the proviso that Wilson be allowed "all the latitude of an independent commander."[34] In other words, Wilson was to take Thomas's place as head of the army's striking force.

Thomas raised no objection since his only goal was the defeat of the Confederacy and he believed Wilson quite fit for an independent command. The cavalry officer had an anecdote to relate in evidence of the morale of his corps. One day he gave a Confederate lady permission to visit Nashville on a shopping expedition, supplying her with the necessary pass and a guard. Two days later one of his officers showed up with the lady's pocketbook containing the pass and $250 in gold which one of his men had found. Wilson put the purse in his desk. When the lady returned to report on her trip, she declared that it had been quite successful on the whole although she had been compelled to borrow some money for her shopping. Wilson then reached into his desk and handed the lady her pocketbook.

As Wilson elaborated the tale: "She received it in surprise and then grew desperately pale as though about to faint. . . . I asked what was the matter. 'Oh, the Confederacy is doomed, the Confederacy is doomed! It can not prevail against an army in which such discipline exists. Had my pocketbook been found by Confederate soldiers, I should never have seen it again.' "[35] Roving Confederate "cavalry"—any outlaw with a horse and a gun—had been the scourge of the South. When Thomas sent a party of officers to discuss an exchange of prisoners with Forrest during the latter part of February, the Confederate leader remarked that "he would esteem it a favor" if his opponent hanged every guerrilla he caught. It was during this conference

34 *Ibid.*, 180.
35 *Ibid.*, 181–82.

at Rienzi that Forrest, confessing his ignorance of any formal school of military tactics, made his famous remark that it was his rule "to get there first with the most men." He certainly did not say "fustest with the mostest," a mawkish rephrasing of the General's own words.[36]

Wilson prepared to make his campaign with a mounted force of 12,500 troopers under division commanders Eli Long, E. M. McCook of the "Fighting McCooks," and Emory Upton. Hatch's division remained behind at Eastport and that of R. W. Johnson at Pulaski to guard against guerrilla depredations. Three batteries of horse artillery, a pontoon train of 30 canvas boats and a supply train of 250 wagons guarded by 1,500 men not yet mounted accompanied the army, which, in Wilson's words, was "perfectly clad and equipped." Delayed by flood waters and bad roads, Wilson did not start to cross the Tennessee River until March 18, leaving the south bank four days later while Canby began his move against Mobile on the Alabama coast. Whether or not the preparations were "ponderous," as had been Grant's concern if Thomas had remained in the field, it was to be a spring campaign.

Since wire communications had been broken, couriers on horseback were to relay news of Wilson's successful rampage through rural and industrial Alabama. While John Croxton's brigade was sent to destroy the public buildings and Confederate government stores at Tuscaloosa, Wilson engaged a much lesser force under Forrest, who tried with all his might to parry a stroke against Selma with its great arsenal of furnaces, foundries, factories, and supply depots. Beaten in almost every encounter during a two-day running fight, Forrest saved his army by dashing into the open country as the Federals stormed the entrenchments about Selma on April 2, seizing 2,700 prisoners, 2,000 horses, many big guns, and tons of munitions. Arms-making machinery was dismantled and smashed, the torch put to factories and government buildings, and round shot rolled into the river.[37] News of the fall of Richmond was spread that same day, as President Jefferson Davis and Lee's army trailed south—

36 Henry, *Forrest,* 424.
37 Piatt, *Thomas,* 616.

Davis to the Deep South to be captured by an alert detachment of Wilson's cavalry. Still awaiting news from Alabama, Thomas ordered one hundred guns fired on Capitol Hill in celebration of the capture of Richmond. It was a joyful day in Nashville for Federal partisans. The Tenth Tennessee Regiment band played "Hail, Columbia" and other patriotic airs. Federal colors in abundance brightened up the dingy city, waving from the Capitol, from the Adams Express office, the St. Cloud Hotel, and the Colonnade Building where the telegraph office was housed— Flag Day in Nashville. Citizens reluctant to join in the festivities were reminded of their duty, and if colors were unavailable on the premises of offices and homes, they were supplied from quartermaster's stores.[38]

A few days later a former itinerant Methodist preacher and Whig newspaper editor of Knoxville, William G. Brownlow, was inaugurated as governor, and a controversial four-years' tenure began. Numbed by creeping despair, citizens loyal to the South awaited the final end of the fettered Confederacy which long since had ceased to protect them. On April 10 they witnessed "great rejoicing" over the surrender of General Lee at Appomattox. Thomas sped wires to the commanding officers at Chattanooga, Knoxville, Memphis, and Murfreesboro, ordering two hundred guns to be fired "at meridian tomorrow at each point in your command." Joyfully hailing the end of the Rebellion, Union-sponsored newspapers announced plans for a great celebration at Nashville to commemorate the raising of the Stars and Stripes over Fort Sumter in Charleston Harbor. A bright sun played over a city in gala array as officers in their finest dress uniforms assembled at noon on the fifteenth to lead a parade from Forts Negley and Wood. But almost at that very moment someone was seen racing out of the telegraph office. A horse and rider dashed to the Capitol, where Thomas, in cheerful mood, was chatting with Governor Brownlow. News of the assassination of Lincoln brought the celebration to a confused halt. Flags were placed at half-mast and the gay decorations were removed or draped in mourning. Once again army representatives patrolled the streets to remind recalcitrant citizens

[38] Wooldridge, *History of Nashville*, 203.

exactly what colors they should display.[39] Throughout the afternoon and until sundown guns on Capitol Hill boomed at intervals of one minute. Thomas busily dictated telegrams to his generals, to Secretary Stanton, and to Andrew Johnson, who had succeeded to the President's chair. "With profound sorrow for the calamity which has befallen the nation," he wired Johnson, "permit me to tender to you as President of the United States assurances of my profound esteem and hearty support."[40]

News from two successful generals trickled into Nashville as the body of Lincoln lay in state in the White House and the nation stewed in its wrath. "Please accept my congratulations," Thomas wired General Canby who had seized Mobile. For the capture of Selma, Wilson was asked to accept "my cordial thanks and heartiest congratulations."[41] Wilson was managing all he had promised and before he had finished would do still more. Following the capture of Selma, he raised the Federal colors over the original Confederate Capitol at Montgomery on April 12; four days later, traveling light, he shot his way into Columbus on the lower Chattahoochee River, seizing 1,200 prisoners and 52 guns plus the Confederate ram *Jackson*, a dozen locomotives, and large quantities of small arms, munitions, supply stores, and cotton.

Thomas's message to Wilson was accompanied by a letter offering a formal surrender to forces under General Richard Taylor, son of President Zachary Taylor, commanding the Confederate Military Division of the West. Terms were to be the same as those offered Lee by Grant: "Rolls of all the men and officers to be made in duplicate. . . . The arms, artillery and public property to be stacked and parked. . . . This will not embrace side-arms of the officers nor their private horses or baggage. . . . Each officer and man will be allowed to return to his home."[42] But since Wilson was miles away at Columbus on the day the letter was written, surrender terms were arranged

39 *Tennessee Historical Quarterly*, March, 1945, 21.
40 Johnson Papers, 58:2613.
41 *Official Records*, 1st Series, XLIX, Part 2, 378–79, 383.
42 *Ibid.*, 379.

between Taylor and Canby at Citronelle, forty miles north of Mobile. While authorizing General Steedman and other officers to accept the surrender of guerrilla bands, Thomas threatened recalcitrants with angry words. Should Brigadier General William T. Wofford persist in his known plans for a raid into East Tennessee, Thomas advised Steedman, "tell him we are prepared, and if he makes the attempt, I will so despoil Georgia that it will be a wilderness 50 years hence."[43]

Wilson, riding hell-for-leather, was racing east from Columbus to Macon, where on April 20 he outlined terms to four sober-faced generals after gathering in 3,500 captives, 60 guns and 3,000 stands of small arms plus the usual stores and supplies, which included several million dollars in Confederate paper money. Some of the worthless currency made a fairly nice light for a cigar. Save for some scattered forces west of the Mississippi, it was the final capitulation of the war. When the surrender order for the entire Confederacy came on May 6, there was talk among Forrest's division of "going to Mexico" and the General himself was dissuaded from going only by the argument of his inspector general, Charles W. Anderson, who declared it his duty to guide his men in the paths of peace.[44]

The soldiers began to return to their farms. Numerous recruits, whom Thomas had been training, were mustered out and sent happily home. The veteran Fourth Corps quit East Tennessee for Nashville, and on May 9 Thomas bade a formal farewell to men who had fought at Shiloh, Stone River, Chickamauga, Chattanooga, Atlanta, Franklin, and Nashville. From a stand erected on the outskirts of the city, the commanding General and a few invited notables watched fifty-four thinned regiments, some numbering scarcely one hundred men, pass in review. "Reverently and affectionately they saluted the old hero as they reached the reviewing stand," wrote one who marched. "Thousands of soldiers . . . never looked upon that strong and kindly face again."[45] In the seclusion of his office next morning,

---

43 *Ibid.*, 395.

44 Henry, *Forrest*, 437.

45 *Tennessee Historical Magazine*, VI, 262.

Thomas, brimming over with sentiment, put on paper words which he never could have summoned while facing his troops:

"The General Commanding the Department takes pride in conveying to the Fourth Army corps the expression of his admiration, excited by their brilliant and martial display at the Review yesterday.

"As the battalions of your magnificent corps swept successfully before the eye, the coldest heart must have warmed with interest in contemplation of these men, who had passed through the varied and shifting scenes of this great, modern tragedy, who had stemmed with unyielding breasts the Rebel tide threatening to engulph the landmarks of Freedom; and who, bearing on their bronzed and furrowed brows the ennobling marks of the years of hardship, suffering and privation, undergone in defense of freedom and the integrity of the Union, could still preserve the light step and wear the cheerful expressions of youth."[46]

The corps boarded steamers for New Orleans, the next post of duty, leaving only the regular garrison at Nashville, every man of which was becoming a passable carpenter, painter, lumberjack, or mechanic in refurbishing the worn-out town. Other detachments were shifted from place to place in the task of restoring the miles of broken railroad and wire communications, some only recently destroyed. To Speaker James R. Hood of the recently elected Tennessee House, Thomas gave assurance that he was prepared to assist the civil authorities in every part of the state, both by protecting them "from personal violence when in the execution of their office, and in holding courts."[47] With much hammering and pounding and fitting things awkwardly into place, the work of rebuilding the South had begun.

[46] *Army and Navy Journal*, June 3, 1865.
[47] *Ibid.*, June 10, 1865.

XVI
Reconstruction Years

THE conscientious execution of ordinary military duties placed Thomas above gifts. His rule was to hold himself wholly independent and to refuse all offerings of value. Thus he intercepted a fund-raising movement among grateful Louisville and Cincinnati citizens by directing that the money be used for the relief of disabled soldiers and the widows and orphans of dead veterans.[1] A postwar command suitable to his rank, however, he would have. General Steedman, returning from an official mission to Washington, displayed a map with military divisions already marked out for the top-ranking major generals. Halleck was to have the Pacific Coast; Sheridan, the territory west of the Mississippi; Sherman, the Midwest and the South; and Meade, the Atlantic Coast down to Georgia. For Thomas, only a department within Sherman's Division of the Mississippi was designated. This would of course, continue him in a subordinate role.

Folding up the map and placing his fist upon it, Thomas gave certain instructions to General John Miller, commanding the Post of Nashville, who had become quite well acquainted with President Johnson during his governorship. "I wish you to take the first train for Washington and tell President Johnson that during the war I permitted the national authorities to do what they pleased with me," Thomas told Miller. "The life of the Nation was then at stake, and it was not proper to press questions of rank, but now that the war is over . . . I demand a command suited to my rank, or I do not want any."[2]

1 *Army and Navy Journal,* February 4, 1865; Van Horne, *Thomas,* 423–24.
2 *Ibid.,* 396.

Miller took the map and went to Washington. There he located the President in the Treasury Building where temporary offices had been set up while Mrs. Lincoln still occupied the White House. Miller produced his map and remarked that in his opinion Thomas should have charge of reconstruction in the various states in which he had served during the war. Johnson seemed fairly willing. "You know my appreciation of General Thomas," he remarked, and drew a pencil along the outer boundaries of Kentucky, Tennessee, Mississippi, Alabama, and Georgia. That, said the President, was to be the new division for Thomas. Johnson's action took considerable territory away from Sherman and made it necessary for War Department heads to engage in a reluctant reshuffling of the commands. Since Sherman had been left only the territory between Pennsylvania and the Mississippi River, his command was now extended to the Rocky Mountains while Sheridan received the Gulf states of Florida, Louisiana, and Texas, which remained from the newly created Division of the Tennessee. Although Mississippi was included in Sheridan's command in the War Department order of June 27, 1865, it was restored to Thomas, upon his inquiry, in the fall.

More Southern states had fallen to the rule of Thomas than to any other military commander. The Virginian whom Southern newspapers had long berated for "disloyalty" had received jurisdiction from the Ohio River to the Gulf. Convinced that professed Rebels were lacking in basic moral fiber, Thomas recommended that Governor Brownlow adopt "strenuous measures" in enforcing punitive laws passed by the Tennessee legislature.[3] This the "Fighting Parson" was pleased to do.

Because both Thomas and Brownlow had suffered much abuse from the Confederacy, they were allied in action even though they were poles apart in basic character. Tall, thin, and smooth-shaven, with a great shock of hair on his head, Brownlow was an austere and fanatical character—a hell-fire preacher as a young circuit rider and a caustic and vituperative penman as editor of the Knoxville *Whig*. He had opposed secession rather than slavery, upholding the "domestic institution" in public

[3] Johnson Papers, 71:5567.

debates in the North. Success had not come easily to Brownlow, and it took a devastating war to place him in power. Beaten by Andrew Johnson in an early Congressional election, he thereafter upheld the Whig opposition in his Knoxville paper until forced to exile in the North, where he happened upon more money than he had ever seen before by lecturing on the horrors attending the rape of East Tennessee. The war over, he became God's chosen instrument to work His will upon a misguided people. For the defeated and resentful, his prescription was further humiliation and embarrassment. His labors with the Tennessee legislature produced a bill by which anyone found wearing a Confederate uniform would be fined from five to fifty dollars, depending upon the rank of the offender—this at a time when thousands of former soldiers had only a Confederate uniform to wear. Although the Parson induced the Tennessee Senate to pass a bill depriving Confederate ministers of the right to perform the marriage ceremony and requiring them to work on the roads and serve in the militia, the measure was rejected by the House. A measure requiring women to swear allegiance to the United States before they could be married failed in the Senate by only one vote.[4] Thomas faithfully supported the Brownlow rule by attempting to muzzle a reviving Confederate press, combating negrophobia, guarding the polls, assisting in arrests, and altogether was as zealous in reconstructing what he termed "many obtuse minds" as if he had been born in Massachusetts—though the effectiveness of the methods used may be open to question.

On the other hand, Thomas would go as far as anyone in obtaining pardons and privileges for former Confederate officers and their kin. The war was not yet over when he tried to convince Secretary Stanton that it was proper to permit the widow of General Richard S. Ewell to remain in Nashville long enough to complete the disposition of her private affairs, but the Secretary was adamant in ordering her immediate return to St. Louis.[5] The General's later correspondence was sprinkled with

[4] E. Merton Coulter, *William G. Brownlow*, 269.

[5] Thomas-Stanton correspondence, April 21–24, 1865, Richard S. Ewell Papers, Library of Congress.

appeals for help in obtaining Presidential pardons and with thanks for those received. He heeded appeals from his old classmate General Paul O. Hebert of Louisiana, from Generals William T. Wofford, Gideon J. Pillow, Josiah Gorgas, and James Longstreet, and from the friends of Alexander H. Stephens, Confederate vice president now languishing in jail.

While Thomas and Brownlow held similar views regarding the advancement of the Federal Union, personal elements of difference were summed up by Navy Secretary Gideon Welles, classed as a "Moderate," in his interesting diary. While Brownlow, to Welles, was a "coarse, vulgar creature," the "fine, soldierly appearance"[6] of Thomas caught his eye during a meeting at the White House in October. "My impressions are," wrote Welles, "that he has, intellectually and as a civilian, as well as a military man, no superior in the service. . . . He has been no courtly carpet officer, to dance attendance on Washington during the War but has nobly done his duty."[7] Thomas received the applause of former fellow officers and other members of the House when escorted to the Speaker's stand during his visit at the Capitol. The General was rocked by solid cheers as if he were facing a gale. Speaker Schuyler Colfax, who stood at the hero's side, saw his hand tremble "like an aspen leaf" as he "shrank from the storm of applause."[8]

Owing chiefly to Brownlow's legislative tactics, the policy of repression, in Thomas's division, was at its worst in Tennessee, although there were protracted storms as well in Kentucky, where General John G. Palmer, commanding the district, was fighting "high-handed," in his own words, the battles of the Negro.[9] Clashes were frequent between returned Confederate soldiers and "loyal citizens," particularly in East Tennessee where the tables had been squarely turned, and the sea of troubles was made more stormy by the enforcement of law by Negro soldiers. The President judiciously ordered these troops from East Tennessee, where a sufficient number of loyal whites

[6] Welles, *Diary*, II, 557.

[7] *Ibid.*, II, 382.

[8] Society of the Army of the Cumberland, 1870 Reunion, *Report*, 89.

[9] Palmer, *A Conscientious Turncoat*, 183.

were maintaining law and order after their own fashion. Thomas believed the Negroes to be doing their job well. "As a general rule the negro soldiers are under good discipline," he wrote the President on September 5. "I have required all commanding officers to keep their commands under good discipline and . . . I believe they have. I believe in the majority of cases of collision between whites and negro soldiers that the white man has attempted to bully the negro, for it is exceedingly repugnant to Southerners to have negro soldiers in their midst & some are so foolish as to vent their anger upon the negro because he is a soldier."[10] However, clashes also had occurred between Negro and white troops, who were "particularly hostile." Despite the difficulties, since all the regular regiments in Kentucky and Tennessee had been ordered to be mustered out, Thomas had no choice but to continue using the Negro troops as guards.

A tour of inspection through Mississippi, Alabama, and Georgia during the fall convinced Thomas that justice to the Negro was generally being observed by civil and military officers and that the worst cases of open rebellion were the Bishop of Alabama and "the women."[11] The Right Reverend Richard Hooker Wilmer, an interesting case of unreconstruction, was considered guilty of misfeasance for having instructed his clergy to omit the prescribed prayer for all those in civil authority as "utterly incongruous under the present state of affairs." He was visited in Mobile by a member of Thomas's staff, who proved no match for him in an argument concerning Church *versus* State. When the officer fell back upon the threat of force, the Bishop remarked, "Suppose our positions reversed. Suppose we had conquered you."[12] Force it had to be. But after Thomas had suspended the Bishop and closed the churches, members continued to meet for worship in private homes throughout the unchastened diocese. It was true Christian martyrdom. "The people," commented the *Historical Magazine* of the Protestant

[10] Johnson Papers, 76:6701.

[11] Van Horne, *Thomas*, 401–402.

[12] T. C. De Leon, *Belles, Beaux and Brains of the Sixties*, 374–75; Richard H. Wilmer, *The Recent Past*, 143–44; Van Horne, *Thomas*, 409–10.

Episcopal Church, "rather enjoyed this military tyranny."[13] About a year later, however, after civil authority had been restored in the state of Alabama, Bishop Wilmer ordered the clergy and laity to resume using the prayer for the President of the United States, who, after all, had now set his face against the Radical persecutors in Congress.

Southern states were being readmitted to the Union when and if their legislatures ratified the Fourteenth Amendment, by which citizenship rights were not to be abridged because of race, color, or previous condition of servitude. Governor Brownlow, during a hot July, was doing his best to secure a legislative quorum in order to vote on the amendment. A special session was convened on the Fourth at Nashville and the Senate promptly ratified it, but the assemblymen who came willingly numbered only fifty-four, whereas fifty-six were necessary for a quorum. The House continued to meet from day to day as excitement and suspense filled the ordinarily languorous city. "I could observe it," remarked Thomas, "from the conversations various persons had with me, and what I read in the newspapers. . . . The comments of the papers were very severe on both sides, and so were the remarks of those persons who conversed with me. . . . It was my opinion that there was a disposition to break up the legislature."[14]

Brownlow requested action by the military arm. Asked to arrest two absent legislative members, Thomas wired General Grant (July 14, 1866) asking whether he should furnish military assistance. Grant passed the wire over to Secretary Stanton, who may have ordered the action *sub rosa* without consulting the President, for it was not until the seventeenth that Johnson saw the telegram. The President then emphatically declared that Thomas should "not meddle with local parties and politics"; but by this time the two required assemblymen had been arrested and seated, ratification pulling through by a vote of forty-three to thirteen. Diarist Welles, who detected the hand of

[13] *Historical Magazine of the Protestant Episcopal Church*, June, 1938, 145–47.

[14] James Welch Patton, *Unionism and Reconstruction in Tennessee*, 217–18.

Stanton in the proceedings, commented: "This is an exhibition of Radical regard for honest principle, for popular opinion, and for changes in the organic law. The change is to be imposed upon the people by fraud, not adopted by choice." The news of Tennessee's affirmation, Welles also noted, "caused great exultation in Congress."[15]

The Radicals, in their rejoicing, could consider that Tennessee had had its come-uppance for a race riot in Memphis which had begun in a quarrel between Negro soldiers and Irish policemen. Three days of savage bloodletting resulted in the deaths of some forty Negroes, and although Thomas made a number of arrests that summer, the grand jury, he reported to Grant, "failed to take any notice whatever of the offenders or of the riot."[16] Other incidents, some fully as grave, symbolized the dangers inherent in reconstruction efforts in suppressed once-sovereign states. A riot attending a procession of freedmen in Norfolk—celebrating the passage of a Civil Rights bill guaranteeing "equal rights" to all citizens—resulted in the deaths of two whites and two Negroes; but "St. Bartholomew's Day of New Orleans," so called, was one of the most sanguinary in the country's peacetime history. The rule of General Sheridan in Louisiana had proved so rigid and harsh as to arouse justifiable suspicion that he had his eye on the Presidency. By engaging in wholesale removals from office, Sheridan served notice that no citizen was eligible to serve in any post unless personally acceptable to the military commander. The blow-off came on July 30, 1866, as a convention met to revise the state constitution and consider the adoption of the Fourteenth Amendment. Troops who had been ordered to guard the hall failed to appear through a misunderstanding of the time of the meeting. A drunken mob drove a procession of Negroes into the building, then stormed it, and when the work was done, 534 colored men and three whites lay dead, including the minister who had offered prayer at the opening of the meeting. Negroes also comprised a large

---

[15] Johnson Papers, 97:11681; Van Horne, *Thomas*, 407; Howard K. Beale, *The Critical Year*, 105; Welles, *Diary*, II, 556–58.

[16] Thomas to Grant, August 15, 1866, Stanton Papers.

majority of the some 150 wounded.[17] There continued, of course, the scattered assaults on Union men and Negroes by former Confederate soldiers in every state, but it was during the summer of 1866 that mob violence reached its apogee.

In August the two southern divisions were discontinued and made departments, and Thomas was permitted to move his headquarters to Louisville, considered a more agreeable city. Some official notice of his services was taken by the Tennessee legislature, which voted $1,000 to have his portrait painted by Artist George Dury of Washington, and a gold medal commemorating the Battle of Nashville was ordered from Tiffany's in New York.[18] The medal was more acceptable than the painting, which was to bring some later embarrassment once a Democratic legislature was elected. An engraved service of silver plate, offered by a group of officers and friends, was somewhat brusquely refused.[19] The General desired no reward. Accepted, however, was a military memento—a jeweled badge of the Army of the Cumberland, the gift of his staff. Thomas returned to Nashville on December 15 to accept the gold medal during a commemorative downpour of rain, which forced scheduled outdoor ceremonies into the Capitol. Governor Brownlow presented the medal with an allusion to the victory at Nashville and "Funeral Rights" for traitors, to which Thomas responded with a speech commending his officers and troops: "I today take pride in saying that no other country on earth ever produced such another army as that which assembled to put down the rebellion. . . . It is with the greatest pleasure that I avail myself today of the opportunity in speaking in praise of those gallant men and officers then under my command."[20]

A more placid mood existed in Kentucky, which had turned away from the Radicals in a Democratic landslide. But since it had remained a sovereign state throughout the war, it bitterly resented the provision that statehood now depended upon

---

17 Robert Selph Henry, *Story of Reconstruction*, 180, 188–89.
18 Van Horne, *Thomas*, 415–17.
19 *Ibid.*, 424; Coppée, *Thomas*, 308.
20 Van Horne, *Thomas*, 415–17.

ratification of the Fourteenth Amendment. Ratification, in Kentucky, would have to wait. Commotions of sorts in other states took up much of the General's time and attention. A few weeks of quiet were broken by the arrest of several citizens of Rome, Georgia, who marked the January 19 anniversary of Georgia's secession by bold displays of the Confederate flag. This symbolism was especially irritating to Thomas, who preferred to view the Stars and Bars as a trophy of war. The arrest of the offenders was ordered. Replying to Rome's mayor, Charles H. Smith, who contended that no disrespect to the United States government was intended, Thomas unleashed his scorn of the Confederacy and all its works.

"The sole cause of this and similar offenses," he fired back, "lies in the fact that certain citizens of Rome, and a portion of the people of the States lately in rebellion, do not and have not accepted the situation, and that is, that the late civil war was a rebellion and history will so record it. Those engaged in it are and will be pronounced rebels; rebellion implies treason; and treason is a crime, and a heinous one too, and deserving of punishment; and that traitors have not been punished is owing to the magnanimity of the conquerors. With too many of the people of the South, the late civil war is called a revolution, rebels are called 'Confederates,' loyalists to the whole country are called d——d Yankees and traitors, and over the whole great crime with its accursed record of slaughtered heroes, patriots murdered because of their true-hearted love of country, widowed wives and orphaned children, and prisoners of war slain amid such horrors as find no parallel in the history of the world, they are trying to throw the gloss of respectability, and are thrusting with contumely and derision from their society the men and women who would not join hands with them in the work of ruining their country. Everywhere in the States lately in rebellion, treason is respectable and loyalty odious. This, the people of the United States, who ended the Rebellion and saved the country, will not permit."[21]

Although Thomas's plain words, backed as they were by strong personal feeling, may have struck with force, it was like

21 *Army and Navy Journal,* March 2, 1867.

pushing back water. Southerners who still felt the righteousness of their cause were not likely to be more co-operative after hearing themselves thus characterized. A secret organization known as the Ku Klux Klan, a trivial movement at the start, was beginning to arouse interest among former Confederate soldiers in Tennessee. The group had led an aimless existence for more than a year when its true possibilities, as a force to instill superstitious terror into the Negro, were discovered. In May, 1867, a thorough reorganization of the secret body took place in Room 10 of the Maxwell House in Nashville. That the Klan now meant business was indicated by the election of Nathan Bedford Forrest as Grand Wizard. Other appointments—Grand Dragons, Grand Titans, Grand Giants, Grand Cyclops, and subordinate Genii, Hydras, Furies, Goblins, Night Hawks, Magi, Monks, Turks, Scribes, Sentinels, and Ensigns—were also made by ordinary members known as Ghouls. The so-called "Invisible Empire" no longer comprised ordinary states, Congressional districts, counties, and towns but was transformed by edict into Realms, Dominions, Provinces, and Dens. Scary regalia was selected—hooded uniforms of black and scarlet, a white flag with a black cross—and the Ghouls tiptoed out of the hotel as secretly as they had come in.[22]

There followed midnight parades "in deathlike stillness," and even a "tournament," after the manner, perhaps, of those in Scott's novels of which Southerners had read many. Cities and towns were decorated with terrifying emblems—a death's head and cross-bones, daggers dripping blood. Odd jobs undertaken by the Klan in Tennessee included various severe beatings administered to Union men and Negroes with warnings against voting; the burning of schoolhouses, the mailing of many threatening letters couched in weird and grotesque terms, the murder of a Baptist minister, and the lynching of a white desperado who was taken from jail.[23] Convinced that the Klan was an armed political machine organized with a view of controlling southern elections through intimidation and actual vio-

[22] Henry, *Forrest*, 442–43; Patton, *Unionism and Reconstruction in Tennessee*, 181.

[23] *Ibid.*, 185–86.

lence, Thomas collected all available evidence of activities in Tennessee and Kentucky and forwarded it to Washington, and although he was abused by the Conservative press, which hastened to deny the truth of the statements, stories of oppression and outrage continued to pour in. A Tennessee law authorizing sheriffs to recruit posses to hunt down Klansmen failed in its purpose because too many officials were members of the order themselves. Still restive under the Brownlow rule, the city of Nashville hatched an election problem in September. In responding to Brownlow's appeal for protection, Thomas hurried to the city to maintain order during a municipal election, bringing with him sufficient troops to avert a clash between army guards and extra policemen who had been called in by Mayor W. Matt Brown. Outnumbered in respect to armed forces, Brown withdrew under protest, and the election was handily won by the Commissioner of Registration, one A. E. Alden, a carpetbagger whom Nashville Conservatives later credited with the theft of $700,000 in less than two years.[24] Nashville was again becoming a prosperous town.

Because Thomas invariably consulted with Washington before taking any authoritative action, he continued in high favor at the White House. Sheridan, the personal friend of Grant, acted first and consulted afterward, the General-in-Chief taking no exception to his numerous removals and arrests. When Sheridan began again to oust duly elected officials from office, Johnson sought his removal over the remonstrance of Grant, who was temporarily occupying the office of secretary of war following the dismissal, that summer, of Stanton. Replying to Grant's protest that Sheridan had performed his civil duties "faithfully and intelligently," Johnson contrasted his record with that of Thomas, whom, the President declared, "has not failed, under the most trying circumstances, to enforce the laws, to preserve peace and order, to encourage the restoration of civil authority, and to promote as far as possible a spirit of reconciliation."[25] So Sheridan was removed to western scenes and Thomas appointed in his place.

24 Coulter, *Brownlow*, 342–43; Welles, *Diary*, III, 211–12; Johnson Papers, 121:17133, 17143, 17170, 17183, 17189.
25 George Fort Milton, *Age of Hate*, 458–59.

Thomas immediately declined the appointment. He would not go farther south. Writing Grant from Lewisburg, West Virginia, where he was visiting one of the curative springs, he insisted that he would be of no greater service to Louisiana and Texas than General Sheridan. No prosecutor or proselyter by choice, Thomas wished to remain where affairs were most quiet. "I fear the reconstruction of those states will be very much retarded if it does not fail altogether by appointing me to that command," he told Grant. "I earnestly hope . . . that General Hancock to whose Department General Sheridan is assigned may be disposed to relieve him than relieve me."[26] To clinch his argument, Thomas enclosed a doctor's certificate testifying to a bad liver, and the reason for his refusal was publicly announced as poor health. When a worried former aide wrote to inquire after details, the General replied that although he had suffered some pain in his side, medicine had given him "great relief." He had protested to Grant "not on the score of health . . . but because of the hostility of the people toward me, making it impossible for me to be of any service . . . in the Southern States."[27] Thomas was satisfied to remain in comparatively friendly surroundings in Louisville, although a chance remark by a former opponent-at-arms seemed to indicate that he was fully not happy nor could be. A meeting in Louisville had been arranged between Thomas and General Hood, who happened to be stopping at the same hotel. As Hood came clattering down the corridor on his crutches, Thomas flung open his door, threw his arm around his old rival, "and helped him in with a tenderness that was touching." The two men occupied themselves for an hour with conversation and occasional silences, and upon returning to his room, Hood remarked: "Thomas is a grand man. He should have remained with us, where he would have been appreciated and loved."[28]

Topics discussed by Thomas and Hood conceivably were the campaigns of Atlanta and Nashville, both of which had left sore spots. Thomas could not complain of lack of special

26 Thomas to Grant, August 22, 1867, Dearborn Collection.
27 Coppée, *Thomas*, 296–97.
28 Piatt, *Thomas*, 51; Van Horne, *Thomas*, 206.

attention from the body politic, mostly Moderates who were looking for a foil against Grant, who was very much in the race for the Presidency. Since early that year, 1867, he had been declining written and verbal suggestions that he permit his name to be used as a choice for high office. Editor Murat Halstead of the Cincinnati *Commercial* considered that there was hope. Thomas, he wrote, "refused the command of the Army of the Cumberland at one time but had come to it later." General Henry M. Cist declared it "a matter of duty" for Thomas to run. Reflecting upon his lack of experience and his distaste for politics, Thomas stuck to his guns. He was utterly disqualified for such a responsible position, he informed Cist, "being but a mere tyro in the science of government."

While political incapacity would not stop others from running, Thomas believed in fundamental preparedness. Furthermore, as an army officer, he had been accustomed to giving orders and seeing them carried out without bickering or palaver, and without having his powers circumscribed by a debating body such as Congress, which was busily overriding the vetoes of President Johnson. "I have not the necessary control over my temper," his letter to Cist continued, "nor have I the faculty of yielding to a policy and working to advance it unless convinced within myself that it is right and honest. My habits of life . . . are such as to make it repugnant to my self respect to have to induce people to do their duty by persuasive measures. If there is anything that enrages me more than another, it is to see an obstinate and self willed man oppose what is right morally, & under the law, simply because, under the law, he cannot be compelled to do what is right. . . . I have no taste whatever for politics, and besides, restrictions have recently been thrown around the President by Congress which virtually deprive him of his just powers and rights. . . . I could never consent to be deprived of rights and privileges guaranteed . . . by the Constitution as long as the Constitution itself remains unaltered. . . . I was very glad to receive your letter as it has afforded me an opportunity to express my sentiments in an unmistakable manner."[29] Although this letter, when published, won Thomas

[29] Cist-Thomas correspondence, March, 1867, Henry E. Huntington Library; Van Horne, *Thomas*, 421–22.

some applause for his principles, which were considered as an example for Grant, they failed nevertheless, to carry weight in this respect. The General-in-Chief was definitely on the side of the Radicals and stood as their obvious choice for 1868.

Thomas occupied a platform seat beside General Sherman as the Society of the Army of the Cumberland held its organization meeting in Cincinnati on February 6 and was elected president of that body by acclamation. Speeches, reminiscences, eulogies, and feasting occupied two full days. At the Burnet House banquet which ended the session, the name of Thomas was heard at the eighth toast, "loud calls were made for the General, the audience rising . . . and drinking his health with the wildest excitement."[30] Thomas arose and mentioned some incidents of the war at Chattanooga and then touched upon a favorite subject, military discipline: "We were tied up . . . we did not have a great deal to eat, we economized our rations and proposed to starve before we gave up that place. . . . We waited patiently, diminished our rations from day to day until they became almost a myth, but the day came when the Army of the Tennessee, on our left, opened the way to relief and final triumph. . . .We have not only broken down one of the most formidable rebellions that ever threatened the existence of any country, but the discipline of the Army of the Cumberland alone has civilized two hundred thousand valuable patriots and citizens. I have traveled a little since the war was over. Wherever I have been . . . I have either seen on the steamboat, engaged in peaceful occupations of merchant sailors, or in the fields along the railroad, engaged in peacefully following the plow and setting an example of industry worthy to be followed by all the country, men innumerable dressed in blue."[31]

Sherman came to Cincinnati wearing three stars. Grant was now serving both as army general and secretary of war. Opportunity remained for Thomas to receive higher rank if he wished. With the reconvening of Congress, a resolution was quickly adopted disapproving the suspension of Secretary

[30] Society of the Army of the Cumberland, First Meeting (1867), *Report*, 83.

[31] *Ibid.*, 83–86; Van Horne, *Thomas*, 425–26.

Stanton, and Grant cheerfully walked out of the War Office, having kept the seat warm for Stanton. The sequel was some acrimonious correspondence between Grant and the White House, and Stanton was again dismissed, although he would not quit now, with the President on the run. While Presidential impeachment was excitedly discussed in Congress, Johnson sent Thomas's name to the Senate for confirmation as brevet lieutenant general and brevet general. What Johnson really meant to do was to oust Grant as army commander, replacing him with Thomas, who would also succeed Stanton. Thomas was familiar with the maneuver, which already had been tried, some months before, on Sherman. Acceptance, he knew, would only widen the breach between the President and Congress. Therefore, on February 22, 1868, he telegraphed Senator Ben Wade, Radical leader from Ohio, that the Senate should refuse to confirm: "My services since the war do not merit so high a compliment, and it is now too late for it to be regarded as a compliment if conferred for services during the war."[32] A wire to Johnson, declining the nomination, was sent the next day. The messages served their purpose. Thomas preserved with the draft of his telegram to Johnson a printed copy of the hymn "Dare To Do Right," sent him by an anonymous admirer from Pittsburgh, and considered the incident closed.

He advised the War Department that he would be glad to receive any orders or instructions to proceed against the Klan, which was being heard from again; but the President decided that since Tennessee had returned to the Union, only the state legislature, under the Constitution, could apply for federal aid. Appeals from Governor Brownlow alone would not suffice. In June, after Congressman Samuel M. Arnall had been threatened by a masked band of men "with pistols and rope in hand," Brownlow importuned Thomas for troops to take over six counties but was refused on the ground that Tennessee should attend to its own policing. Brownlow called a special session of the legislature, the state guard was strengthened, and a more

[32] *Army and Navy Journal*, February 29, 1868; Van Horne, *Thomas*, 420.

rigid anti-Klan law, providing fines and prison sentences for nocturnal marauders, was passed.[33]

The more repression, however, the more force was needed to keep the lid on the pot, particularly since the undisciplined state guard proved hopeless. To the relief of most law-abiding Tennesseans, who regarded the guardsmen as a public nuisance, Thomas was authorized to send troops into twenty-one counties to maintain order at the fall elections. No incidents of special consequence were reported; but after the troops had been withdrawn, the newspapers again began to be filled with accounts of Klan outrages. Ultimately—no one knows exactly when—the force of public opinion began to be felt, and General Forrest concluded it wise to dissolve the order in Tennessee. Klan methods had proved too well suited to freebooters, outlaws, and citizens with private grudges who set out on unauthorized projects. Spreading to other states, the order died slowly, a victim of his own secrecy and dark-of-the-night operations.

Thomas's mission in the South was nearly done. Wearing a blue military cape and peaked, broad-brimmed hat, he appeared in Washington in November to preside at the inquiry into the conduct of General Alexander B. Dyer, army ordnance chief during the latter years of the war. Dyer was another native Virginian who had remained loyal to the Union, and his military career, fortunately, had been without stain. After serving in Florida and Mexico, he had administered affairs at the Springfield National Armory with industry and efficiency, and had introduced the same competent method to army headquarters at Washington. But dishonest contractors and disgruntled inventors turned in so many complaints to Congress that it insisted on an official inquiry, which, as searchingly conducted by Thomas, lasted nearly six months. The parade of complainants and witnesses to the stand was interrupted by a reunion of the western armies in Chicago on the fourth anniversary of the Battle of Nashville. Thomas, appointed chairman, sat on the platform between Sherman and President-elect Grant. Noisy conviviality among some 2,000 former officers and soldiers

[33] Johnson Papers, 134:19963; *Army and Navy Journal*, November 28, 1868; Henry, *Story of Reconstruction*, 328–29; Coulter, *Brownlow*, 357.

drowned out most of the speech-making at the great banquet held in Chamber of Commerce Hall. "Hubbub and turmoil were indescribable and apparently uncontrollable," one eyewitness related. Sherman, who presided at the banquet, introduced a number of one-time generals and practiced orators, including several members of Congress, but with some "it was mere dumb pantomime, with others . . . merely the handing of manuscripts to the reporters."

There was one definite break in the clamor, according to an admirer of Thomas. When he was introduced by Sherman as the "determined soldier . . . the beloved commander . . . the Rock of Chickamauga," the company leaped up and spent itself in cheering—"such a storm of applause as hardly once in a century falls upon human ears." The outburst gave way to two minutes of quiet attention, and as Thomas finished his brief speech with a toast "To the Citizens of Chicago," the pandemonium was renewed again to continue far into the night.[34]

Grant impassively smoked his cigar, well satisfied that he had the hero of the evening and the favorite of President Johnson in his grip. The military hierarchy under the new administration was already decided upon. Sherman was next in line as general of the army, and although Congress was threatening to abolish this post, Grant would find a way to stop that. Passing over Halleck, who did not expect promotion, and over Meade, who did, the President-elect made it known that Sheridan was "fully entitled" to the lieutenant-generalship which would become vacant upon the elevation of Sherman. The names of both Meade and Thomas had been discussed at Chicago as likely prospects, but Grant had already published his views in his official report written after the war. General W. W. Averell, a cavalry officer with Sheridan, discussed the report briefly in a letter to a former associate. "I think his [Grant's] attempt at justice to Meade and his subsequent division of the A[rmy] of P[otomac] by giving Sheridan command of the Cavalry and two Corps of infantry rather mixed and his meager praise of Thomas which he takes some pains to discount afterwards is rather Curious when contrasted with his Constant and uncondi-

34 Military Historical Society of Massachusetts, *Papers*, X, 198.

tional praise of Sheridan," wrote Averell. "How difficult it is to beliefe in any History after seeing a page or two of our own made!"[35] Thomas took the news of Sheridan's appointment calmly: "His commission as Major General was older than mine, and . . . I always supposed the President would exercise the right to appoint his friend to an office in preference to another whom he did not particularly like," he explained to former aide Robert H. Ramsey following Grant's inauguration. He strongly felt that Grant had never forgiven him for having commanded the army at Corinth, but considering the nature of the new Cabinet appointments, it was obvious that the President could never like or accept men such as Meade or Thomas, preferring a rough-hewn and cruder mold.

The well-born Virginian was not to get anywhere with Grant. Still occupied with the Dyer inquiry in late March, Thomas learned that General Halleck was to be transferred from the West Coast and that Schofield would be assigned the Military Division of the Pacific. Thomas, who commanded only a department, angrily reminded Sherman that his rank "should not be degraded . . . that if this program were carried out, to give his junior a division . . . he would publicly protest against it."[36] Thomas particularly wanted the Division of the Atlantic so that he could live in the East, but this was to be Meade's. His second choice, the Division of the Missouri, was the assignment of Lieutenant General Sheridan. Sherman, who seemed worried, obtained a promise from Grant that Schofield should make way for Thomas at San Francisco. All that Grant had to do then was to retain Schofield as secretary of war and reorganize Thomas's former department into the Division of the South with Halleck in command. Thomas could not help but feel that Grant was "vindictive."[37] A. K. McClure, who attended the opera one evening with Thomas, regarded the situation in this wise: "I doubt whether anyone ever heard him utter a single complaint but it was obvious to those who knew him well that

[35] McClure, *Lincoln and Men of War Times*, 332–33; R. S. Thorndike (ed.), *The Sherman Letters*, 324–25.

[36] Van Horne, *Thomas*, 434.

[37] *Ibid.*, 435.

he felt humiliated and heartsore at the treatment he had received from the military power of the Government."[38]

"General Thomas is a man of uncommon executive ability . . . is modest, unassuming, affable . . . a truly great man, and his coming here will prove a real acquisition to the official circles of the Pacific States," heralded the San Francisco *Alta*.[39] Traveling across the country by rail, with stops at Chicago, Omaha, and Promontory Point, Utah, where the spreading east-west lines now almost met, Thomas and his party took only seven days and ten hours to reach San Francisco. An old friend of Florida days, General Erasmus Darwin Keyes, who met the party, was shocked to observe a profound change in Thomas's countenance, although he had not yet reached his fifty-third birthday. "White lines bordered his lips and his eyes had lost their wonted fires. . . . He made no complaint but applied himself with customary strictness to duty."[40]

The assignment to the Pacific was taken up with travel from one remote post to another, and with another trip across the continent and back, Thomas was to log some 14,000 miles in one year. Starting out on June 15, the Commander visited the forts in Nevada, Arizona, Southern California, Idaho, and Washington Territory; then debarked on a cruise to recently purchased Alaska and its islands, where seals could be seen "lying in winrows for two or three miles."[41] Returning to headquarters at the corner of Kearny and Sutton streets on September 16, Thomas wrote Sherman that he could recommend no change in the number of troops stationed in Alaska until laws had been passed regulating the killing of fur-bearing animals and intercourse with the natives. "If it is desirable to perpetuate the fur seal and sea otter it will be necessary for Congress to [regulate] . . . the manner of killing these animals indiscriminately," he advised. "Up to this time the gold hunters have had friendly intercourse with the natives but should important dis-

38 McClure, *Lincoln and Men of War Times,* 343.
39 San Francisco *Alta,* March 18, 1864.
40 Keyes, *Fifty Years' Observation of Men and Events,* 167.
41 San Francisco *Alta,* September 17, 1869.

coveries of gold be made, there will be a rush of adventurers to the Territory and the usual depredations will soon follow. . . . The Aleutians are a civilized race, very industrious, docile & amiable [but] they have a weakness for whiskey, and already the whiskey dealers have demoralized all to whom they have access. . . . Gold has been found . . . but as yet in no very large quantities."[42]

Thomas returned to the East to report to the War Office in person and brought his wife back with him in November. The General's aides, who were beginning to be concerned over his health, were glad to see the gracious lady accompanying him. Although Thomas was entitled to an administration of peace and contentment, after continuous military service for nearly thirty years, a series of aggravations now caused his blood pressure to rise—first a proposal by a Democratic member of the Tennessee House to sell the commissioned portrait which hung in the state library. Although the motion failed by a large majority, Thomas angrily offered to purchase the painting for $1,000, its original cost. Still smarting over the "insult," which would have troubled few others, he vowed he would return the gold medal which the legislature had awarded him as soon as he could get it out of deposit in New York.[43] This letter of rebuke was hardly in the mails when a statement by gossiping General Halleck that Grant had demanded the Virginian's removal in favor of Schofield just before the Battle of Nashville appeared in western newspapers. That he had come close to being displaced was something which Thomas had never known but had always suspected.

Possibly fearing that the administration would be criticized, Schofield or someone close to him attempted to defend General Grant. On March 12, 1870, an anonymous letter bearing the headline: "Secrets of History . . . Was Grant's Order a Blunder?" was printed in the New York *Tribune.* Its studied argument that the Nashville campaign had really been won at Franklin,

[42] Thomas to Sherman, September 21, 1869, War Department Files, National Archives.

[43] Van Horne, *Thomas,* 437–39; *Army and Navy Journal,* November 25, 1869; January 29, 1870.

where "the enemy had been whipped until there was very little fight in him" amazed many former soldiers of the Army of the Cumberland. Schofield would have been much better off had he only kept quiet, but now the storm was loosed. Heated replies to his argument began to fill newspaper columns in many cities, and the unhappy Secretary of War was to be berated for errors of omission and downright falsehood for the better part of a year. Wrote "Another Man" in defense of the hero of Nashville: "No one who knows what that army was and what its failings were will dare dispute the fact that Thomas's removal would have proved a great if not fatal error, and that a very large part of the enthusiasm, vim, and heartiness with which the battle of Nashville was fought was due to the fact that in the current words of the men in the ranks: 'This is Old Pap's fight, and we're going to win it for him.' "[44]

Thomas, looking grim, took the criticism and the detailed reply, which filled two newspaper columns, and prepared to make some comment of his own. During the forenoon of March 28, Colonel Alfred L. Hough, his chief aide, left him to his writing but returned to headquarters about three hours later to discover that the General was very ill. Stricken as his task was almost finished, Thomas reached the outer door of his office, opened it, and called, "I want air," and immediately fell. Three physicians were summoned, arriving in turn. After rallying in response to stimulants, Thomas complained of a pain about his right temple, "a bad sign," one of the doctors remarked in an aside to Hough. Thomas insisted on getting up from his couch but soon lay down again. After Mrs. Thomas arrived, there was an attempt at conversation. Observing later that the General was speaking to him, Hough put his ear down and heard him say that he felt easier, with no pain. "He looked up to Mrs. Thomas who leaned down to him, and he spoke to her," related Hough. "Shortly after this I saw him struggle, with a convulsive movement about his chest, and try to rise, which he could not do. I called the physicians from the outer room, and one of them told me . . . it was apoplexy. . . . He was unconscious and gradually sank until twenty-five minutes past seven o'clock

44 New York *Tribune*, March 19, 1817.

when he died. He did not struggle, only giving a convulsive spasm at the last moment."[45]

The body was removed to the General's rooms at the Lick House and immediately embalmed. Groups of citizens discussed the news next day, some shaking their heads. "Since the death of the martyred President Lincoln there has not been so universal an expression of grief and sorrow in San Francisco as yesterday," the *Alta* commented. The body lay in state at the Lick House, the face exposed to view through a glass. No public demonstration was permitted by the widow. Following an Episcopal service, the remains were borne to a crape-festooned railroad car at Oakland, and as each gun from Alcatraz Island spoke, guns responded from the British frigate *Zealous,* then in the harbor, her flags flapping at half-mast.[46] The train moved slowly across the continent followed by the echo of guns at every near-by army post and with a great demonstration of pomp at Chicago.

Meantime President Grant, Generals Sherman, Sheridan, and Meade, Cabinet members (save Schofield), a joint committee from Congress, the governor of New York and his staff, the state Senate and Assembly, and thousands of soldiers and former veterans were gathering in Troy. "The escort will be a battalion of eight companies and General Meade is authorized to use two companies . . . from Willet's Point, two companies . . . from Governor's Island, and the band from West Point," read the official order of General-in-Chief Sherman dated April 3. "All officers of the Army who can be spared from duty, all civil officers of the General and State Governments, members of the Volunteer armies, civil societies, and citizens generally, are invited to be present to manifest their respect."[47] Twenty-five railway cars drawn by two locomotives brought the National Guard from Utica. "Never before in the history of Troy were so many strangers in the city," commented the local *Times.*[48]

Yet among the thousands who came, no member of the General's own family was present. "Our brother George died

[45] Van Horne, *Thomas,* 442–43; San Francisco *Alta,* March 29, 1870.
[46] *Ibid.,* April 1, 1870.
[47] Van Horne, *Thomas,* 447.
[48] Troy (N. Y.) *Times,* April 8, 1870.

to us in '61," his sisters told their neighbors. Although the family fortunes were at low ebb, presents sent them by the General had been returned unopened, and requests that they send the handsome gift sword presented by the citizens of Southampton County had been returned unanswered.[49]

The Right Reverend Bishop Doane and four assisting clergymen conducted solemn services in St. Paul's Episcopal Church.[50] Then the coffin was borne from the church, and the waiting military guard awoke to the sharp command "Attention!" repeated along near-by streets. Rifles were slung to shoulders, shuffled into their places, four brass bands played their dirges, and 140 carriages bearing the President of the United States and a distinguished company rolled past the thousands of citizens standing with bared heads. The echo of tolling bells and minute guns drifted over the city; horses freakishly danced and were swung with tight rein into place. Bishop Doane intoned the Episcopal ritual at the grave: "Man that is born of a woman hath but a short time to live and is full of misery. . . . In the midst of life we are in death. . . ." Rifles in precision blasted their farewell volleys as frightened sparrows flew wildly above.

In quiet Oakwood Cemetery a massive granite tomb surmounted by an American eagle now marks the burial place. Amid the hum of passing motor cars in Washington, a bronze equestrian monument graces the intersection known as Thomas Circle; here the Rock of Chickamauga, astride a great horse, sees no teeming traffic but gazes silently over the Potomac River toward his native South.

49 Squires, *Days of Yester-Year*, 195.
50 A. J. Weise, *History of the City of Troy*, 254–55.

Bibliography

MANUSCRIPT SOURCES

Frederick H. Dearborn Collection, New York City.

Duncan Papers, United States Military Academy Library, West Point.

Ewell Papers, Johnson Papers, Porter Papers, Sherman Papers, and Stanton Papers, Library of Congress, Washington, D. C.

Thomas Papers, Henry E. Huntington Library, San Marino, California (microfilm deposited in the New York Public Library).

Miscellaneous Thomas Papers, Chicago Historical Society Library; California State Library, Sacramento; Library of Congress; and Pennsylvania Historical Society Library, Philadelphia. Many of these have been photostated and deposited in the New York Public Library.

War Department Files, National Archives, Washington, D. C.

PERIODICALS

Anderson, Colonel Thomas M. "General George H. Thomas," Military Service Institution *Journal*, Vol. LVI (January-February, 1915), 37–42.

Army and Navy Chronicle, 1840–41.

Army and Navy Journal, 1865–70.

Byers, S. H. M. "Some More War Letters," *North American Review*, Vol. CXLIV (April, 1887), 374–80.

Crane, R. C. "Major George H. Thomas on the Trail of Indians in 1860," West Texas Historical Association *Year Book*, Vol. XX (October, 1944), 77–84.

Crimmins, Colonel M. L. "An Episode in the Texas Career of General David E. Twiggs," *Southwestern Historical Quarterly,* Vol. XLI (October, 1937), 167–73.

———. "Major George H. Thomas in Texas," West Texas Historical Association *Year Book,* Vol. XIV (October, 1938), 73–82.

Gist, W. W. "The Battle of Franklin," *Tennessee Historical Magazine,* Vol. VI (October, 1920), 213–65.

Hay, Thomas R. "The Battle of Spring Hill," *ibid.,* Vol. VII (April, 1921), 74–91.

Horn, Stanley F. "Nashville during the Civil War," *Tennessee Historical Quarterly,* Vol. IV (March, 1945), 3–22.

"Isle of Wight County Records," *William and Mary Quarterly,* Vol. VII, No. 4 (April, 1899), 205–316.

Johnson, Lewis. "General Thomas's First Victory," *United Service Journal,* Vol. XIII (October, 1895), 385–99.

Johnston, General Joseph E. "Opposing Sherman's Advance to Atlanta," *Century Magazine,* Vol. XII, n.s. (August, 1887), 584–96.

"Major Connolly's Letters to His Wife," Illinois State Historical Library *Publication No. 35* (1928), 217–438.

Maloney, Alice Bay. "Some Oatman Documents," California Historical Society *Quarterly,* Vol. XXI (June, 1942), 107–12.

"Notes & Queries," Southern Historical *Papers,* Vol. X (November, 1882), 524–25; Vol. XII (December, 1884), 568.

Piatt, Donn. "The General Who Heard Mass before Battle," *The Collector,* January–February, 1942, 33–36, 49–52.

Sherman, General W. T. "Old Shady, with a Moral," *North American Review,* Vol. CXLVII (October, 1888), 361–68.

Stone, Colonel Henry. "Hood's Invasion of Tennessee," *Century Magazine,* Vol. XII, n.s. (August, 1887), 597–616.

Tucker, Gardiner C. "Richard Hooker Wilmer, Second Bishop of Alabama," *Historical Magazine of the Protestant Episcopal Church,* Vol. VII (June, 1938), 144–48.

United Service Journal, January 18, 1851.

Wells, Colonel E. T. "The Campaign of Chickamauga," *United Service Journal,* Vol. XVI, n.s. (September, 1896), 217–27.

GENERAL SOURCES

Baird, Charles W. *History of the Huguenot Emigration to America.* New York, 1885. 2 vols.

Banks, R. W. *Battle of Franklin.* New York, 1908.

Battles and Leaders of the Civil War. New York, 1884. 4 vols.

Beale, Howard K. *The Critical Year.* New York, 1930.

Beatty, John. *Memoirs of a Volunteer (The Citizen Soldier).* Cincinnati, 1879, and New York, 1946.

Bennett, L. G. *The 36th Illinois.* Aurora, Ill., 1876.

Berry, Thomas. *Four Years with Morgan and Forrest.* Oklahoma City, 1914.

Bickham, W. D. *Rosecrans' Campaign with the 14th Army Corps.* Cincinnati, 1869.

Bishop, Judson W. *Story of a Regiment.* St. Paul, 1890.

Boddie, John Bennett. *Seventeenth Century Isle of Wight County.* Chicago, 1938.

Boynton, H. B. *Sherman's Historical Raid.* Cincinnati, 1875.

Bradford, Gamaliel. *Union Portraits.* Boston and New York, 1916.

Briant, C. G. *History of the 6th Indiana Regiment.* Indianapolis, 1891.

Calendar of Virginia State Papers. Vol. XI.

Canfield, S. S. *History of the 21st Ohio Regiment.* Toledo, 1893.

Carleton, James Henry. *The Battle of Buena Vista.* New York, 1848.

Chickamauga and Chattanooga National Park Commission. *The Campaign for Chattanooga.* 1896. Pamphlet.

Chittenden, L. E. *Recollections of President Lincoln.* New York, 1891.

Cist, H. M. *Army of the Cumberland.* New York, 1882.

Conyngham, David P. *Sherman's March Through the South.* New York, 1865.

Cope, Alexis. *The 15th Ohio.* Columbus, 1916.

Coppée, Henry. *General Thomas.* New York, 1893.

Coulter, E. Merton. *Civil War and Readjustment in Kentucky.* Chapel Hill, N. C., 1926.

Cox, Jacob. *Battle of Franklin.*

———. *Military Reminiscences.* New York, 1900. 2 vols.

Cullum, George W. *Biographical Register of Officers and Cadets of the U. S. Military Academy.* Boston, 1891. 8 vols.

Dana, Charles A. *Recollections of the Civil War.* New York, 1913.

Dawson, G. *Life and Services of General John A. Logan.* Chicago, 1888.

De Leon, T. C. *Belles, Beaux and Brains of the Sixties.* New York, 1909.

De Peyster, John Watts. *General George H. Thomas.* New York, 1875. Pamphlet.

Doubleday, Rhoda (ed.). *Journal of Major Philip Norbourne Barbour.* London, 1936.

Drewry, William Sidney. *The Southampton Insurrection.* Washington, 1900.

Duffield, H. M. *Address at Dedication of Monuments.* 1895. Pamphlet.

Dyer, Brainerd. *Zachary Taylor.* Baton Rouge, La., 1946.

Eisenchiml, Otto, and Newman, Ralph. *The American Iliad.* Indianapolis, 1947.

Force, M. F. *General Sherman.* New York, 1899.

Freeman, Douglas Southall. *Robert E. Lee.* New York, 1934-35. 4 vols.

French, Samuel G. *Two Wars.* Nashville, 1901.

Giddings, L. *Sketches of the Campaign in Northern Mexico.* New York, 1853.

Grant, U. S. *Personal Memoirs.* Hartford, Conn., 1885.

Green, Wharton J. *Recollections and Reflections.* Raleigh, N. C., 1906.

Hall, Clifton R. *Andrew Johnson.* Princeton, 1916.

Hamilton, Holman. *Zachary Taylor.* Indianapolis, 1941.

Hannaford, E. *Story of a Regiment.* Cincinnati, 1868.

Hartpence, William R. *The 51st Indiana Volunteers.* Cincinnati, 1894.

Hay, Thomas R. *Hood's Tennessee Campaign.* New York, 1925.

Haynie, J. H. *The 19th Illinois.* Chicago, 1912.

Hazen, W. H. *Narrative of Military Service.* Boston, 1885.

Hebert, Walter E. *Fighting Joe Hooker.* Indianapolis, 1944.

Hedley, F. Y. *Marching Through Georgia.* Chicago, 1890.

Henkels, Stan V. *Catalogue of Autographed Manuscripts* No. 1379, October 15, 1925.

Henry, Robert Selph. *"First with the Most" Forrest.* Indianapolis, 1944.

———. *Story of the Confederacy.* Indianapolis, 1931, 1936.

———. *Story of Reconstruction.* Indianapolis, 1938.

Henry, W. S. *Campaign Sketches of the War with Mexico.* New York, 1847.

Hergesheimer, Joseph. *Sheridan.* Boston, 1931.

High, Edwin W. *The 68th Indiana.* Metamora, Ind., 1902.

Hitchcock, Henry. *Marching with Sherman.* New Haven, Conn., 1927.

Hood, John B. *Advance and Retreat.* New Orleans, 1880.

Hopkins, Timothy. *The Kelloggs in the Old World and the New.* San Francisco, 1903. 3 vols.

Horn, Stanley B. *The Army of Tennessee.* Indianapolis, 1941.

Howard, Oliver Otis. *Autobiography.* New York, 1907. 2 vols.

Howe, Henry. *Historical Collections of Virginia.* Charleston, S. C., 1945.

Howe, M. A. DeWolfe (ed.). *Home Letters of General Sherman.* New York, 1909.

Johnson, Richard W. *Memoir of Major General George H. Thomas.* Philadelphia, 1881.

———. *A Soldier's Reminiscences.* Philadelphia, 1886.

Johnston, W. Preston. *Albert Sidney Johnston.* New York, 1878.

Joint Committee on the Conduct of the War. *Supplemental Report,* 1866. 2 vols.

Jones, Jenkin Lloyd. *An Artilleryman's Diary.* Madison, Wis., 1914.

Jones, John William. *Life and Letters of Robert E. Lee.* New York, 1906.

Kenly, John R. *Memoirs of a Maryland Volunteer.* Philadelphia, 1873.

Keyes, Erasmus D. *Fifty Years' Observation of Men and Events.* New York, 1885.

Lewis, Lloyd. *Sherman: Fighting Prophet.* New York, 1932.

McClure, Alexander K. *Lincoln and Men of War Times.* Philadelphia, 1892.

————. *Recollections of Half a Century*. Salem, Mass., 1902.

Meade, George (ed.). *Life and Letters of George Gordon Meade*. New York, 1913. 2 vols.

Merrill, Samuel. *The 70th Indiana Volunteer Infantry*. Indianapolis, 1900.

Military Historical Society of Massachusetts *Papers*. Vol. VII, *Campaigns in Kentucky and Tennessee, 1862–64* (1908); Vol. VIII, *The Mississippi Valley, Tennessee, Georgia, Alabama, 1861–64* (1910); Vol. X, *Critical Sketches of Some Federal and Confederate Commanders* (1895).

Military Order of the Loyal Legion of the U. S., District of Columbia Commandery, Indiana Commandery, New York Commandery, Oregon Commandery. *War Papers, Recollections,* and other publications.

Milton, George Fort. *The Age of Hate*. New York, 1930.

Nicholay, J. G., and Hay, John. *Complete Works of Abraham Lincoln*. New York, 1905. 12 vols.

Official Records of the War of the Rebellion. Washington, 1880–1901.

Owens, Hamilton. *Baltimore on the Chesapeake*. Garden City, N. Y., 1941.

Palmer, George T. *A Conscientious Turncoat*. New Haven, Conn., 1941.

Palmer, John M. *Personal Recollections*. Cincinnati, 1901.

Park, Roswell. *Sketch of the History and Topography of West Point*. Philadelphia, 1840.

Patton, James Welch. *Unionism and Reconstruction in Tennessee*. Chapel Hill, N. C., 1934.

Perry, Henry F. *History of the 38th Indiana Regiment*. Palo Alto, Calif., 1906.

Phisterer, Frederick. *The Regular Brigade of the 14th Corps*. Albany, N. Y., 1863.

Piatt, Donn, and Boynton, H. V. *General George H. Thomas*. Cincinnati, 1891.

Porter, Horace. *Campaigning with Grant*. New York, 1897.

Price, George. *Across the Continent with the Fifth Cavalry*. New York, 1883.

Reid, S. C. *Scouting Expedition of McCulloch's Texas Rangers.* Philadelphia, 1847.

Rhodes, James Ford. *History of the United States.* New York, 1920. 8 vols.

Richardson, A. D. *The Secret Service.* Hartford, Conn., 1865.

Ridpath, J. C. *Life of James A. Garfield.* Cincinnati, 1882.

Rister, Carl Coke. *Robert E. Lee in Texas.* Norman, Okla., 1946.

Robinson, Will H. *Story of Arizona.* Phoenix, 1919.

Rodenbough, Theo F. (ed.). *The Army of the United States.* New York, 1896.

Rodgers, Andrew D. *John Torrey.* Princeton, N. J., 1942.

Rogers, Augustus C. *Sketches of Representative Men North and South.* New York, 1873.

Royse, Isaac H. C. *History of the 115th Illinois Volunteers.* Terre Haute, Ind., 1900.

Rustling, James F. *Men and Things I Saw in Civil War Days.* New York, 1899.

Sandburg, Carl. *Abraham Lincoln: The War Years.* New York, 1939. 4 vols.

———. *Storm over the Land.* New York, 1942.

Schmitt, Martin F. (ed.). *General Crook: His Autobiography.* Norman, Okla., 1946.

Schofield, John M. *Forty-six Years in the Army.* New York, 1897.

Scott, John. *The 32nd Iowa Volunteers.* Nevada, Iowa, 1896.

Shanks, W. F. G. *Personal Recollections of Distinguished Generals.* New York, 1866.

Sheridan, Philip H. *Personal Memoirs.* New York, 1892.

Sherman, John. *Recollections.* New York, 1895.

Sherman, William T. *Personal Memoirs.* New York, 1891. Fourth edition.

Smith, Justin H. *The War with Mexico.* New York, 1919. 2 vols.

Snow, Edward R. *Castle Island.* Andover, Mass., 1935. Pamphlet.

Society of the Army of the Cumberland. *Reports of the Meetings.* 1867–93.

Sprague, John T. *The Florida War.* New York, 1848.

Squires, W. H. T. *The Days of Yester-Year.* Portsmouth, Va., 1928.

Stanley, D. S. *Personal Memoirs*. Cambridge, Mass., 1917.

Stephenson, N. W. *Texas and the Mexican War*. New Haven, Conn., 1921.

Stevenson, Alexander F. *The Battle of Stone's River*. Boston, 1884.

Taylor, Benjamin F. *Mission Ridge and Lookout Mountain*. New York, 1872.

Thorndike, R. S. (ed.). *The Sherman Letters*. New York, 1894.

U. S. Military Academy Library. *Bulletin No. 1, Cadet Life Before the Mexican War*. West Point, N. Y., 1945. Pamphlet.

Van Horne, T. B. *History of the Army of the Cumberland*. Cincinnati, 1875. 3 vols.

———. *Major General George H. Thomas*. New York, 1882.

Vance, Wilson. *Stone's River*. New York, 1914.

Villard, Henry. *Memoirs*. Boston, 1904. 2 vols.

Weise, A. J. *History of the City of Troy*. Troy, N. Y., 1876.

Welles, Gideon. *Diary*. Boston, 1911. 3 vols.

Wiley, Bell Irvin. *The Life of Johnny Reb*. Indianapolis, 1943.

Williams, John Lee. *The Territory of Florida*. New York, 1837.

Wilmer, Richard H. *The Recent Past*. New York, 1887.

Wilson, Goodridge. *Smythe County History and Tradition*. Kingsport, Tenn., 1932.

Wilson, James H. *Life of Charles A. Dana*. New York, 1907.

———. *Life of John A. Rawlins*. New York, 1916.

———. *Under the Old Flag*. New York, 1912. 2 vols.

Wooldridge, John. *History of Nashville*. Nashville, 1890.

Wyeth, Dr. John Allen. *With Sabre and Scalpel*. New York, 1914.

Index

107; Alabama and Tennessee campaigns (1862), 107–10; answers Governor Johnson, 108–109; declines army command, 112–13; Perryville campaign, 114–16; merits weighed at Washington, 117; defends Buell, 118–19; nicknames of, 121, 179; Murfreesboro campaign, 122–25; at Stone's River, 125–36; at Murfreesboro, 138–43; Tullahoma campaign, 144–46; advance to Chickamauga, 148–56; in battle, 158–76; at Chattanooga, 177–93; named to A. of C. command, 182; at Missionary Ridge, 194–200; quoted on Bragg, 192; on battle of Missionary Ridge, 200; on use of Negro troops, 204; invades Georgia, 207; strategy of, 207–209; operations under Sherman, 210–39; sent to Chattanooga, 242; commands at Nashville, 243 ff.; fortifies city, 249; strategy for battle, 251–54, 261; prepares for enemy, 254–56; criticized, 255, 257–60; battle preparations, 261; defeats Hood, 262–67; pursues enemy, 271–74; promoted, 275; relations with Grant, 275; selects winter quarters, 276; his army dispersed, 277; directs Wilson's campaign, 278–79; celebrates victory, 281; surrender terms, 282; final review, 283; final order, 284; insists on suitable postwar command, 285; reconstruction assignments and activities, 286–300; criticizes Southern attitude, 293; fights Ku Klux Klan, 295; declines to run for president, 297; speech at A. of C. meeting, 298; at Chicago meeting, 301; assigned to West Coast, 302; reports on Alaska, 303–304; answers newspaper criticism, 305; death, 305–306; funeral at Troy, N. Y., 306–307
Thomas, John: 6–8
Thomas, Judith: 3, 5–7
Thomas, Mary Rochelle: 8
Thomas, Robert: 8

Thornton, Seth B.: 26
Thruston, Gates P.: 268, 178
Travis, Joseph: 7
Trenton, Georgia: 150
Trimble, Carey A.: 77
Triune, Tennessee: 124
Troy, New York: 50, 306
Tullahoma, Tennessee: 138, 146, 243
Turchin, John B.: 175, 189, 199
Turner, Nat: insurrection of, 5–7
Tuscaloosa, Alabama: 278, 280
Tuscumbia, Alabama: 107, 247, 249
Twiggs, David Emanuel: 51; in Mexican War, 30, 35; anecdotes concerning, 46; quarrels with Thomas, 56–57; Thomas reports on, 63; surrenders Texas, 63, 65

Upton, Emory: 280

Van Cleve, H. P.: 122, 124, 182; at Stone's River, 128–29, 133–35; at Chickamauga, 160, 163, 168–69; criticized, 178–79
Vanderveer, Ferdinand: 158, 173
Van Dorn, Earl: with Second U. S. Cavalry, 55, 58–59; Civil War service, 108–109, 117, 141
Van Vliet, Stewart: at West Point, 9–10; in Florida, 17–18, 20; at Ft. Moultrie, 22
Vera Cruz, Mexico: 43–44
Vicksburg, Mississippi: home of Benjamin Thomas, 4, 62; campaign of, 141–42, 146, 275; mentioned, 73, 205
Victoria, Mexico: 36
Villa Gran, Mexico: 38
Vining's Station, Georgia: 226
Virginia Military Institute: 63–64

Wade, Ben: 299
Wade, Richard D. A.: 18–19
Wagner, George D.: 222
Walker, W. H. T.: 159, 161, 207
Wallace, Lew: 104
Walnut Springs, Mexico: Taylor camps at, 31, 38
Wartrace, Tennessee: 136, 138
Washington, George: 67; Thomas compared with, 9, 121, 178, 185

Washington, D. C.: 72, 76, 307;
  Thomas visits, 9, 63, 288, 301
Waterloo, Alabama: 377–78
Watervliet Arsenal, New York: 18
Wauhatchie, Tenn.: action at, 189
Webster, Edward: 30, 32–33
Weir, Robert W.: 49
Welles, Gideon: quoted, 179, 288,
  290–91
West Point (U. S. Military academy):
  Thomas admitted, 8–9; cadet life
  at, 9–14, 120; Thomas teaches at,
  48–50
Wheeler, Joseph: 123, 125, 165, 207,
  229, 242
Whipple, William D.: 48, 221–22, 259
Wilder, J. T.: 152–53
Willard, J. P.: 161
Williams, Alpheus S.: 215
Williams, John Lee: 14
Williams, Seth: 49
Williamsport, Maryland: 72
Willich, August: 126, 175
Wilmer, Richard H.: 289–90
Wilson, James Harrison: quoted,
  185–86, 258–59, 267, 273, 278–79;
  meets Thomas, 185; U. S. cavalry
leader, 250, 254–55, 261; charac-
  terizes Grant, 258; fights at Nashville, 262–65; pursues Hood, 269–
  71; strengthens cavalry force, 278;
  sweeps through South, 280–83
Winchester, Tennessee: 136
Winchester, Virginia: 73–75, 269,
  274
Withers, Jones W.: 135
Wofford, William T.: 283, 288
Wood, Thomas J.: 122, 124, 211, 234,
  261, 278; advances to Nashville
  and Shiloh, 102–103; at Stone's
  River, 128–29; characterized, 140;
  at Chickamauga, 160, 163, 165,
  167–71; at Chattanooga, 194–95,
  198–99; operations in Georgia, 217,
  227; at Nashville, 254, 258; action
  at, 263–66; pursues Hood, 270
Worth, William Jenkins: 19; in
  Mexican War, 30–31, 34–35, 38

Yaryan, John L.: quoted, 131

Zollicoffer, Felix: campaigns in
  West, 79, 85, 88–89; killed at Mill
  Springs, 98; Thomas forwards
  body, 100

ROCK OF CHICKAMAUGA

The Life of General George H. Thomas

HAS BEEN SET ON THE LINOTYPE

IN TEN-POINT BASKERVILLE

WITH TWO POINTS BETWEEN

LINES.

UNIVERSITY OF OKLAHOMA PRESS

NORMAN